Sudanese Colloquial Arabic for Beginners

SIL International®
First Edition, 1979, SIL U.K.
Second Edition, 1980, SIL U.K.
Third Edition, 2002, SudMedia, Khartoum
Second Impression, 2003

Fourth Edition, 2016
SIL International®

Managing Editor
Eric Kindberg

Volume Editors
Bonnie Brown
Mary Huttar
Barbara Shannon

Production Staff
Lois Gourley, Production Director
Karoline Fisher, Compositor
Judy Benjamin, Compositor
Barbara Alber, Cover Design

Cover Image
Photo by Christine Perkins, used with permission

Sudanese Colloquial Arabic for Beginners

Andrew M. Persson and Janet R. Persson
with
Ahmad Hussein

SIL International®
Dallas, TX

Library of Congress Control Number: 2016961502
ISBN: 978-1-55671-378-1

Copies of this and other publications of SIL International® may be obtained through distributors such as Amazon, Barnes & Noble, other worldwide distributors and, for select volumes, www.sil.org/resources/publications:

SIL International Publications
7500 W. Camp Wisdom Road
Dallas, TX 75236-5629 USA

General inquiry: publications_intl@sil.org
Pending order inquiry: sales_intl@sil.org
www.sil.org/resources/publications

Contents

Acknowledgements

We would like to express our thanks to Mr. Philip Gordon, without whose knowledge of Sudanese Arabic this book could not have been written; to our colleagues of the Summer Institute of Linguistics in Sudan, for their encouragement; and to our neighbours and friends in East Banat, Omdurman, whose hospitality and patience made our learning of their language such a pleasant experience.

Andrew and Janet Persson May 1979

Many thanks to Mr. Yusif Osman Hassan for his invaluable assistance with the revisions. We also acknowledge Mr. Douglas Sampson for producing the Arabic-English glossary which was added to the Second Edition.

Andrew and Janet Persson September 2003

Introduction

1 Sudanese Colloquial Arabic

This course has been written to help those who, like the authors, have come from abroad to Sudan and want to be able to talk to their Sudanese colleagues, friends, and neighbours in their everyday language. It uses the Arabic spoken in Khartoum and Omdurman, as this is understood in most parts of Sudan. Students who live outside the metropolis should be aware of differences in their local dialect and adapt to them. Even within the metropolitan dialect there are differences between the ways Sudanese from different backgrounds speak. Each student should therefore be guided by the way his or her own teacher speaks.

It is important to realise that this spoken, colloquial Arabic is a different form of the language from the Arabic that is written. Written Arabic is referred to in English as 'Modern Standard Arabic' and is called *al fuṣHa* by Sudanese. Modern Standard Arabic is used both for writing and for formal speeches and broadcasts. It is common to the whole Arabic-speaking world. Each Arabic-speaking country, however, has its own colloquial form of Arabic for everyday conversation, with its distinctive pronunciation, grammatical rules and vocabulary. There is some overlap between the written and spoken forms of Arabic, especially as the spoken language often borrows new words from Modern Standard; but in order to learn to read and write properly, it is necessary to study Modern Standard Arabic as a separate language. Colloquial Arabic is not normally written, except for recording folk stories. Many Arabic speakers do not even think of it as a language that has grammar.

2 How to use this course

The lessons in this course are designed to be used either in a class situation with a trained teacher or by individuals with a Sudanese friend acting as 'teacher.' It is not a reference grammar or a 'teach-yourself' book. Most of the material in the course has been written in Arabic as well as Roman script in order to help Sudanese teachers who may find the Arabic text easier to read.

Each lesson contains a dialogue, some explanation and drills on new grammatical points, suggestions for role play and conversation practice, and a vocabulary of new words in the order in which they occur in the lesson. With each of the first twelve lessons there are also some pronunciation drills.

Preparation

Before each lesson you, the student, need to do some preparation. Read through the English translation of the dialogue so that you know what it is about. Then make sure that you understand what the purpose of each drill is in that lesson. If you are studying with a private teacher decide how much of the lesson you want to cover in your next session with your teacher. You do not have to complete a whole lesson at one go. It can be spread out over several sessions. Note down any questions you have for your teacher. It is more useful to learn what you want to know than to memorise a lot of words that are irrelevant to you.

Dialogue

This is the most important part of the lesson for gaining fluency. First, the student should listen as the teacher reads the whole dialogue through. Then, the teacher should read it again with the student repeating each sentence or part of a sentence after him, taking care to imitate the pronunciation and intonation as closely as possible. Finally, the teacher should read the whole dialogue through once again. Parts of some dialogues could also be memorized for use in practical situations.

Grammar drills

The student should read through the explanations and examples beforehand, and then work through the drills with the teacher. Each drill should be performed in accordance with the instructions, and if possible, extra drills could be constructed along the lines of those in the lessons.

Role play

The idea of a role play is to help the students to relate what they learn to real life. The dialogue and drills are of no use unless they teach a person to speak to their neighbours. It doesn't matter if students make grammatical mistakes in the role play. The vital thing is that they should talk and interact with each other and their teacher *in Arabic*—so that they lose their self-consciousness and feel that it is natural to speak Arabic.

Some of these role plays can be followed up by an outing to somewhere like a restaurant or museum for a real-life experience.

Conversation practice

From Lesson 6 onward, most lessons contain suggestions for conversation practice. Like the Role Play in each lesson, these suggestions help students actually speak the language. However, they are more structured than is a role play. Some of them involve practising a particular construction or set of expressions. Others involve preparing a set dialogue with the teacher's help in order to use it afterward with Sudanese friends and acquaintances in specific situations.

Vocabulary

The vocabulary for each lesson should be learned by heart. It is impossible to make any sort of conversation unless one can remember basic vocabulary without any conscious effort.

Pronunciation drills

These are designed to help the student pronounce correctly the words he learns, so that he will be understood. Instructions for the pronunciation drills are given in section 3 of this introduction.

However, no one will learn to speak Sudanese Arabic simply by studying this course. From the time they have completed the first lesson, all students must put into practice what they have learned by speaking Arabic with their Sudanese friends, shopkeepers, and anyone else they meet in daily life. The Sudanese are renowned for their friendliness and hospitality and no foreigner need fear a rebuff if he tries out the little Sudanese Arabic he knows. He will find that especially those who do not know any English will be delighted to talk with someone who is trying to learn their language.

3 Pronunciation of Sudanese Arabic

The sounds

The following table gives the sounds of Sudanese Arabic as they are represented in this course in Roman and Arabic scripts. The International Phonetic Alphabet (IPA) symbols are given for the benefit of students who have some training in phonetics, along with a brief description of the sounds not found in English for the benefit of others. However, for all the sounds, the most important principle is to watch and listen as the Sudanese teacher reads the words in the drills and then to imitate the teacher's speech. Even the simplest sounds may be pronounced with subtle differences from the way they are in one's mother tongue or dialect of English, and only by careful imitation will the learner come to sound like a Sudanese.

Consonants

Roman	Arabic	IPA	Description
b	ب	b	
d	د	d̪	like the English sound but with the tip of the tongue touching the back of the front teeth
ḍ	ض	dˤ	like d but with the root of the tongue drawn back towards the position for 9 (see below)
f	ف	f	
g	ق	ɡ	
gh	غ	ɣ	like kh (see below) but voiced like g
h	ه	h	
H	ح	ɦ/ħ	like h but produced in the throat rather than in the mouth. The root of the tongue is pushed back into the throat. (This sound is not just an h produced with more force.)
j	ج	ʤ	generally softer than English j
k	ك	k	
kh	خ	x	like the ch in Scottish “loch” or German “Dach”
l	ل	l	
m	م	m	
n	ن	n̪	like the English sound but with the tip of the tongue touching the back of the front teeth
r	ر	r	a rolled r
s	س	s̪	like the English sound but with the tip of the tongue touching the back of the front teeth
ṣ	ص	sˤ	like s but with the root of the tongue drawn back towards the position for 9 (see below)
sh	ش	ʃ	as English sh
t	ت	t̪	like the English sound but with the tip of the tongue touching the back of the front teeth
ṭ	ط	tˤ	like t but with the root of the tongue drawn back towards the position for 9 (see below)
y	ي	j	
w	و		
z	ز	z̪	like the English sound but with the tip of the tongue touching the back of the front teeth
9	ع	ʕ	produced at the same position in the throat as H. (Try saying the vowel a as in “father” progressively deeper and further back in the throat, until the root of the tongue cannot go any further back without blocking the throat. With the tongue in this position you will produce the sound 9.)
’ *	ء	ʔ	the glottal stop
ẓ *	ظ	zˤ	like z but with the root of the tongue drawn back towards the position for 9

* These sounds are rare in Sudanese Arabic.

Vowels

Roman	Arabic	IPA	Description
a		a	Since the pronunciation of the vowel sounds in English differs greatly between different English dialects, it is important not to read these letters as if they were English, but to listen and imitate the Sudanese teacher reading the drills.
aa	ا	aa	
ee	ى	ee	
i		i	
ii	و	ii	
oo	ى	oo	
u		u	
uu	و	uu	

The pronunciation drills

The pronunciation drills are designed to give practice in recognizing and pronouncing accurately each of the sounds, beginning with the simpler ones. The drills are of two types, 'Listen and Repeat' drills for the simpler ones, and 'Contrast drills' for the more difficult sounds.

Listen and Repeat drills

Stage 1: Listen to the list read through once or twice.
Stage 2: Repeat each word after the teacher.

Contrast drills

Stage 1: recognizing the difference between two similar sounds.

Listen as the teacher reads:

a) the first of the two lists (see Lesson 4.4)
b) the second list
c) the first list again but inserting before the last word one word from the second list. For example, using lists (section 4.4 c and d), he could read: *sharig, yamsik, jilid, daris, katiir, mumkin*
d) the second list, but inserting before the last word one word from the first list, e.g. using lists (section 4.4 c and d): *katiir, gadiim, jadiid, tagiil, sharig, yamiin*
e) Steps c) and d) should be repeated, inserting different words until the student can recognize the odd word standing out as different.

Stage 2: producing the different sounds correctly.

Repeat each word after the teacher as he reads:

a) the first of the two lists
b) the second list
c) alternate words from the two lists, for example, using lists (section 4.4 c and d): *sharig, katiir, yamsik, gadiim, jilid, jadiid,...*
d) words from both lists at random

Initial familiarisation

The pronunciation drills are located at the end of each lesson so that the learner can work on them concurrently with the grammar. It is unwise to try to master all the sounds completely before embarking on any conversation. However, since many of the sounds have to be used before they are dealt with in pronunciation drills, a list of examples of each sound is given here.

باب
بيض
بدرى

دقيق
دروس
دخل

ضيف
ضرورى
ضَهَر

فوق
فطور
فهم

قروش
قهوة
قفة

غنم
غرب
غسّل

هناك
هوا
هدوم

حلو
حمار
حيوان

جبنة
جواب
جيران

كتير
كبرى
كمان

خدام
خمسة
خلاص

لبن
ليمون
لسع

موية
مدرسة
ممكن

ناس
نحن
ناشف

راجل
ركب
راس

سمك
سوق
ساعة

صابون
صندوق
صورة

شراب
شمال
شوف

تانى
تلاته
تكسى

طيب
طوالى
طلب

واحد
وين
ولد

يمين
ينوم
يوم

زول
زبون
زراف

عربى
عيان
عرف

Before starting Lesson 1 the teacher should read this consonant and vowel wordlist to the student and then the student should repeat each item after the teacher. Accurate pronunciation cannot be expected at this stage but this exercise will begin to familiarise the student with the sounds.

Consonant wordlist

b
baab — door
beeḍ — eggs
badri — early

d
dagiig — flour
duruus — lessons
da<u>kh</u>al — he entered

ḍ
ḍeef — visitor
ḍaruuri — necessary
ḍahar — back

f
foog — over
faṭuur — breakfast
fihim — he understood

g
guruu<u>sh</u> — money
gahwa — coffee
guffa — basket

<u>gh</u>
<u>gh</u>anam — goats
<u>gh</u>arib — west
<u>gh</u>assal — he washed

h
hinaak — there
hawa — air
hiduum — clothes

H
Hilu — pleasant
Humaar — donkey
Hayawaan — animal

j
jibna — cheese
jawaab — letter
jeeraan — neighbours

k
katiir — much
kubri — bridge
kamaan — also

<u>kh</u>
<u>kh</u>addaam — servant
<u>kh</u>amsa — five
<u>kh</u>alaaṣ — finished

l
laban — milk
leemuun — lime
lissa9 — yet

m
mooya — water
madrasa — school
mumkin — possible

n
naas — people
niHna — we
naa<u>sh</u>if — dry

r
raajil — man
rikib — he rode
raas — head

s
samak — fish
suug — market
saa9a — hour

ṣ
ṣaabuun — soap
ṣanduug — box
ṣuura — photo

<u>sh</u>
<u>sh</u>araab — drink
<u>sh</u>imaal — left
<u>sh</u>uuf — look

t
taani — again
talaata — three
taksi — taxi

ṭ
ṭaiyib — alright
ṭawwaali — straight on
ṭalab — he asked

w
waaHid — one
ween — where?
walad — boy

y
yamiin — right
yanuum — he sleeps
yoom — day

z
zool — person
zabuun — customer
zaraaf — giraffe

9
9arabi — Arabic
9ayyaan — ill
9irif — he knew

سؤال	ظرف
اتأخر	بايظ
مؤجر	موظف
درس	جيب
اهلا	بيرة
لحم	فيل
حاجة	موز
تالت	زول
ساكن	يوم
بيت	سكر
ليل	ممكن
عيش	اخت
جدّ	شوف
ملح	سوق
انت	قول

’ *	
su’aal	question
it’akhkhar	he was late
mu’ajjir	tenant

ẓ *	
ẓarif	envelope
baayiẓ	not working
muwaẓẓaf	employee

* As these sounds are rare in Sudanese Arabic they are not dealt with in the pronunciation drills.

Vowel wordlist

a	
daris	lesson
ahlan	welcome
laHam	meat
aa	
Haaja	thing
taalit	third
saakin	living
ee	
beet	house
leel	night
9eesh	bread
i	
jidd	grandfather
miliH	salt
inta	you (masc.)

ii	
jiib	bring
biira	beer
fiil	elephant
oo	
mooz	bananas
zool	person
yoom	day
u	
sukkar	sugar
mumkin	possible
ukhut	sister
uu	
shuuf	look
suug	market
guul	say

Stress or accent

Each word in Sudanese Arabic has one syllable that is stressed (accented) more than the others. The stress usually falls on the first syllable of a word if the word only contains short syllables. If it contains any long syllables the stress falls on the last long syllable. (A long syllable is one with a vowel *aa, ee, ii, oo, uu,* or with any vowel followed by two consonants.)

When suffixes are added to words this often causes the stress to change from one syllable to another, so it is always important to listen for the stress on words and imitate it carefully together with the pronunciation of the consonants and vowels.

الدرس الاول

حوار : فى الدكان

س : سيد الدكان ز : زبونة

ز ازيك.

س اهلا.

ز انت كويس؟

س الحمد لله. انت كويسة؟

ز كويسة. فى صابون؟

س فى. عاوزة كم؟

ز جيب اتنين. فى ملح؟

س ملح ما فى.

ز دا شنو؟

س دا سكر. عاوزة سكر؟

ز ايوه. الكيس بكم؟

س الكيس باربعة الف.

ز طيب جيب واحد.

س عاوزة حاجة تانى؟

ز لا خلاص. شكرا.

س شكرا. مع السلامة.

تمرين

١,١,١

ازَيك	ازيِك	ازيكم
كويس	كويسة	كويسين

الحمد لله

انتَ انتِ

ad daris al awwal

Hiwaar: fi d dukkaan

s: siid ad dukkaan z: zabuuna

z: izzeeyyak.
s: ahlan.
z: inta kwaiyis?
s: al Hamdu lillaa. inti kwaiysa?
z: kwaiysa. fii ṣaabuun?
s: fii. 9aawza kam?
z: jiib itneen. fii miliH?
s: miliH maa fii.
z: da shinuu?
s: da sukkar. 9aawza sukkar?
z: aiwa. al kiis bee kam?
s: al kiis bee arba9a alif.
z: ṭaiyib. jiib waaHid.
s: 9aawza Haaja taani?
z: la', khalaaṣ. shukran.
s: shukran. ma9a s salaama.

Lesson 1

Dialogue: At the shop

s: shopkeeper c: customer (lady)

c: How are you?
s: Welcome.
c: Are you well?
s: Yes, thank God. Are you well?
c: Yes, I'm well. Is there soap?
s: There is. How much do you want?
c: Give me two. Is there salt?
s: There's no salt.
c: What is that?
s: That's sugar. Do you want sugar?
c: Yes. How much is a bag?
s: A bag is 4,000 pounds.
c: Okay. Give me one.
s: Do you want anything more?
c: No, that's all. Thank you.
s: Thank you. Good-bye.

Notes on the dialogue

1. The Sudanese currency is officially dinars, in Arabic *diinaar*, and all transactions in banks and offices should be in dinars. However, in everyday speech people still use the old currency of the pound, in Arabic *jineeh.* ten pounds equal one dinar. So in the dialogue, when the shopkeeper quotes a price of 4,000 he means 4,000 pounds, not 4,000 dinars. In dinars it would be 400. The general word for 'money' is *guruush*.
2. Since this book was revised in 2002, the Sudanese currency has changed back to the pound *jineeh* and the value of the *jineeh* has also changed, so the reader will need to make adjustments to prices given in the book.

1.1 Drills: tamriin

1.1.1 Greetings

In the Sudanese culture greetings are important. You should observe how often the Sudanese shake hands and what greetings are used to whom and on what occasions. Some of these greetings have different masculine and feminine forms. Two like that are given here:

a) *izzeeyyak*: to a man; *izzeeyyik*: to a woman; *izzeeyyakum*: plural
b) *kwaiyis*: to or of a man; *kwaiysa*: to or of a woman; *kwaiysiin*: plural
c) *al Hamdu lillaa* is the usual reply to *inta kwaiyis*

Note also that Arabic has two words for 'you' (singular): *inta* when addressing a man and *inti* to a woman.

Teacher and student or the students in pairs should practice the greetings exchange given in the dialogue (from *izzeeyyak...kwaiysa*, also *shukran* and *ma9a s salaama*), using the correct forms as they address a man or a woman.

السلام عليكم   عليكم السلام

١,١,٢

دا شنو؟	دا عيش	دا زيت
دا ملح	دا شاى	دا بيض
دا سكر	دا دقيق	دا لحم
دا صابون	دا لبن	دا كيس

دا ملح؟   ايوه، دا ملح   لا، دا ما ملح   (والى آخره)

١,١,٣

في ملح   في سكر (والى آخره)

في ملح؟   ايوه، ملح في   لا، ملح ما في (والى آخره)

١,١,٤

عاوز لحم؟	ايوه، عاوز لحم	عاوزة عيش؟	ايوه، عاوزة عيش
عاوز لبن؟	ايوه، عاوز لبن	عاوزة شاى؟	ايوه، عاوزة شاى
عاوز زيت؟	لا، ما عاوز زيت	عاوزة ملح؟	لا، ما عاوزة ملح
عاوز بيض؟	لا، ما عاوز بيض	عاوزة كيس؟	لا، ما عاوزة كيس

Another common greeting is *as salaamu 9aleekum,* with its reply *9aleekum as salaam.* This is the universal greeting in the Arab world and not peculiar to Sudan. In Sudan it is more formal than the other greetings and is used mostly to people one doesn't know or in formal situations like a meeting or classroom. Practice saying it with your teacher so that you get the correct pronunciation.

1.1.2 'This is ____' type of sentences

The purpose of this drill is for you to learn how to make sentences of the type, 'This is ____,' e.g. 'This is sugar.' Note that in Arabic there are no words for 'is' and 'are.' The sentence consists of the word *da* 'this' and the word for the item, e.g. *da sukkar,* 'This is sugar'. The teacher should read each sentence and let the students repeat it after him. (See the vocabulary at the end of the lesson for new words.)

da shinuu?	da 9eesh	da zeet
da miliH	da shay	da beeḍ
da sukkar	da dagiig	da laHam
da ṣaabuun	da laban	da kiis

Now the teacher should repeat the sentences but this time turn them into questions, e.g. *da miliH?* 'Is this salt'? Notice the difference of intonation. You can also supply an answer to each question, e.g. *aiwa, da miliH,* 'Yes, this is salt', or *la' da maa miliH,* 'No, this is not salt'.

Now bring out pictures of salt, sugar, etc., or actual samples of them and practice the same sentences with their variations using pictures or samples. This will help you learn the vocabulary.

1.1.3 'There is ____' type of sentences

Note that *fii* 'there is' may come either before or after the noun. Follow the same procedure as for drill 1.1.2. First the teacher should read out *fii miliH, fii sukkar,* etc. as statements, with the student repeating each sentence after him. Then these statements can be turned into questions by changing the intonation, and answers supplied, e.g. *aiwa, fii miliH* or *aiwa, miliH fii* or *la', miliH maa fii,* etc.

1.1.4 'I want'

As with the greetings, you will find that certain common expressions have different forms for masculine, feminine, and plural. Later in the course you will see how they fit into the general structure of the language, but in the meantime you can learn some of these expressions on their own. One of these is a term for 'want' or 'would like.' In the dialogue the shopkeeper asks the lady customer, *9aawza kam?* using the feminine because he is addressing a woman. The customer, referring to herself, would also use the feminine, e.g. *9aawza sukkar* 'I want sugar'. Note that in Arabic it is not always necessary to have a pronoun in the sentence. You can say *inti 9aawza sukkar?* or just *9aawza sukkar?* if the meaning is clear from the context. The masculine of *9aawza* is *9aawz* and the plural, *9aawziin.*

As you did for drills 1.1.2 and 1.1.3, repeat the sentences after the teacher and then practice in pairs.

9aawz laHam?	aiwa, 9aawz laHam	9aawza 9eesh?	aiwa, 9aawza 9eesh
9aawz laban?	aiwa, 9aawz laban	9aawza shaay?	aiwa, 9aawza shaay
9aawz zeet?	la', maa 9aawz zeet	9aawza miliH?	la', maa 9aawza miliH
9aawz beeḍ?	la', maa 9aawz beeḍ	9aawza kiis?	la', maa 9aawza kiis

عاوزين سكر؟	ايوه، عاوزين سكر
عاوزين صابون؟	لا، ما عاوزين صابون
عاوزين واحد؟	ايوه، عاوزين واحد
عاوزين اتنين؟	لا، ما عاوزين اتنين

١,١,٥

جيب جيبى جيبوا

كلمات

درس	سكر
ال	كيس
اول	بى ب
حوار	اربعة
دكان	الف
سيد الدكان	طيب
زبونة	واحد
زبون	حاجة
ازيك	تانى
اهلا	لا
انتَ انتِ	خلاص
كويس كويسة	شكرا
الحمد لله	مع السلامة
فى	دينار
صابون	تمرين
عاوز عاوزة	عيش
كم	لبن
جيب	زيت
اتنين	دقيق
ملح	شاى
ما	بيض
دا	لحم
شنو	قروش
ايوه	
فى	

تمرين الاصوات

هوا	زيارة
جواب	بيوت
دوا	نايم
سوا	دايما

9aawziin sukkar?	aiwa, 9aawziin sukkar
9aawziin ṣaabuun?	la', maa 9aawziin ṣaabuun
9aawziin waaHid?	aiwa, 9aawziin waaHid
9aawziin itneen?	la', maa 9aawziin itneen

1.1.5 *jiib* 'bring'

jiib means 'bring' but is also used for 'give me.' Like *9aawz* it has a feminine form, *jiibi*, and a plural, *jiibu.* Practice *jiib, jiibi*, and *jiibu* with some of the nouns you have learned.

1.2 Role play

Teacher and students can act out the parts of a shopkeeper and customers. It may help to have some actual items on the table. Then, when the students feel confident about the phrases and vocabulary, they should go out to a market or small shop where English is not spoken and actually buy something.

1.3 Vocabulary: kalmaat

daris	lesson	sukkar	sugar
al	the	kiis	bag (paper, plastic)
awwal	first	bee, bi	by, for
Hiwaar	conversation	arba9a	four
dukkaan	shop	alif	thousand
siid ad dukkaan	shopkeeper	ṭaiyib	alright, okay
zabuuna	customer (female)	waaHid	one
zabuun	customer (male)	Haaja	thing
izzeeyyak	how are you?	taani	again, more
ahlan	welcome	la'	no
inta (m), inti (f)	you (sg.)	<u>kh</u>alaaṣ	finished
kwaiyis (m), kwaiysa (f)	good, well	<u>sh</u>ukran	thank you
al Hamdu lillaa	thank God	ma9a s salaama	good-bye
fii	there is, are	diinaar	dinar,
ṣaabuun	soap		10 Sudanese pounds
9aawz (m), 9aawza (f)	want	tamriin	practice
kam	how much, many	9ee<u>sh</u>	bread
jiib	bring	laban	milk
itneen	two	zeet	oil
miliH	salt	dagiig	flour
maa	not	<u>sh</u>aay	tea
da	this, that	beeḍ	eggs
<u>sh</u>inuu	what?	laHam	meat
aiwa	yes	guruu<u>sh</u>	money
fii, fi	at, in		

1.4 Pronunciation drills: w, y, <u>sh</u>, g, f

Listen and repeat drills (see Introduction, section 3)

(a) w

hawa	air
jawaab	letter
dawa	medicine
sawa	together

(b) y

ziyaara	visit
biyuut	houses
naayim	sleeping
daayman	always

قفف
كفاية
سافر
شفت

وقف
لقيت
بقى
يقوم

مش
بشوف
ناشف
بشيل

(c) f

gufaf	baskets
kifaaya	enough
saafar	he travelled
shufta	I looked

(d) sh

masha	he went
bashuuf	I look
naashif	dry
bashiil	I take

(e) g

wagaf	he stood up
ligiit	I found
biga	he became
yaguum	it departs

الدرس التانى

حوار : الزيارة

ر : راجل (خواجة)　　ض : ضيف (سودانى)　　م : مرة

ر　اهلا.

ض　ازيك.

ر　انت شديد؟

ض　الحمد لله.　كيف انت؟

ر　كويس　اتفضل.

ض　انت عارف العربى كويس.

ر　شوية بس. اتفضل .

ض　انا درست انجليزى　فى المدرسة لكن الانجليزى صعب.

ر　العربى برضو صعب.

م　(المرة بتدخل)　اهلا وسهلا.

ض　ازيك. انت كويسة؟

ر　(للمرة) جيبى ليمون واعملى قهوة. (للضيف) فطرت؟

ض　لسع.

ر　انا شربت القهوة بدرى لكن ما فطرت.

م　اتفضل.　دا الليمون.　خلاص، الفطور جاهز.

ض　الفطور كويس.　شكرا.

م　عفوا.

تمرين

١,١,٢

شديد

اتفضل

عفوا

ad daris at taani

Hiwaar: az ziyaara

r: raajil (khawaaja) ḍ: ḍeef (suudaani)
m: mara

r: ahlan.
ḍ: izzeeyyak.
r: inta shadiid?
ḍ: al Hamdu lillaa. keef inta?
r: kwaiyis. itfaḍḍal.
ḍ: inta 9aarif 9arabi kwaiyis.
r: shwaiya bass. itfaḍḍal.
ḍ: ana darasta ingliizi fi l madrasa laakin al ingliizi ṣa9ab.
r: al 9arabi barḍu ṣa9ab.

(al mara bitadkhul.)

m: ahlan wa sahlan.
ḍ: izzeeyyik. inti kwaiysa?
r: (li l mara) jiibi leemuun u a9mili gahwa. (li ḍ ḍeef) faṭarta?
ḍ: lissa9.
r: ana shiribta l gahwa badri laakin maa faṭarta.
m: itfaḍḍal, da l leemuun. khalaaṣ, al faṭuur jaahiz.
ḍ: al faṭuur kwaiyis. shukran.
m: 9afwan.

Lesson 2

Dialogue: Visiting

m: man (foreigner) v: visitor (Sudanese)
w: woman

m: Welcome.
v: How are you?
m: Are you well?
v: Thank God, yes. And how are you?
m: Well. Come in.
v: You know Arabic well.
m: Only a little. Sit down.
v: I studied English at school but English is difficult.
m: Arabic is difficult as well.

(The woman comes in.)

w: Welcome.
v: How are you? Are you well?
m: (to the woman) Bring us some lemonade and make coffee. (to the visitor) Have you had breakfast?
v: Not yet.
m: I drank coffee early but haven't had breakfast.
w: Please go ahead, here's the lemonade. Breakfast is all ready.
v: The breakfast is good. Thank you.
w: You're welcome.

Notes on the dialogue

1. *bee, lee,* and *fii* become *bi, li,* and *fi* when followed by the definite article, e.g. *li l mara, fi l beet.*
2. The Sudanese eat breakfast, *faṭuur,* mid-morning. Lunch, *ghada,* is about 3 or 4 o'clock and supper, *9asha,* about 9 p.m. Of course, there are many personal variations on this.

2.1 Drills: tamriin

2.1.1 Greetings

Some new greetings and polite expressions are given in this dialogue.

1. *shadiid* has roughly the same meaning, when used as a greeting, as *kwaiyis*. It has feminine and plural forms, which are given in the vocabulary.
2. *itfaḍḍal* also has feminine and plural forms. It cannot be translated by one English phrase but serves as an invitation to do something, e.g. to come in if one is standing at the gate, to sit down when one enters a house, to eat or drink what is placed before one, or to feel free to leave when one gets up to go.
3. *9afwan* is simply the polite reply to *shukran*.

٢,١,٢

الليمون وين؟	دا الليمون	الليمون فى الكباية
العيش وين؟	دا العيش	العيش فى القفة
البيض وين؟	دا البيض	البيض فى الكيس
البيت وين؟	دا البيت	البيت فى العمارات

٢,١,٣

انتَ وين؟	انا فى البيت
انتِ وين؟	انا فى المدرسة
انتوا وين؟	نحن فى الخرطوم
انتَ كويس؟	ايوه، انا كويس
انتِ كويسة؟	ايوه، انا كويسة
انتوا كويسين؟	ايوه، نحن كويسين

٢,١,٤

انتَ فطرت؟	ايوه، انا فطرت	لا، انا ما فطرت
انتِ فطرتى؟	ايوه، انا فطرت	لا، انا ما فطرت
انتوا فطرتوا؟	ايوه، نحن فطرنا	لا، نحن ما فطرنا
انت درست العربى؟	ايوه، انا درست العربى	لا، انا ما درست العربى
انت درستى العربى؟	ايوه، انا درست العربى	لا، انا ما درست العربى
انتوا درستوا العربى؟	ايوه، نحن درسنا العربى	لا، نحن ما درسنا العربى
انت شربت موية؟	ايوه، انا شربت موية	لا، انا ما شربت موية
انت شربتى موية؟	ايوه، انا شربت موية	لا، انا ما شربت موية
انتوا شربتوا موية؟	ايوه، نحن شربنا موية	لا، نحن ما شربنا موية
انت سمعت؟	ايوه، انا سمعت	لا، انا ما سمعت
انت سمعتى؟	ايوه، انا سمعت	لا، انا ما سمعت
انتوا سمعتوا؟	ايوه، نحن سمعنا	لا، نحن ما سمعنا
انت قفلت الباب؟	ايوه، انا قفلت الباب	لا، انا ما قفلت الباب
انت قفلتى الباب؟	ايوه، انا قفلت الباب	لا، انا ما قفلت الباب
انتوا قفلتوا الباب؟	ايوه، نحن قفلنا الباب	لا، نحن ما قفلنا الباب

Practise the greetings exchange as you did in Lesson 1.

2.1.2 The definite article

The definite article in Sudanese Arabic is *al* but when it follows a word ending in a vowel the *a* is dropped, e.g. *fi al beet* 'in the house' becomes *fi l beet.*

Say the following sentences after your teacher. Note that *ween* means 'where' and the first sentence means 'Where is the lemonade?' *al leemuun fi l kubbaaya* means 'The lemonade is in the glass'.

al leemun ween?	da l leemuun	al leemuun fi l kubbaaya
al 9eesh ween?	da l 9eesh	al 9eesh fi l guffa
al beeḍ ween?	da l beeḍ	al beeḍ fi l kiis
al beet ween?	da l beet	al beet fi l 9amaaraat

2.1.3 Personal pronouns

You have already learned the words for 'you' singular: *inta* (masc.) and *inti* (fem.). In this lesson we add *ana* 'I', *niHna* 'we', and *intu* 'you (plural).' Practise the following question and answer drill in pairs.

inta ween?	ana fi l beet
inti ween?	ana fi l madrasa
intu ween?	niHna fi l kharṭuum
inta kwaiyis?	aiwa, ana kwaiyis
inti kwaiysa?	aiwa, ana kwaiysa
intu kwaiysiin?	aiwa, niHna kwaiysiin

2.1.4 Verbs: the past tense

Arabic has two main forms of the verb, one of which can be regarded for practical purposes as a past tense. As a pattern we can take the verb *faṭar* 'to have breakfast'. In this lesson only the 1st and 2nd persons are introduced. So we have *ana faṭarta* meaning 'I had breakfast', *inta faṭarta* meaning 'you had breakfast' and so on. Repeat the following drill after the teacher until you have memorized it. Then the teacher should ask one of the questions in the drill and see if the student can answer correctly, and so on.

inta faṭar-ta?	aiwa, ana faṭar-ta	la', ana maa faṭar-ta
inti faṭar-ti?	aiwa, ana faṭar-ta	la', ana maa faṭar-ta
intu faṭar-tu?	aiwa, niHna faṭar-na	la', niHna maa faṭar-na

Now repeat the same drill with these other verbs, some of which occur in the dialogue: *daras* 'to study', *shirib* 'to drink', *simi9* 'to hear', *gafal* 'to shut', *fataH* 'to open'.

inta darasta l 9arabi?	aiwa, ana darasta l 9arabi	la', ana maa darasta l 9arabi
inti darasti l 9arabi?	aiwa, ana darasta l 9arabi	la'. ana maa darasta l 9arabi
intu darastu l 9arabi?	aiwa, niHna darasna l 9arabi	la', niHna maa darasna l 9arabi
inta shiribta mooya?	aiwa, ana shiribta mooya	la', ana maa shiribta mooya
inti shiribti mooya?	aiwa, ana shiribta mooya	la', ana maa shiribta mooya
intu shiribtu mooya?	aiwa, niHna shiribna mooya	la', niHna maa shiribna mooya
inta simi9ta?	aiwa, ana simi9ta	la', ana maa simi9ta
inti simi9ti?	aiwa, ana simi9ta	la', ana maa simi9ta
intu simi9tu?	aiwa, niHna simi9na	la', niHna maa simi9na
inta gafalta l baab?	aiwa, ana gafalta l baab	la', ana maa gafalta l baab
inti gafalti l baab?	aiwa, ana gafalta l baab	la', ana maa gafalta l baab
intu gafaltu l baab	aiwa, niHna gafalna l baab	la', niHna maa gafalna l baab

انت فتحت الشباك؟	ايوه، انا فتحت الشباك	لا، انا ما فتحت الشباك
انت فتحتى الشباك؟	ايوه، انا فتحت الشباك	لا، انا ما فتحت الشباك
انتوا فتحتوا الشباك؟	ايوه، نحن فتحنا الشباك	لا، نحن ما فتحنا الشباك

٢,١,٥

انا، موية.....انا شربت موية

انتَ....العربى	انتوا....فى المدرسة
نحن....الباب	نحن....القهوة
انتِ....لبن	انتِ....فى البيت
انا....بدرى	انتَ....فى الخرطوم

كلمات

تانى
زيارة
راجل
خواجة
خواجية
ضيف
ضيفة
سودانى
سودانية
شديد شديدة شديدين
كيف
اتفضل اتفضلى اتفضلوا
عارف
عربى
شوية
بس
درس
انجليزى
مدرسة
لكن
صعب
برضو
مرة
دخل
ل
ليمون
و
اعملى
قهوة
فطر
لسع
انا
شرب
بدرى
فطور
جاهز
عفوا
غدا
عشا
وين
كباية
قفة
بيت
العمارات
انتوا
نحن
الخرطوم
موية
سمع
قفل
فتح
باب
شباك

inta fataHta <u>sh</u> <u>sh</u>ubbaak?	aiwa, ana fataHta <u>sh</u> <u>sh</u>ubbaak	la', ana maa fataHta <u>sh</u> <u>sh</u>ubbaak
inti fataHti <u>sh</u> <u>sh</u>ubbaak?	aiwa, ana fataHta <u>sh</u> <u>sh</u>ubbaak	la', ana maa fataHta <u>sh</u> <u>sh</u>ubbaak
intu fataHtu <u>sh</u> <u>sh</u>ubbaak?	aiwa, niHna fataHna <u>sh</u> <u>sh</u>ubbaak	la', niHna maa fataHna <u>sh</u> <u>sh</u>ubbaak

2.1.5 More practice on verbs

Fill in the gaps in the following sentences with one of the verbs from drill 2.1.4 in the correct form. For example, *ana ____ mooya → ana <u>sh</u>iribta mooya*. This can be done orally with the teacher.

inta_____9arabi		intu_____fi l madrasa
niHna____l baab		niHna_____gahwa
inti_____laban		inti_____fi l beet
ana_____badri		inta_____fi l <u>kh</u>arṭuum

2.2 Role play

Act out the parts of a foreigner visiting a Sudanese neighbour or being visited by them. Start visiting your own neighbours. It is quite acceptable for you to knock on a neighbour's door and say that you have come to greet them; or you can start to greet them when you meet them in the street. Hospitality is highly valued in Sudanese society and it is not uncommon for a foreigner to be invited into the house of a total stranger out of sheer friendliness.

2.3 Vocabulary: kalmaat

taani	second	a9mili	make! (f)
ziyaara	visit	gahwa	coffee
raajil	man	faṭar	to have breakfast
<u>kh</u>awaaja	foreigner (male)	lissa9	not yet
<u>kh</u>awaajiiya	foreigner (female)	ana	I
ḍeef	visitor, guest (male)	<u>sh</u>irib	to drink
ḍeefa	visitor (female)	badri	early
suudaani	Sudanese (male)	faṭuur	breakfast
suudaaniiya	Sudanese (female)	jaahiz	ready
<u>sh</u>adiid (m), <u>sh</u>adiida (f),	well	9afwan	reply to "thank you"
<u>sh</u>adiidiin (pl)		<u>gh</u>ada	lunch
keef	how	9a<u>sh</u>a	supper
itfaḍḍal (m),	(see drill in 2.1.1)	ween	where?
itfaḍḍali (f),		kubbaaya	drinking glass, cup
itfaḍḍalu (pl)		guffa	basket
9aarif	know, knowing	beet	house
9arabi	Arabic	al 9amaaraat	the New Extension,
<u>sh</u>waiya	a little		suburb of Khartoum
bass	only	intu	you (plural)
daras	to study	niHna	we
ingliizi	English	al <u>kh</u>arṭuum	Khartoum
madrasa	school	mooya	water
laakin	but	simi9	to hear
ṣa9ab	difficult	gafal	to shut
barḍu	also	fataH	to open
mara	woman	baab	door, gate
da<u>kh</u>al	to enter	<u>sh</u>ubbaak	window
lee, li	to, for		
leemuun	lemon, lime		
u, w	and		

تمرين الاصوات

مكنة	شمال	بنات
شكى	ليمون	جنينة
ساكن	سمك	سنة
اكلت	نمرة	ينوم
قبيلة	زرقا	
لبن	زيت	
جبل	زول	
ابدا	زيارة	

2.4 Pronunciation drills: k, m, n, b, z

Listen and repeat drills

k		**m**		**n**	
makana	engine	shimaal	left	banaat	girls
shaka	he complained	leemuun	limes	jineena	garden
saakin	living	samak	fish	sana	year
akalta	I ate	nimra	number	yanuum	he sleeps

b		**z**	
gabiila	tribe	zarga	blue
laban	milk	zeet	oil
jabal	hill	zool	person
abadan	never	ziyaara	visit

الدرس التالت

حوار : فى الباب

ر : راحل و : ولد خ : خدام

ر يا ولد، احمد ساكن هنا؟

و ايوه. البيت جنب الدكان.

ر شكرا. (هو بيدق الباب والخدام بيفتح)

ر احمد موجود؟

خ لا، هو سافر امبارح.

ر سافر وين؟

خ سافر شندى وزينب سافرت كمان.

ر هم ركبوا الباص ولا القطر؟

خ ركبوا الباص.

ر فى زول عيان فى شندى؟

خ لا، واحد من الاخوان رجع من برا.

ر الاولاد موجودين؟

خ لا، مرقوا هسع.

ر معليش. الساعة كم؟

خ الساعة خمسة.

ر شكرا. مع السلامة.

خ مع السلامة.

اهلا، يا نفيسة

الزيت واللبن

مرقوا هسع فطرهسع

تمرين

٣,١,١

ad daris at taalit — Lesson 3

Hiwaar: fi l baab — Dialogue: At the gate

r: raajil w: walad k: khaddaam	m: man b: boy s: man-servant
r: ya walad, aHmad saakin hina?	m: Boy, does Ahmad live here?
w: aiwa. al beet jamb ad dukkaan.	b: Yes. The house next to the shop.
r: shukran.	m: Thank you.
(hu bidugg al baab w al khaddaam biyaftaH.)	(He knocks at the gate and the servant opens it.)
r: aHmad moojuud?	m: Is Ahmad here?
k: la', hu saafar umbaariH.	s: No, he travelled yesterday.
r: saafar ween?	m: Where has he gone?
k: saafar shandi u zeinab saafarat kamaan.	s: He's gone to Shendi and Zeinab has also gone.
r: hum rikbu l baaṣ walla l gaṭar?	m: Did they take the bus or the train?
k: rikbu l baaṣ.	s: They took the bus.
r: fii zool 9ayyaan fii shandi?	m: Is someone ill in Shendi?
k: la', waaHid min al akhwaan raja9 min barra.	s: No, one of the brothers has returned from abroad.
r: al awlaad moojuudiin?	m: Are the children at home?
k: la', maragu hassa9.	s: No, they have just gone out.
r: ma9leesh. as saa9a kam?	m: Never mind. What's the time?
k: as saa9a khamsa.	s: It's 5 o'clock.
r: shukran. ma9a s salaama.	m: Thank-you. Good-bye.
k: ma9a s salaama.	s: Good-bye.

Notes on the dialogue

1. *ya* is a word placed in front of people's names or term of address when you speak to them directly, e.g. *ahlan, ya nafiisa,* "Welcome, Nafisa."
2. *u* 'and' when followed by the definite article becomes *w*, e.g. *az zeet w al laban* 'the oil and the milk'.
3. *hassa9* 'now' is used where English has 'just' in a sentence, such as *maragu hassa9* 'they have just gone out' or *faṭar hassa9* 'he has just had breakfast'.

3.1 Drills: tamriin

3.1.1 The past tense completed

In this lesson we introduce the 3rd person of the past tense. A few points about the past tense should be noted.

1. This tense can be used to translate both the English past tenses, e.g. 'he studied' and 'he has studied' would both be *daras.*
2. The 3rd person masculine singular of the past tense is the form of the verb quoted in the vocabularies, e.g. *daras, saafar,* etc.
3. The vowels of the past tense are always *a-a* or *i-i.* When the vowels are *i-i,* the second *i* is dropped if the ending begins with a vowel, i.e. in the 3rd feminine singular and 3rd plural, e.g. *shirib + at → shirbat; rikib + u → rikbu.*

درست	درسنا
درست	درستوا
درستى	
درس	درسوا
درست	

فطرت (والى آخره) مرقت رجعت سافرت ركبت سمعت

هى، سافر هى سافرت (والى آخره)

٣,١,٢

هو درس شنو؟	هو درس العربى
هو درس العربى وين؟	هو درس العربى فى الخرطوم
هو ركب شنو؟	هو ركب الباص
هو ركب الباص امبارح؟	لا، هو ما ركب الباص امبارح
هى رجعت من وين؟	هى رجعت من شندى
هى رجعت من شندى مع الاولاد؟	لا، هى ما رجعت من شندى مع الاولاد
هى شربت شنو؟	هى شربت قهوة
هى شربت قهوة بدرى؟	ايوه، هى شربت فهوة الساعة سته
هم قفلوا الباب؟	ايوه، هم قفلوا الباب كويس
هم قفلوا الباب كيف؟	هم قفلوا الباب من برا
هم سافروا شندى؟	لا، هم سافروا الخرطوم
هم سافروا الخرطوم الساعة تلاتة؟	لا، هم سافروا الخرطوم الساعه اربعة
القطر وقف؟	ايوه، القطر وقف
الولد مرق هسع؟	ايوه، الولد مرق مع الخدام
المرة فتحت الباب؟	لا، المرة ما فتحت الباب
الاخوان فطروا مع احمد؟	لا، الاخوان فطروا فى البيت

٣,١,٣

Repeat the following drill until you have memorized it.

	Singular	**Plural**
1st	daras-ta	daras-na
2nd m	daras-ta	daras-tu
2nd f	daras-ti	
3rd m	daras	daras-u
3rd f	daras-at	

Now try the same drill with other verbs: *faṭar* 'to have breakfast', *marag* 'to go out', *raja9* 'to return', *saafar* 'to go on a journey', *rikib* 'to ride', *simi9* 'to hear'.

As a third step the teacher should name a pronoun and verb and let the student give the appropriate form of the verb, e.g. teacher says *hi* and *saafar*; student replies *hi saafarat*.

3.1.2 More practice on the past tense

Repeat the following sentences after the teacher. They are set out as questions and answers.

hu daras <u>sh</u>inuu?	hu daras al 9arabi.
hu daras al 9arabi ween?	hu daras al 9arabi fi l <u>kh</u>arṭuum.
hu rikib <u>sh</u>inuu?	hu rikib al baaṣ.
hu rikib al baaṣ umbaariH?	la', hu maa rikib al baaṣ umbaariH.

hi raja9at min ween?	hi raja9at min <u>sh</u>andi.
hi raja9at min <u>sh</u>andi ma9a l awlaad?	la', hi maa raja9at min <u>sh</u>andi ma9a l awlaad.
hi <u>sh</u>irbat <u>sh</u>inuu?	hi <u>sh</u>irbat gahwa.
hi <u>sh</u>irbat gahwa badri?	aiwa, hi <u>sh</u>irbat gahwa s saa9a sitta.

hum gafalu l baab?	aiwa, hum gafalu l baab kwaiyis.
hum gafalu l baab keef?	hum gafalu l baab min barra.
hum saafaru <u>sh</u>andi?	la', hum saafaru l <u>kh</u>arṭuum.
hum saafaru l <u>kh</u>arṭuum as saa9a talaata?	la', hum saafaru l <u>kh</u>arṭuum as saa9a arba9a.

al gaṭar wagaf?	aiwa, al gaṭar wagaf.
al walad marag hassa9?	aiwa, al walad marag ma9a l <u>kh</u>addaam.
al mara fataHat al baab?	la', al mara maa fataHat al baab.
al a<u>kh</u>waan faṭaru ma9a aHmad?	la', al a<u>kh</u>waan faṭaru fi l beet.

Now in pairs or round the class, using the vocabulary you have learned, ask each other questions and provide appropriate answers, not necessarily from the above sentences.

3.1.3 More on the definite article

As we saw, the definite article is *al*, but when it comes before a noun which begins with a consonant pronounced with the tip of the tongue the *l* is changed into that same letter, e.g. *al + raajil* 'the man' becomes *ar raajil*. The following is a list of the letters pronounced with the tongue tip: *t, d, ṭ, ḍ, s, z, ṣ, ẓ, sh, j, n, r, l*. In Arabic these are known as 'sun letters.' Before the remaining letters of the alphabet, called in Arabic 'moon letters,' the definite article appears as *al*.

التانى	البيت
الدكان	الفطور
الطربيزة	الولد
الضيف	الملح
السكر	الكباية
الزيارة	القهوة
الصابون	الخرطوم
الظرف	الغنم
الشاى	الهوا
الجبنة	الحاجة
الناس	العربى
الراجل	اليوم
الليموم	

بيت البيت (والى آخره)

٣,١,٤

انت ساكن وين؟	انا ساكن فى الخرطوم
انت ساكنة وين؟	انا ساكنة فى الخرطوم
انتوا ساكنين وين؟	نحن ساكنين فى الخرطوم
هو ساكن هنا؟	لا، هو ما ساكن هنا
هى ساكنة هنا؟	لا، هى ما ساكنة هنا
هم ساكنين هنا؟	لا، هم ما ساكنين هنا
انت عيان؟	ايوه، انا عيان
انت عيانة؟	ايوه، انا عيانة
انتوا عيانين؟	ايوه، نحن عيانين
هو عيان؟	لا، هو ما عيان
هى عيانة؟	لا، هى ما عيانة
هم عيانين؟	لا، هم ما عيانين
هو موجود؟	لا، هو مرق هسع
الراجل موجود؟	ايوه، هو موجود
احمد موجود؟	ايوه، اتفضل
الضيفة موجودة؟	ايوه، هى موجودة
الخواجية موجودة؟	لا، هى مرقت هسع
الاولاد موجودين؟	ايوه، هم موجودين
الاخوان موجودين؟	لا ، هم مرقوا هسع

The teacher should read the list below vertically and then horizontally, the student repeating after him.

at taani	al beet
ad dukkaan	al faṭuur
aṭ ṭarabeeza	al walad
aḍ ḍeef	al miliH
as sukkar	al kubbaaya
az ziyaara	al gahwa
aṣ ṣaabuun	al kharṭuum
aẓ ẓarif	al ghanam
ash shaay	al hawa
aj jibna	al Haaja
an naas	al 9arabi
ar raajil	al yoom
al leemuun	

Now the teacher can pick nouns at random and let the student give the correct form of the definite article with the noun, e.g. teacher says *beet* and student replies *al beet.*

3.1.4 *saakin, 9ayyaan,* and *moojuud*

These are three more useful words which follow the same pattern as *9aawz,* i.e. they have a masculine form, given above, a feminine form ending in *-a,* and a plural ending in *-iin. saakin* means 'live', e.g. *ana saakin fi l 9amaaraat* means 'I live in the New Extension/Amarat'. *9ayyaan* means 'ill', and *moojuud* means 'present', e.g. *hu moojuud* means 'he is present/here'. Repeat the following sentences after the teacher.

inta saakin ween?	ana saakin fi l kharṭuum *(or name the place where you live)*
inti saakna ween?	ana saakna fi l kharṭuum.
intu saakniin ween?	niHna saakniin fi l kharṭuum.
hu saakin hina?	la', hu maa saakin hina.
hi saakna hina?	la', hi maa saakna hina.
hum saakniin hina?	la', hum maa saakniin hina.
inta 9ayyaan?	aiwa, ana 9ayyaan.
inti 9ayyaana?	aiwa, ana 9ayyaana.
intu 9ayyaaniin?	aiwa, niHna 9ayyaaniin.
hu 9ayyaan?	la', hu maa 9ayyaan.
hi 9ayyaana?	la', hi maa 9ayyaana.
hum 9ayyaaniin?	la', hum maa 9ayyaaniin.
hu moojuud?	la', hu marag hassa9.
ar raajil moojuud?	aiwa, hu moojuud.
aHmad moojuud?	aiwa, itfaḍḍal.
aḍ ḍeefa moojuuda?	aiwa, hi moojuuda.
al khawaajiiya moojuuda?	la', hi maragat hassa9.
al awlaad moojuudiin?	aiwa, hum moojuudiin.
al akhwaan moojuudiin?	la', hum maragu hassa9.

كلمات

تالت
ولد
خدام
خدامة
ساكن
هنا
جنب
دق
موجود
سافر
امبارح
كمان
هم
ركب
باص
ولا
قطر
زول
عيان
من
اخوان (اخو)

رجع
برا
اولاد
مرق
هسع
معليش
ساعة
خمسة
هو
هى
ستة
وقف
مع
جبنة
ظرف
طربيزة
غنم
ناس
هوا
يوم

تمرين الاصوات

جبنة
جاب
جسم
جمل

يجيب
سجوك
بيجى
راجل

رقد
ركب
راس
راجل

مَرَة
شراب
شركة
فرش

خبر
خدروات
خفيف
خور

اخد
اخت
اخيرا
اخدر

غلب
غالى
غدا
غنم

لغة
شغل
مغرب
يغلب

3.2 Role play

Act out the parts of someone calling at a house and having a conversation at the gate with the person who opens the gate.

3.3 Vocabulary: kalmaat

taalit	third
walad	boy
khaddaam	servant (male)
khaddaama	servant (female)
saakin	living
hina	here
jamb	beside
dagga	to knock
moojuud	present, here
saafar	to travel
umbaariH	yesterday
kamaan	also
hum	they
rikib	to ride, get on
baaṣ	bus
walla	or
gaṭar	train
zool	person
9ayyaan	ill
min	from, among
akhwaan	brothers (sg. akhu)
raja9	to return
barra	outside, abroad
awlaad	children
marag	to go out
hassa9	now, just
ma9leesh	never mind, sorry
saa9a	hour, watch
khamsa	five
hu	he
hi	she
sitta	six
wagaf	stop, stand
ma9a	with
jibna	cheese
ẓarif	envelope
ṭarabeeza	table
ghanam	goat
naas	people
hawa (m)	air
yoom	day

3.4 Pronunciation drills: j, r, kh, gh

Listen and repeat drills with consonants at the beginning of the word, then in the middle of the word.

a) j

jibna	cheese
jaab	he brought
jisim	body
jamal	camel

b) j

yajiib	he brings
sujuuk	sausages
biiji	he will come
raajil	man

c) r

ragad	he lay down
rikib	he rode
raas	head
raajil	man

d) r

mara	woman
sharaab	a drink
sharika	company
farish	bed

e) kh

khabar	news
khudrawaat	vegetables
khafiif	light
khoor	river bed

f) kh

akhad	he took
ukhut	sister
akhiiran	finally
akhdar	green

g) gh

ghalab	he won
ghaali	expensive
ghada	lunch
ghanam	goat

h) gh

lugha	language
shughul	work
mughrib	sunset
yaghlib	he wins

الدرس الرابع

حوار: التكسى

أ : أمين ح : حسن س : سواق

ا شوف. العربية ما ماشة كل كل.

ح صلحت المكنة؟

ا صلحت المكنة وغيرت الزيت لكن البطارية بايظة.

ح معليش. ما ضرورى. فى تكسى هنا. (هو بيوقف تكسى)

ا نحن ماشين امدرمان. بكم لامدرمان؟

س بسبعة الف.

ا دا كتير. بخمسة؟

س لا، خمسة شوية.

ا طيب. بستة كويس؟

س خلاص. كويس. اتفضلوا. (هم بيركبوا والتكسى بيقوم)

ح بعد الكبرى بشارع الموردة.

س كويس.

ح لو سمحت لف شمال، بعدين طوالى ... لو سمحت، لف يمين جنب المدرسة.

ا الشارع داك بعد السوق ... قدام شوية.

ح خلاص، أقيف هنا. شكرا. مع السلامة.

تمرين

٤،١،١

ad daris ar raabi9 — Lesson 4

Hiwaar: at taksi — Dialogue: The taxi

a: amiin H: Hassan s: sawwaag	A: Amin H: Hassan d: driver
a: shuuf. al 9arabiiya maa maasha kullu kullu.	A: Look, the car won't go at all.
H: ṣallaHta l makana?	H: Did you repair the engine?
a: ṣallaHta l makana u ghayyarta z zeet laakin al baṭṭaariiya baayẓa.	A: I repaired the engine and changed the oil but the battery's dead.
H: ma9leesh. maa ḍaruuri. fii taksi hina.	H: Never mind. It's not necessary. There's a taxi here.
(hu biwaggif taksi.)	(He stops a taxi.)
a: niHna maashiin umdurmaan. bee kam lee umdurmaan?	A: We are going to Omdurman. How much to Omdurman?
s: bee sab9a alif.	d: Seven thousand.
a: da katiir. bee khamsa?	A: That's a lot. How about five thousand?
s: la', khamsa shwaiya.	d: No, five is too little.
a: ṭaiyib. bee sitta kwaiyis?	A: Okay, is six all right?
s: khalaaṣ. kwaiyis. itfaḍḍalu.	d: Done. All right. Get in.
(hum biyarkabu w at taksi biguum.)	(They get in and the taxi sets off.)
H: ba9d al kubri bee shaari9 al moorada.	H: After the bridge take the Moorada road.
s: kwaiyis.	d: Good.
H: law samaHta, liff shimaal, ba9deen ṭawwaali... law samaHta, liff yamiin jamb al madrasa.	H: Please turn left, then straight on...turn right beside the school.
a: ash shaari9 daak ba9d as suug...giddaam shwaiya.	A: That street after the market... a little further.
H: khalaaṣ, agiif hina. shukran. ma9a s salaama.	H: Okay, stop here. Thank you. Good-bye.

4.1 Drills: tamriin

4.1.1 Some variations in the verb in the past tense

You may have noticed that nearly all the verbs that have occurred in the dialogues so far have just three consonants. This is not chance. A large majority of Arabic words do have three basic consonants. It is useful to know what the three basic consonants of a word are, because one often finds words of related meaning with the same three consonants but a different arrangement of vowels, or one of the consonants doubled, or some other variation, e.g. *daris* 'lesson', *daras* 'to study', *darras* 'to teach', *mudarris* 'teacher', *diraasa* 'the study'.

The basic type of verb is the one you have learned already. Here are introduced two variations on it:

a) The middle of the three consonants is doubled. This is also a common type, e.g. *ṣallaH* 'to repair', *ghayyar* 'to change', *ghassal* 'to wash', etc.
b) The first *a* is doubled, e.g. *saafar* 'to travel', *saa9ad* 'to help',

Note that these variations always have *a-a* as vowels in the past tense.

Repeat the following sentences after the teacher with attention to good pronunciation. Then, using them to start from, make new sentences by changing one part of the sentence at a time, e.g. *ana ṣallaHta l makana* 'I have repaired the engine' becomes *inta ṣallaHta l makana* 'you have repaired the engine'; *as sawwaag ṣallaH al makana* 'the driver has repaired the engine', etc. You could change *al walad ghayyar al mooya* 'the boy changed the water' to *al walad shirib al mooya* 'the boy drank the water', and so on.

انا صلحت المكنة
انا صلحت العربية
انا صلحت البيت

انت سافرتى امبارح؟
انت سافرتى بدرى؟

الولد غير الزيت
الولد غير البطارية
الولد غير الموية

نحن ساعدنا الراجل
نحن ساعدنا السواق

المرة غسلت العدة
المرة غسلت الكباية
المرة غسلت البلاط

٤,١,٢

اللحم كويس	الجبنة كويسة
الفطور جاهز	القهوة جاهزة
التكسى بايظ	العربية بايظة
القطر ماشى	العربية ماشة
الولد عيان	المرة عيانة

عيش العيش كويس

التكسى وقف العربية وقفت

٤,١,٣

ana ṣallaHta l makana
ana ṣallaHta l 9arabiiya
ana ṣallaHta l beet

al walad ghayyar az zeet
al walad ghayyar al baṭṭaariiya
al walad ghayyar al mooya

al mara ghassalat al 9idda
al mara ghassalat al kubbaaya
al mara ghassalat al balaaṭ

inti saafarti umbaariH?
inti saafarti badri?

niHna saa9adna r raajil
niHna saa9adna s sawwaag

4.1.2 Masculine and feminine

As with some European languages like French and Spanish, all nouns in Arabic belong to one of two groups, known as masculine and feminine, e.g. *9eesh* 'bread' is masculine and *jibna* 'cheese' is feminine. It is easy in Arabic to tell to which group a word belongs.

a) Some nouns are masculine or feminine by meaning because they refer to persons, e.g. *raajil* 'man' is masculine and *mara* 'woman' is feminine.
b) Nouns that end in *-a* and do not refer to male persons are feminine, e.g. *mooya* 'water', *jibna* 'cheese', etc. There are a few exceptions which will be noted in the vocabularies and glossary.
c) With a few exceptions which will be noted, all other words are masculine, e.g. *zeet* 'oil', *gaṭar* 'train', etc.

Like the pronouns, the masculine nouns go with the masculine form of adjectives and feminine nouns with the feminine form. Listen and repeat the following drill after the teacher.

al laHam kwaiyis
al faṭuur jaahiz
at taksi baayiẓ
al gaṭar maashi
al walad 9ayyaan

aj jibna kwaiysa
al gahwa jaahza
al 9arabiiya baayẓa
al 9arabiiya maasha
al mara 9ayyaana

Now the teacher should say a noun, any noun known to the students, and let them pair it with an appropriate adjective, e.g. teacher says *9eesh* and student replies *al 9eesh kwaiyis.*

Note that with verbs masculine nouns take the 3rd person singular masculine, and feminine nouns take the 3rd person singular feminine even when they refer to things, e.g. *at taksi wagaf,* but *al 9arabiiya wagafat.*

4.1.3 *maashi* 'going'

maashi means 'going', and follows the same pattern as *saakin,* e.g. *hu maashi s suug* 'he is going to the market', *hi maasha s suug* 'she is going to the market', *hum maashiin as suug* 'they are going to the market'.

انت ماشى وين؟	انا ماشى البيت
انت ماشة وين؟	انا ماشة الخرطوم
انتوا ماشين وين؟	نحن ماشين امدرمان
هو ماشى وين؟	هو ماشى الدكان
هى ماشة وين؟	هى ماشة السوق
هم ماشين وين؟	هم ماشين المدرسة

٤,١,٤

درس، دروس	مدرسة، مدارس
دكان، دكاكين	بيت، بيوت
زبون، زباين	باب، ابواب
زبونة، زبونات	كباية، كبابى
كيس، اكياس	قفة، قفف
حاجه، حاجات	ولد، أولاد
راجل، رجال	خدام، خدامين
ضيف، ضيوف	خدامة، خدامات
ضيفة، ضيفات	باص، باصات
خواجة، خواجات	قطر، قطرات
خواجية، خواجيات	ظرف، ظروف
سودانى، سودانيين	طربيزة، طربيزات
سودانية، سودانيات	شباك، شبابيك
	يوم، ايام

كلمات

رابع
تكسى، تكاسى
سواق، سواقين
شوف، شوفى، شوفوا
عربية، عربات
لو سمحت
ماشى، ماشة، ماشين

صلح
مكنة، مكنات
غيّر
بطارية، بطاريات
بايظ، بايظة
ضرورى
وقّف
امدرمان
سبعة
كتير

Repeat after the teacher:

inta maashi ween?	ana maashi l beet.
inti maasha ween?	ana maasha l kharṭuum.
intu maashiin ween?	niHna maashiin umdurmaan.
hu maashi ween?	hu maashi d dukkaan.
hi maasha ween?	hi maasha s suug.
hum maashiin ween?	hum maashiin al madrasa.

4.1.4 Note on grammar

Plurals of nouns: From this Lesson on, the plurals of nouns will be given after their singulars in the vocabularies. You should learn both together. There is no single way of forming plurals from singulars in Arabic; some nouns have an ending such as *-iin* or *-aat,* and others change the vowels. But the basic consonants generally remain the same (see drill 4.1.1 on verbs).

Listed here are nouns introduced in Lessons 1–3 with their plurals.

daris, duruus	lesson	madrasa, madaaris	school
dukkaan, dakaakiin	shop, store	beet, biyuut	house
zabuun, zabaayin	customer (m)	baab, abwaab	door
zabuuna, zabuunaat	customer (f)	kubbaaya, kabaabi	cup
kiis, akyaas	bag	guffa, gufaf	basket
Haaja, Haajaat	thing	walad, awlaad	boy
raajil, rujaal	man	khaddaam, khaddaamiin	servant (m)
ḍeef, ḍuyuuf	visitor (m)	khaddaama, khaddaamaat	servant (f)
ḍeefa, ḍeefaat	visitor (f)	baaṣ, baaṣaat	bus
khawaaja, khawaajaat	foreigner (m)	gaṭar, gaṭraat	train
khawaajiiya, khawaajiiyaat	foreigner (f)	ẓarif, ẓuruuf	envelope
suudaani, suudaaniyiin	Sudanese (m)	ṭarabeeza, ṭarabeezaat	table
suudaaniiya, suudaaniyaat	Sudanese (f)	shubbaak, shabaabiik	window
		yoom, ayyaam	day

4.2 Role play

Act out the parts of a taxi driver and some people wishing to ride in his taxi, as in the dialogue. You may be limited as to how much bargaining you can do because numbers are not introduced until Lesson 5. But sometimes gestures can work as well as words.

Follow up your classroom practice with a real taxi ride, but do know the price and the route beforehand so that you can give the driver instructions. Alternatively, you could ask your teacher or a Sudanese friend to take you somewhere by taxi and listen to how they do it.

4.3 Vocabulary: kalmaat

raabi9	fourth	ṣallaH	to repair
taksi, takaasi	taxi	makana, makanaat	engine
sawwaag, sawwaagiin	driver	ghayyar	to change
shuuf (m),	look!	baṭṭaariiya, baṭṭaariiyaat	battery
shuufi (f),		baayiẓ (m),	not working
shuufu (pl)		baayẓa (f)	
9arabiiya, 9arabaat	car	ḍaruuri	necessary
law samaHta	please	waggaf	to stop (something)
maashi (m),	going	umdurmaan	Omdurman
maasha (f),		sab9a	seven
maashiin (pl)		katiir	many, much, often

كل كل	قام
بعد	قدام
كبرى، كبارى	داك
شارع، شوارع	اقيف
لف	غسّل
شمال	ساعد
بعدين	عدة
طوالى	بلاط
يمين	ممكن
سوق، اسواق	

تمرين الاصوات

بيت	زول
ليل	خور
زيت	نوم
جيران	لون
ليمون	نوتة

شرق	كتير
يمسك	قديم
جلد	جديد
درس	تقيل
ممكن	يمين

كتب	شهور
جُزر	دروس
بطن	جنوب
سخن	بيوت
اخت	قروش

kullu kullu	at all	gaam	to depart, set off
ba9d	after	giddaam	further, in front
kubri, kabaari	bridge	daak	that
shaari9, shawaari9	street	agiif	stop!
liff	turn!	ghassal	to wash
shimaal	left	saa9ad	to help
ba9deen	and then, later	9idda	kitchen utensils
ṭawwaali	straight on, continually	balaaṭ	floor
yamiin	right	mumkin	possible
suug, aswaag	market, shops		

4.4 Pronunciation drills: ee, oo, i, ii, u, uu

Lists (a) and (b) are Listen and Repeat drills with *ee* and *oo* words

(a) ee		**(b) oo**	
beet	house	zool	person
leel	night	khoor	river bed
zeet	oil	noom	sleep
jeeraan	neighbours	loon	color
leemuun	limes	noota	notebook

Contrast Drills

See Introduction, section 3 Contrast drills for instructions. Lists (c) and (d) are contrasting *i* and *ii* in second syllable; lists (e) and (f) are contrasting *u* and *uu* in second syllable.

(c) i		**(d) ii**	
sharig	east	katiir	many
yamsik	he holds	gadiim	old
jilid	leather	jadiid	new
daris	lesson	tagiil	heavy
mumkin	possible	yamiin	right

(e) u		**(f) uu**	
kutub	books	shuhuur	months
juzur	islands	duruus	lessons
baṭun	belly	januub	south
sukhun	hot	biyuut	houses
ukhut	sister	guruush	money

الدرس الخامس

حوار : فى المطعم

ر : راجل　　م : مرة　　و : ولد

ر　فى محل فاضى؟

و　فى طربيزات هناك جنب الباب داك.

ر　(للمرة) الطربيزة دى كويسة؟

م　لا، دى قريبة من الباب. ديك أحسن

ر　طيب، اتفضلى. انت دايرة حاجة باردة؟

م　دايرة عصير برتكان.

ر　(للولد) أسمع. جيب اتنين عصير ، واحد برتكان وواحد جوافة.

و　حاضر ، يا سيد.

ر　فى لستة؟

و　ايوه، فى. (جايب اللستة)

م　السمك محمر؟

و　ايوه.

ر　(للمرة) اكلتى كباب؟ الكباب هنا مخصوص.

م　طيب. عاوزة كباب ببطاطس محمر وسلطة اسود.

ر　انا داير شوربة وجداد مشوى.

و　يعنى واحد كباب ببطاطس محمر وواحد شوربة وواحد جداد مشوى. ما فى سلطة اسود اليلة.

(الولد بيجيب الاكل)

م　الاكل لزيز ، مش كدا؟

ر　ايوه، لزيز جدا.

تمرين

٥,١,١

دا سمك	السمك دا لزيز
دا لحم	اللحم دا لزيز
دا بيض	البيض دا لزيز
دا كباب	الكباب دا لزيز
دى شوربة	الشوربة دى لزيزة

ad daris al <u>kh</u>aamis

Hiwaar: fi l maṭ9am

r: raajil   m: mara   w: walad

r: fii maHall faaḍi?
w: fii ṭarabeezaat hinaak jamb al baab daak.
r: (li l mara) aṭ ṭarabeeza di kwaiysa?
m: la', di gariiba min al baab. diik aHsan.

r: ṭaiyib, itfaḍḍali. inti daayra Haaja baarda?

m: daayra 9aṣiir burtukaan.
r: (li l walad) asma9. jiib itneen 9aṣiir, waaHid
   burtukaan u waaHid jawaafa.
w: Haaḍir, ya seeyid.
r: fii lista?
w: aiwa, fii. (jaayib al lista)
m: as samak muHammar?
w: aiwa.
r: (li l mara) akalti kabaab? al kabaab hina
   ma<u>kh</u>ṣuuṣ.
m: ṭaiyib. 9aawza kabaab bee baṭaaṭis
   muHammar u salaṭat aswad.
r: ana daayir <u>sh</u>oorba u jidaad ma<u>sh</u>wi.
w: ya9ni, waaHid kabaab bee baṭaaṭis
   muHammar u waaHid <u>sh</u>oorba u waaHid
   jidaad ma<u>sh</u>wi. maa fii salaṭat aswad alleela.

   (al walad bijiib al akil)
m: al akil laziiz, mu<u>sh</u> kida?
r: aiwa, laziiz jiddan.

Lesson 5

Dialogue: At the restaurant

m: man   w: woman   x: waiter

m: Is there an empty place?
x: There are tables over there next to that door.
m: (to the woman) Is this table all right?
w: No, this one is too near the door. That one's
   better.
m: Okay, have a seat. Would you like something
   cold to drink?
w: I'd like an orange juice.
m: (to the waiter) Waiter! Bring us two juices,
   one orange and one guava.
x: Certainly, sir.
m: Is there a menu?
x: Yes, there is. (brings the menu)
w: Is the fish fried?
x: Yes.
m: (to the woman) Have you eaten kebab? The
   kebab here is a speciality.
w: Fine. I'll have kebab with fried potatoes and
   aubergine salad.
m: I'll have soup and grilled chicken.
x: So that's one kebab with fried potatoes, one
   soup, and one grilled chicken. There's no
   aubergine salad today.

   (The waiter brings the food.)
w: The food is delicious, isn't it?
m: Yes, very good indeed.

Note on the dialogue

The word *walad,* which usually means 'boy' is also used to refer to a waiter or a man servant of any age.

5.1 Drills: tamriin

5.1.1 'This' and 'that'

In Lesson 1 you learned how to say 'this is ___.' In this lesson we introduce the type of sentence 'this
__ is __', e.g. 'this fish is good.' In Arabic *as samak da* 'this fish' has the word for 'this' after 'fish' and
the definite article in front of it. *da* has a feminine form, *di.* 'That' is *daak* (masc.) and *diik* (fem.).

Repeat the following drill after the teacher.

da samak	as samak da laziiz
da laHam	al laHam da laziiz
da beeḍ	al beeḍ da laziiz
da kabaab	al kabaab da laziiz
di <u>sh</u>oorba	a<u>sh</u> <u>sh</u>oorba di laziiza
di jibna	aj jibna di laziiza

دى جبنة	الجبنة دى لزيزة
دى سلطة	السلطة دى لزيزة
دى قهوة	القهوة دى لزيزة
الدقيق داك احسن	القفة ديك احسن
اللبن داك احسن	الكباية ديك احسن
الزيت داك احسن	الطربيزة ديك احسن
الظرف داك احسن	المكنة ديك احسن

اكل جيب الاكل دا (والى آخره)

٥,١,٢

اسمع، جيب موية	اسمعى، جيبى موية	اسمعوا، جيبوا موية
اسمع، جيب قهوة	اسمعى، جيبى قهوة	اسمعوا، جيبوا فهوة
اسمع، جيب شاى	اسمعى، جيبى شاى	اسمعوا، جيبوا شاى
اسمع، جيب ليمون	اسمعى، جيبى ليمون	اسمعوا، جيبوا ليمون
شوف العربية	شوفى العربية	شوفوا العربية
شوف الكبرى	شوفى الكبرى	شوفوا الكبرى
شوف السوق	شوفى السوق	شوفوا السوق
شوف الناس	شوفى الناس	شوفوا الناس
تعال، يا سيد	تعالى، يا منى	تعالوا، يا جماعة
تعال، يا ولد	تعالى، يا بت	تعالوا، يا اولاد
تعال، يا احمد	تعالى، يا آمال	

٥,١,٣

تعال، يا جون

جيبى موية، يا ميرى (والى آخره)

٥,١,٤

صفر	خمسة	عشرة
واحد	ستة	حداشر
اتنين	سبعة	اطناشر
تلاتة	تمنية	
اربعة	تسعة	

الساعة كم؟..........الساعة سبعة (والى آخره)

di salaṭa	as salaṭa di laziiza
di gahwa	al gahwa di laziiza
ad dagiig daak aHsan	al guffa diik aHsan
al laban daak aHsan	al kubbaaya diik aHsan
az zeet daak aHsan	aṭ ṭarabeeza diik aHsan
aẓ ẓarif daak aHsan	al makana diik aHsan

Now the teacher should say a noun and let the student make a sentence using the noun with 'this' or 'that', e.g. teacher says *akil*, student replies *jiib al akil da,* and so on.

5.1.2 Useful expressions: 'look,' 'listen' and 'come'

In Lesson 1 you learned *jiib*. Three other useful words like *jiib* are *shuuf* 'look, see', *asma9* (literally, 'hear, listen', and used to attract someone's attention, such as the waiter's in the restaurant) and *ta9aal* 'come here'. All of these words have masculine, feminine, and plural forms, like *jiib.*

Repeat the following drill after the teacher, across the columns:

asma9, jiib mooya	asma9i, jiibi mooya	asma9u, jiibu mooya
asma9, jiib gahwa	asma9i, jiibi gahwa	asma9u, jiibu gahwa
asma9, jiib shaay	asma9i, jiibi shaay	asma9u, jiibu shaay
asma9, jiib leemuun	asma9i, jiibi leemuun	asma9u, jiibu leemuun
shuuf al 9arabiiya	shuufi l 9arabiiya	shuufu l 9arabiiya
shuuf al kubri	shuufi l kubri	shuufu l kubri
shuuf as suug	shuufi s suug	shuufu s suug
shuuf an naas	shuufi n naas	shuufu n naas
ta9aal, ya seeyid	ta9aali, ya muna	ta9aalu, ya jamaa9a
ta9aal, ya walad	ta9aali, ya bitt	ta9aalu, ya awlaad
ta9aal, ya aHmad	ta9aali, ya aamaal	

5.1.3 Action drill

Using the words *ta9aal* 'come', *jiib* 'bring', *shuuf* 'look', take it in turns to give instructions to others in the class, e.g. one person says, *"ta9aal, ya John,"* and John has to come; then John says, *"jiibi mooya, ya Mary,"* and Mary has to bring water, and so on.

5.1.4 Counting and telling the time

Learn the numbers 0–12, of which you already know some, as given below:

0 ṣifir	5 khamsa	10 9ashara
1 waaHid	6 sitta	11 Hidaashar
2 itneen	7 sab9a	12 iṭnaashar
3 talaata	8 tamanya	
4 arba9a	9 tis9a	

You may sometimes hear 11 and 12 abbreviated to *Hidaar* and *iṭnaar.*

The teacher can take a clock, or a clock face drawn on a board or sheet of paper, and set the hands at different hours in order to drill the students on telling the time. At this stage they can only tell the hours, e.g. teacher sets the hands at 7 o'clock and asks "*as saa9a kam*"; student replies "*as saa9a sab9a.*" Note that 1 o'clock is *as saa9a waaHda* (not *as saa9a waaHid*).

تلاتة وربع
تلاتة وتلت
تلاتة ونص
اربعة الا تلت
اربعة الا ربع

كلمات

خامس
مطعم، مطاعم
محل، محلات
دى
قريب، قريبة
ديك
احسن
داير، دايرة، دايرين
بارد، باردة
عصير
برتكان
جوافة
اسمع، اسمعى، اسمعوا
حاضر
سيد
لستة، لستات
سمك

محمر، محمرة
اكَل
كباب
مخصوص
بطاطس
سلطة
اسود
شوربة
جداد
مشوى
الليلة
لزيز، لزيزة
مش كدا
جدا
تعال، تعالى، تعالوا
جماعة
ربع
تلت
نص

تمرين الاصوات

هجوم	حلو	خير
هوا	حاجة	خاف
هناك	حمار	خور
هنا	حكاية	خفيف
هاكى	حجز	خمسة

Here are the expressions for the fractions of an hour commonly used. When they are learned you can bring them into the drill.

3:15	talaata u rubu9
3:20	talaata u tilit
3:30	talaata u nuṣṣ
3:40	arba9a illa tilit
3:45	arba9a illa rubu9

5.2 Role play

Play the parts of a waiter taking orders from customers in a restaurant. The teacher can supply more vocabulary as needed. Then go out one evening to a small restaurant, perhaps by the river, in order to practice what you have learned.

5.3 Vocabulary: kalmaat

khaamis	fifth	muHammar (m), muHammara (f)	fried
maṭ9am, maṭaa9im	restaurant		
maHall, maHallaat	place	akal	to eat
faaḍi (m), faaḍya (f)	empty	kabaab	kebab
hinaak	there	makhṣuuṣ	special
di	this (f)	baṭaaṭis	potatoes
gariib (m), gariiba (f)	near	salaṭa	salad
diik	that (f)	aswad	aubergine, eggplant
aHsan	better	*sh*oorba	soup
daayir (m), daayra (f), daayriin (pl)	want	jidaad	chicken
		ma*sh*wi	grilled
baarid (m), baarda (f)	cold	alleela	today
9aṣiir	juice	laziiz (m), laziiza (f)	delicious
burtukaan	orange, oranges	mush kida	isn't that so?
jawaafa	guava, guavas	jiddan	very
asma9 (m), asma9i (f), asma9u (pl)	listen!	ta9aal (m), ta9aali (f), ta9aalu (pl.)	come here!
Haaḍir	okay (response to command or request)	jamaa9a	group of people
		rubu9	a quarter
seeyid	sir, Mr.	tilit	a third
lista, listaat	menu, list	nuṣṣ	half
samak	fish		

5.4 Pronunciation drills: h, H, kh

Contrast drills

Follow instructions as in Introduction section 3 Contrast drills.
Lists (a) and (b) contrasting *h* and *H* at the beginning of words
Lists (d) and (e) contrasting *h* and *H* in the middle of words
Lists (b) and (c) contrasting *H* and *kh* at the beginning of words
Lists (e) and (f) contrasting *H* and *kh* in the middle of words

(a) h		**(b) H**		**(c) kh**	
hiduum	clothes	Hilu	pleasant	kheer	good
hawa	air	Haaja	thing	khaaf	he feared
hinaak	there	Humaar	donkey	khoor	river bed
hina	here	Hikaaya	story	khafiif	light
haaki	here it is	Hajiz	booking	khamsa	five

فهم	تحت	اخت
اهل	لحم	اخد
قهوة	بحر	اخوان
كهربة	احمر	اخدر
دهب	نحل	اخيرا

(d) h		**(e) H**		**(f) kh**	
fihim	he understood	tiHit	under	ukhut	sister
ahal	family	laHam	meat	akhad	he took
gahwa	coffee	baHar	river	akhwaan	brothers
kahraba	electricity	aHmar	red	akhdar	green
dahab	gold	naHal	bee	akhiiran	finally

اسئلة لمراجعة الدروس

من ١ الى ٥

١ انت فطرت الساعة تمنية الليلة؟

٢ الولد ماشى وين؟

٣ اكلت سمك محمر من السوق؟

٤ احمد ركب الباص الساعة كم؟

٥ سيد الدكان قفل الدكان الساعة تسعة؟

٦ الراجل دا داير شنو؟

٧ انت عاوز قهوة ولا شاى؟

٨ درست العربى هنا؟

٩ انتوا ماشين البيت قبل الساعة واحدة؟

١٠ الاولاد عيانين؟

١١ الساعة كم هسع؟

١٢ الضيوف مرقوا وين؟

١٣ قى عيش وجبنة فى الطربيزة؟

١٤ انتو ساكنين فى الشارع دا؟

١٥ السواق صلح العربية؟

١٦ الشاى جاهز؟

١٧ فى كبرى قريب من هنا؟

١٨ المرة دايرة كباب ولا جداد؟

١٩ المحل جنب الباب فاضى؟

٢٠ السكر بكم هسع؟

Revision questions for Lessons 1–5

Listen as the teacher asks the following questions, one by one, and answer either from your own experience or with a fictitious answer. The questions in the 2nd person are framed in the 2nd person masculine, but can be put in the 2nd person feminine where appropriate, e.g. question 1., *inta faṭarta s saa9a tamanya alleela?* can be changed to *inti faṭarti s saa9a tamanya alleela?* when addressed to a woman.

1. inta faṭarta s saa9a tamanya alleela?
2. al walad maashi ween?
3. akalta samak muHammar min as suug?
4. aHmad rikib al baaṣ as saa9a kam?
5. siid ad dukkaan gafal ad dukkaan as saa9a tis9a?
6. ar raajil da daayir shinuu?
7. inta 9aawz gahwa walla shaay?
8. darasta l 9arabi hina?
9. intu maashiin al beet gabli s saa9a waaHda?
10. al awlaad 9ayyaaniin?
11. as saa9a kam hassa9?
12. aḍ ḍuyuuf maragu ween?
13. fii 9eesh u jibna fi ṭ ṭarabeeza?
14. intu saakniin fi sh shaari9 da?
15. as sawwaag ṣallaH al 9arabiiya?
16. ash shaay jaahiz?
17. fii kubri gariib min hina?
18. al mara daayra kabaab walla jidaad?
19. al maHall jamb al baab faaḍi?
20. as sukkar bee kam hassa9?

الدرس السادس

حوار : فى البيت

أ : الام　　ا : ايمان　　م : محمد

أ　يا ايمان، الاولاد وين؟

ا　ممحد قاعد فى الصالون وصادق قاعد يلعب برا.

أ　محمد قاعد يعمل شنو فى الصالون؟

ا　قاعد يكتب.

أ　كويس. انتى قطعتى البطاطس؟

ا　ايوه، قطعت البطاطس وقاعدة اغسل العدة.

أ　طيب. انا ماشة السوق.

(محمد بجيب ورقة)

م　يأمَى، انا رسمت سمك. شوفى. دا البحر ودا السمك فى البحر.

أ　ايوه. انت شاطر. كمان كتبت حاجة؟

م　كتبت دا كله، لكن القلم بايظ. جيبى تانى من الدكان.

تمرين

٦,١,١

هو قاعد فى الصالون	انا قاعدة فى البيت
الولد قاعد فى كرسى	البت قاعدة فى كرسى
الولد قاعد برا	البت قاعدة برا
الولد قاعد فى العربية	البت قاعدة فى العربية
انت قاعد فى البيت؟	لا، انا ما قاعد فى البيت
انت قاعدة فى البيت؟	لا، انا ما قاعدة فى البيت
انتوا قاعدين فى البيت؟	لا، نحن ما قاعدين فى البيت

٦,١,٢

ادرس	ندرس
تدرس	تدرسوا
تدرسى	
يدرس	يدرسوا
تدرس	

ad daris as saadis — Lesson 6

Hiwaar: fi l beet (1) — Dialogue: At home (1)

u:	al umm i: iimaan m: muHammad	M:	mother I: Iimaan (girl) b: Muhammad (boy)
u:	ya iimaan, al awlaad ween?	M:	Iimaan, where are the boys?
i:	muHammad gaa9id fi ṣ ṣaaluun, u ṣaadig gaa9id yal9ab barra.	I:	Muhammad is sitting in the living room and Saadig is playing outside.
u:	muHammad gaa9id ya9mil shinuu fi ṣ ṣaaluun?	M:	What is Muhammad doing in the living room?
i:	gaa9id yaktib.	I:	He's writing.
u:	kwaiyis. inti gaṭa9ti l baṭaaṭis?	M:	Good. Have you cut up the potatoes?
i:	aiwa, gaṭa9ta l baṭaaṭis u gaa9da aghassil al 9idda.	I:	Yes, I've cut up the potatoes and am doing the washing up.
u:	ṭaiyib. ana maasha s suug.	M:	Fine. I'm going to the market.
	(muHammad bijiib waraga)		(Muhammad brings a piece of paper)
m:	yumma, ana rasamta samak. shuufi. da l baHar u da s samak fi l baHar.	b:	Mummy, I've drawn some fish. Look! That's the river and that's the fish in the river.
u:	aiwa, inta shaaṭir! kamaan katabta Haaja?	M:	Yes, aren't you clever! Did you write something as well?
m:	katabta da kullu, laakin al galam baayiẓ. jiibi taani min ad dukkaan.	b:	I wrote all that, but the pen has broken. Bring another from the shop.

6.1 Drills: tamriin

6.1.1 *gaa9id* 'sitting' or 'staying'

This is a word that means 'sitting' or 'staying,' e.g. *hu gaa9id fi ṣ ṣaaluun* 'he is sitting in the living room' or *ana gaa9da fi l beet* 'I stay at home', meaning 'I don't go out to work'. It is like *saakin,* having the feminine *gaa9da* and plural *gaa9diin.*

Repeat the sentences below with the teacher:

al walad gaa9id fii kursi.	al bitt gaa9da fii kursi.
al walad gaa9id barra.	al bitt gaa9da barra.
al walad gaa9id fi l 9arabiiya.	al bitt gaa9da fi l 9arabiiya.
inta gaa9id fi l beet?	la', ana maa gaa9id fi l beet.
inti gaa9da fi l beet?	la', ana maa gaa9da fi l beet.
intu gaa9diin fi l beet?	la', niHna maa gaa9diin fi l beet.

6.1.2 Verbs: the imperfect

The imperfect has a variety of uses, which will be introduced gradually in the next few lessons. Look at the table of the imperfect of the verb *daras* 'to study'. (See section 2.1.4 for the perfect verb form, like *daras.*)

	Singular		**Plural**	
1st	a-drus	I study	na-drus	we study
2nd m	ta-drus	you study	ta-drus-u	you study
2nd f	ta-drus-i	you study		
3rd m	ya-drus	he studies	ya-drus-u	they study
3rd f	ta-drus	she studies		

فطر، يفطر؛ شرب، يشرب؛ قفل، يقفل؛ فتح، يفتح؛ رجع، يرجع؛ مرق، يمرق؛ سمع، يسمع

اغسل	نغسل
تغسل	تغسلوا
تغسلى	
يغسل	يغسلوا
تغسل	

صلح، يصلح؛ غير، يغير؛ سافر، يسافر؛ ساعد، يساعد

٦,١,٣

انا قاعد ادرس العربى	انا ما قاعد ادرس العربى
انا قاعد اعمل قهوة	انا ما قاعد اعمل قهوة
انا قاعد اغسل العدة	انا ما قاعد اغسل العدة
انا قاعدة ادرس العربى	انا ما قلعدة ادرس العربى
انا قاعدة اعمل قهوة	انا ما قاعدة اعمل قهوة
انا قاعدة اغسل العدة	انا ما قاعدة اغسل العدة
انت قاعد تدرس العربى	انت ما قاعد تدرس العربى
انت قاعد تعمل قهوة	انت ما قاعد تعمل قهوة
انت قاعد تغسل العدة	انت ما قاعد تغسل العدة

You'll notice that all forms consist of two parts: the verb stem, *drus*, and one or two bits to indicate the person, e.g. the 2nd f. sing. has *ta* before the verb stem and *i* after it.

The stem of the imperfect consists of the same consonants as the stem of the past tense (see section 2.1.4) but has different vowels, e.g. *daras – drus.* For all verbs like *daras* the pattern is the same for the imperfects: two consonants-vowel-consonant, but the vowel may be *a, i,* or *u,* e.g. *shirib – shrab, gafal – gfil,* etc. It is therefore necessary to learn both stems for every verb, and from now on both will be given in the vocabularies for each lesson. The imperfect is given in the 3rd m. sing., e.g. *yadrus.*

Repeat the table of the imperfect of *daras* until you know it by heart.

Then drill the imperfect of other verbs: *faṭar, yafṭur; shirib, yashrab; gafal, yagfil; fataH, yaftaH; raja9, yarja9; marag, yamrug; simi9, yasma9.*

The two variations on the basic verb, i.e. *ghassal* and *saafar* (see Lesson 4), take the same person indicators in the imperfect except in the 3rd m. sing. and 3rd pl. where *ya* becomes *yi*, e.g. *yighassil* 'he washes'. The vowels of these verbs in the imperfect stem are always *a - i*, e.g. *yisaafir* 'he travels', *yighayyir* 'he changes', etc. (See the table below.) The *i* drops out in verbs like *saafar*, but not in verbs like *ghassal*, when the ending begins with a vowel, i.e. in the 2nd feminine singular and 2nd and 3rd plural, e.g. *tasaafri, tasaafru, yisaafru.*

	Singular		**Plural**	
1st	aghassil	I wash	naghassil	we wash
2nd m	taghassil	you wash	taghassilu	you wash
2nd f	taghassili	you wash		
3rd m	yighassil	he washes	yighassilu	they wash
3rd f	taghassil	she washes		

Drill the imperfect with *ghassal, yighassil; ṣallaH, yiṣalliH; ghayyar, yighayyir; saafar, yisaafir; saa9ad, yisaa9id.*

6.1.3 The use of the imperfect--the present continuous

As a general rule the imperfect is not used on its own but with some other word or in a special phrase. In this lesson it is introduced with *gaa9id,* which in this case does not have its own meaning of 'sitting', but simply gives the imperfect a present continuous meaning, e.g. 'I am drinking', 'he is opening the door'.

Repeat the following sentences after the teacher. On the left are positive statements, e.g. 'I am studying Arabic,' and on the right are the corresponding negative statements, e.g. 'I am not studying Arabic.' This may seem a rather boring drill, but if you can once get the imperfect into your head you will have mastered a large part of Sudanese Arabic verbs.

ana (m) gaa9id adrus al 9arabi	ana maa gaa9id adrus al 9arabi
ana gaa9id a9mil gahwa	ana maa gaa9id a9mil gahwa
ana gaa9id aghassil al 9idda	ana maa gaa9id aghassil al 9idda
ana (f) gaa9da adrus al 9arabi	ana maa gaa9da adrus al 9arabi
ana gaa9da a9mil gahwa	ana maa gaa9da a9mil gahwa
ana gaa9da aghassil al 9idda	ana maa gaa9da aghassil al 9idda
inta gaa9id tadrus al 9arabi	inta maa gaa9id tadrus al 9arabi
inta gaa9id ta9mil gahwa	inta maa gaa9id ta9mil gahwa
inta gaa9id taghassil al 9idda	inta maa gaa9id taghassil al 9idda

انت قاعدة تدرسى العربى	انت ما قاعدة تدرسى العربى
انت قاعدة تعملى قهوة	انت ما قاعدة تعملى قهوة
انت قاعدة تغسلى العدة	انت ما قاعدة تغسلى العدة
هو قاعد يدرس العربى	هو ما قاعد يدرس العربى
هو قاعد يعمل قهوة	هو ما قاعد يعمل قهوة
هو قاعد يغسل العدة	هو ما قاعد يغسل العدة
هى قاعدة تدرس العربى	هى ما قاعدة تدرس العربى
هى قاعدة تعمل قهوة	هى ما قاعدة تعمل قهوة
هى قاعدة تغسل العدة	هى ما قاعدة تغسل العدة
نحن قاعدين ندرس العربى	نحن ما قاعدين ندرس العربى
نحن قاعدين نعمل قهوة	نحن ما قاعدين نعمل قهوة
نحن قاعدين نغسل العدة	نحن ما قاعدين نغسل العدة
انتوا قاعدين تدرسوا العربى	انتوا ما قاعدين تدرسوا العربى
انتوا قاعدين تعملوا قهوة	انتوا ما قاعدين تعملوا قهوة
انتوا قاعدين تغسلوا العدة	انتوا ما قاعدين تغسلوا العدة
هم قاعدين يدرسوا العربى	هم ما قاعدين يدرسوا العربى
هم قاعدين يعملوا قهوة	هم ما قاعدين يعملوا قهوة
هم قاعدين يغسلوا العدة	هم ما قاعدين يغسلوا العدة

انت قاعد تسمع الراديو هسع؟	لا، انا قاعد اشرب قهوة هسع
انت قاعدة تسمعى الراديو هسع؟	لا، انا قاعدة اشرب قهوة هسع
انتوا قاعدين تسمعوا الراديو هسع؟	لا، نحن قاعدين نشرب قهوة هسع
هو قاعد يسمع الراديو هسع؟	لا، هو قاعد يشرب قهوة هسع
هى قاعدة تسمع الراديو هسع؟	لا، هى قاعدة تشرب قهوة هسع
هم قاعدين يسمعوا الراديو هسع؟	لا، هم قاعدين يشربوا قهوة هسع

كلمات

سادس
ام، امهات
لعب، يلعب
عمل، يعمل
كتب، يكتب
قطع، يقطع
ورقة
يأمَى

قاعد
صالون، صوالين
شاطر، شاطرة، شاطرين
كل
قلم، اقلام
بت، بنات
كرسى، كراسى

inti gaa9da tadrusi l 9arabi	inti maa gaa9da tadrusi l 9arabi
inti gaa9da ta9mili gahwa	inti maa gaa9da ta9mili gahwa
inti gaa9da taghassili l 9idda	inti maa gaa9da taghassili l 9idda
hu gaa9id yadrus al 9arabi	hu maa gaa9id yadrus al 9arabi
hu gaa9id ya9mil gahwa	hu maa gaa9id ya9mil gahwa
hu gaa9id yighassil al 9idda	hu maa gaa9id yighassil al 9idda
hi gaa9da tadrus al 9arabi	hi maa gaa9da tadrus al 9arabi
hi gaa9da ta9mil gahwa	hi maa gaa9da ta9mil gahwa
hi gaa9da taghassil al 9idda	hi maa gaa9da taghassil al 9idda
niHna gaa9diin nadrus al 9arabi	niHna maa gaa9diin nadrus al 9arabi
niHna gaa9diin na9mil gahwa	niHna maa gaa9diin na9mil gahwa
niHna gaa9diin naghassil al 9idda	niHna maa gaa9diin naghassil al 9idda
intu gaa9diin tadrusu l 9arabi	intu maa gaa9diin tadrusu l 9arabi
intu gaa9diin ta9milu gahwa	intu maa gaa9diin ta9milu gahwa
intu gaa9diin taghassilu l 9idda	intu maa gaa9diin taghassilu l 9idda
hum gaa9diin yadrusu l 9arabi	hum maa gaa9diin yadrusu l 9arabi
hum gaa9diin ya9milu gahwa	hum maa gaa9diin ya9milu gahwa
hum gaa9diin yighassilu l 9idda	hum maa gaa9diin yighassilu l 9idda

A further drill for the imperfect with *gaa9id* is as follows: on the left are questions, e.g. 'Are you listening to the radio at the moment?' and on the right are answers in the form of 'No, I am drinking coffee at the moment.' Repeat them after the teacher, paying attention to intonation.

inta gaa9id tasma9 ar raadyu hassa9?	la', ana gaa9id ashrab gahwa hassa9
inti gaa9da tasma9i r raadyu hassa9?	la', ana gaa9da ashrab gahwa hassa9
intu gaa9diin tasma9u r raadyu hassa9?	la', niHna gaa9diin nashrab gahwa hassa9
hu gaa9id yasma9 ar raadyu hassa9?	la', hu gaa9id yashrab gahwa hassa9
hi gaa9da tasma9 ar raadyu hassa9?	la', hi gaa9da tashrab gahwa hassa9
hum gaa9diin yasma9u r raadyu hassa9?	la', hum gaa9diin yashrabu gahwa hassa9

6.1.4 Conversation practice: 'What are you doing?'

Now take it in turns to ask each other *inta gaa9id ta9mil shinuu?* or *inti gaa9da ta9mili shinuu?* "What are you doing?" and the other person replies, "I am drinking tea" or "I am opening the door" or whatever else they choose.

6.2 Role play

Imagine you are at home in your family and act out the parts of different members of the family talking to each other about what they are doing or where they are going. The teacher can supply some extra phrases to help you.

6.3 Vocabulary: kalmaat

saadis	sixth	gaa9id	sitting (see Drills 1 & 3)
umm, ummahaat	mother	ṣaaluun, ṣawaaliin	living room
li9ib, yal9ab	to play	shaaṭir (m), shaaṭra (f), shaaṭriin (pl)	clever
9amal, ya9mil	to do		
katab, yaktib	to write	kullu	all
gaṭa9, yagṭa9	to cut with a knife	galam, aglaam	pen, pencil
waraga	piece of paper	bitt, banaat	girl
yumma	Mummy	kursi, karaasi	chair

رسم، يرسم	راديو، روادى
بحر	
درس، يدرس	رجع، يرجع
دخل، يدخل	مرق، يمرق
فطر، يقطر	صلح، يصلح
شرب، يشرب	غير، يغير
سمع، يسمع	غسل، يغسل
قفل، يقفل	ساعد، يساعد
فتح، يفتح	
ركب، يركب	

تمرين الاصوات

آثار	عادة	غالى
اهل	عروس	غلب
اسنان	عربى	غنم
ايجار	عيون	غدا
اسود	عيش	غربى

قعد	لغة
لعب	شغل
ساعة	اغانى
كعب	يغير
ساعد	مغرب

وجع	مرة
دفع	قرا
سمع	بمبى
هسع	دوا
مشروع	يمشوا

rasam, yarsum	to draw	raadyu, rawaadi	radio
baHar	river, sea		

Repeat of verbs already introduced with their imperfect stem:

daras, yadrus	to study	raja9, yarja9	to return
dakhal, yadkhul	to enter	marag, yamrug	to go out
faṭar, yafṭur	to have breakfast	ṣallaH, yiṣalliH	to repair
shirib, yashrab	to drink	ghayyar, yighayyir	to change
simi9, yasma9	to hear	ghassal, yighassil	to wash
gafal, yagfil	to shut	saa9ad, yisaa9id	to help
fataH, yaftaH	to open		
rikib, yarkab	to ride, get on		

6.4 Pronunciation drills: *9*, gh

Contrast Drills

Follow instructions in Introduction, section 3.
Lists (a) and (b) contrasting *9* at the beginning of words with words beginning with a vowel.
Lists (b) and (c) contrasting *9* and *gh* at the beginning of words.
Lists (d) and (e) contrasting *9* and *gh* in the middle of words.
Lists (f) and (g) contrasting *9* at the end of words with words ending in a vowel.

(a) -		**(b) 9**		**(c) gh**	
aasaar	ruins	9aada	custom	ghaali	expensive
ahal	family	9aruus	bride	ghalab	he won
asnaan	teeth	9arabi	Arabic	ghanam	goat
iijaar	rent	9iyuun	eyes	ghada	lunch
aswad	black	9eesh	bread	gharbi	western

(d) 9		**(e) gh**	
ga9ad	he sat down	lugha	language
li9ib	he played	shughul	work
saa9a	watch	aghaani	songs
ka9ab	bad	yighayyir	he changes
saa9ad	he helped	mughrib	sunset

(f) 9		**(g) -**	
waja9	pain	mara	woman
dafa9	he paid	gara	he read
simi9	he heard	bambi	pink
hassa9	now	dawa	medicine
mashruu9	project	yamshu	they go

Further practise on *9* will be given in Lesson 12, Pronunciation drills.

الدرس السابع

حوار : الخواجة

س : سوداني   خ : خواجة

س   ازى الحال.

خ   اهلا وسهلا.

س   الله يبارك فيك.

خ   ان شاء الله انت شديد؟

س   شديد، الحمد لله. انتوا ساكنين هنا؟

خ   ايوه، نحن ساكنين في البيت دا.

س   يا سلام، نحن جيران. انا ساكن فى الشارع داك. ليكم كم شهر فى السودان؟

خ   تلاتة شهور بس.

س   قريب، والله. السودان كويس؟

خ   كويس جدا. انت من هنا اصلا؟

س   لا، انا مولود فى كوستى لكن سكنت فى الخرطوم قبل عشرين سنة. انتوا من وين؟

خ   من برطانيا.

س   سمعت برطانيا بلد سمح. انت بتعمل شنو فى السودان؟

خ   بدرس فى الجامعة. بتعرف الجامعة؟

س   طبعا. المرة شغالة كمان؟

خ   ايوه، هى سكرتيرة فى السفارة. انت موظف؟

س   لا، انا مكنيكى. بصلح العربات. عن ازنك، انا ماشى الشغل. نتلاقى فى وكت تانى، مع السلامة.

خ   الله يسلمك.

تمرين

٧,١,١

ازى الحال

الله يبارك فيك

الله يسلمك

ad daris as saabi9 — Lesson 7

Hiwaar: al khawaaja — Dialogue: The foreigner

s:	suudaani k: khawaaja	S:	Sudanese f: foreigner
s:	izzeey al Haal.	S:	How do you do?
k:	ahlan wa sahlan.	f:	Welcome.
s:	allaa yibaarik fiik.	S:	God bless you.
k:	in shaa' allaa inta shadiid?	f:	I trust you are well? (literally, by God's will you are strong?)
s:	shadiid, al Hamdu lillaa. intu saakniin hina?	S:	Well, thank God. Do you live here?
k:	aiwa, niHna saakniin fi l beet da.	f:	Yes, we live in this house.
s:	ya salaam, niHna jeeraan. ana saakin fi sh shaari9 daak. leekum kam shahar fi s suudaan?	S:	Goodness me, we're neighbors. I live in that street. How many months have you been in Sudan?
k:	talaata shuhuur bass.	f:	Only three months.
s:	gariib, wallaahi. as suudaan kwaiyis?	S:	Not long, my God. Do you like Sudan?
k:	kwaiyis jiddan. inta min hina aṣlan?	f:	It's very nice. Are you from here originally?
s:	la', ana mawluud fii koosti laakin sakanta fi l kharṭuum gabli 9ishriin sana. intu min ween?	S:	No, I was born in Kosti but I've lived in Khartoum for 20 years. Where are you from?
k:	min bariṭaanya.	f:	From Britain.
s:	simi9ta bariṭaanya balad samiH. inta bita9mil shinuu fi s suudaan?	S:	I have heard Britain is a fine country. What are you doing in Sudan?
k:	badarris fi j jaam9a. bita9rif aj jaam9a?	f:	I'm teaching at the university. Do you know the university?
s:	ṭab9an. al mara shaghghaala kamaan?	S:	Of course. Is your wife working too?
k:	aiwa, hi sikirteera fi s safaara. inta muwaẓẓaf?	f:	Yes, she's a secretary in the embassy. Are you a civil servant?
s:	la', ana makaniiki. baṣalliH al 9arabaat. 9an iznak, ana maashi sh shughul. nitlaaga fii wakit taani. ma9a s salaama.	S:	No, I'm a mechanic. I repair cars. Excuse me, I'm going to work. We'll meet another time. Good-bye.
k:	allaa yisallimak.	f:	Good-bye.

7.1 Drills: tamriin

7.1.1 Some new greetings

Revise the greetings you learned in Lessons 1 and 2. Now you can add the following to your repertoire:

a) *izzeey al Haal:* This is similar to *izzeeyak,* i.e. an introductory and not too formal greeting.
b) *allaa yibaarik fiik:* This means literally 'God bless you' and is a polite reply to other greetings.
c) *allaa yisallimak* (m), *allaa yisallimik* (f): This means literally 'God give you safety' but is really just another way of saying good-bye.

Practise the greetings exchange in pairs, using the new greetings, and remembering to distinguish between masculine and feminine forms.

٧,١,٢

ليك كم شهر في السودان؟
ليكى كم سنة فى السودان؟
ليكم كم سنة فى السودان؟

٧,١,٣

بدرس	بندرس
بتدرس	بتدرسوا
بتدرسى	
بيدرس	بيدرسوا
بتدرس	

فطر: بفطر بتفطر (والى آخره)
لعب، كتب، سمع

٧,١,٤

بغسّل	بنغسّل
بتغسّل	بتغسّلوا
بتغسّلى	
بيغسّل	بيغسّلوا
بتغسّل	

7.1.2 Useful expressions: 'How long?', 'Excuse me' and 'By God's will'

A question foreigners are often asked by Sudanese is 'How long have you been in Sudan?' In Arabic, as you heard in the dialogue, this is *leekum kam shahar fi s suudaan?,* literally, 'to you how many months in the Sudan?' *leekum* is the plural, *leek* masculine and *leeki* feminine. *sana* 'year' or *usbuu9* 'week' may be substituted for *shahar.* Note that *kam* is always followed by the singular noun. If you want to say, 'I have been three years in Sudan,' in Arabic that is *leey talaata siniin fii s suudaan.*

Repeat the following sentences after the teacher until you can say them easily. Then practise in pairs, one asking the question and the other providing an answer, using only the numbers 1–10 (excluding 2) and the words for 'week,' 'month,' and 'year.' The plural of *shahar* is *shuhuur*, the plural of *sana* is *siniin* and the plural of *usbuu9* is *asaabii9*, e.g. one says, *leek kam shahar fi s suudaan?* and the other replies, *talaata shuhuur.*

leek kam shahar fi s suudaan?
leeki kam sana fi s suudaan?
leekum kam sana fi s suudaan?

The expression 'excuse me' *9an iznak* (m), *9an iznik* (f), *9an iznakum* (pl). This is the polite thing to say when taking leave of someone or when asking them to move so you can pass.

'By God's will': *in shaa' allaa* is a phrase you will hear constantly in the mouths of Sudanese, owing to the belief that all events are conditional on God's will and therefore one cannot hope anything or predict anything that goes contrary to his will. For some people it is an expression of genuine faith but for others it becomes a way of avoiding responsibility.

7.1.3 Verbs: the imperfect with *bi-*

Look at the table below. You'll see it is like the imperfect with the addition of *bi-*.

	Singular	Plural
1st	b-adrus	bi-nadrus
2nd m	bi-tadrus	bi-tadrusu
2nd f	bi-tadrusi	
3rd m	bi-yadrus	bi-yadrusu
3rd f	bi-tadrus	

bi- gives a habitual or repetitive meaning to the imperfect, e.g. *badrus* implies that I study regularly, habitually, in contrast to *gaa9id adrus*, which means that 'I am studying at this moment'.

In Khartoum you will often hear, as an alternative to *biyadrus* and *biyadrusu*, the forms *bidrus* and *bidrusu.* It is good to be familiar with both.

Drill the above table, first with *daras* and then with other verbs: *faṭar, yafṭur*; *li9ib, yal9ab*; *katab, yaktib*; *simi9, yasma9.*

7.1.4 *ghassal* and *saafar* with *bi-*

When *bi-* is added to the imperfect of verbs like *ghassal* and *saafar,* the form of the person indicators changes slightly. See the table below and compare it with the table of the imperfect of *ghassal* in Lesson 6.

	Singular	Plural
1st	b-a-ghassil	bi-n-ghassil
2nd m	bi-t-ghassil	bi-t-ghassil-u
2nd f	bi-t-ghassil-i	
3rd m	bi-ghassil	bi-ghassil-u
3rd f	bi-t-ghassil	

صلح: بصلح بتصلح (والى آخره)

غيّر، درّس، سافر، ساعد

انت، كتب انت بتكتب (والى آخره)

كلمات

سابع
ازى الحال
الله يبارك فيك
ان شاء الله
يا سلام
جار، جيران
جارة، جارات
ليك، ليكى، ليكم
شهر، شهور
السودان
قبل
عشرين
سنة، سنين
برطانيا
بلد، بلدان
سمح، سمحة
درّس، يدرّس
جامعة، جامعات
عرف، يعرف
طبعا
اسبوع، اسابيع

شغال، شغالة، شغالين
سكرتيرة
سفارة، سفارات
موظف، موظفين
موظفة، موظفات
مكنيكى، مكنيكية
والله
اصلا
مولود، مولودة، مولودين
سكن، يسكن
عن ازنك
شغل
اتلاقى، يتلاقى
وكت
الله يسلمك
لى

تمرين الاصوات

ساهل	صاحب
سلام	صغير
سمك	صفق
سوق	صورة
سنين	صفر

Drill this table with *ghassal* and then with other verbs: *ṣallaH, yiṣalliH; ghayyar, yighayyir; darras, yidarris; saafar, yisaafir; saa9ad, yisaa9id.*

Now the teacher can say a pronoun and a verb and let the student supply the right form of the imperfect with *bi-*, e.g. teacher says *inta – katab,* student replies *inta bitaktib.*

7.1.5 Telling about yourself

With the teacher's help the student should make up a short dialogue based on the one in this lesson but applying to him or herself, to be memorised and used in actual conversation with Sudanese friends and neighbors. Include information about how long you have been in Sudan, your job, where you live and what nationality you are.

7.2 Role play

Act out the parts of a Sudanese and a foreigner telling each other about themselves. You can use material from the dialogue and the drills and can also ask the teacher for additional expressions.

7.3 Vocabulary: kalmaat

saabi9	seventh
izzeey al Haal	(see Drill 1)
allaa yibaarik fiik	(see Drill 1)
in shaa' allaa	by God's will
ya salaam	goodness me!
jaar, jeeraan	neighbor (man)
jaara, jaaraat	neighbor (woman)
leek (m), leeki (f), leekum (pl)	to you
shahar, shuhuur	month
as suudaan	Sudan
gabli	before, ago
9ishriin	20
sana, siniin	year
bariṭaanya	Britain
balad, buldaan	country
samiH(m), samHa(f)	beautiful
darras, yidarris	to teach
jaam9a, jaam9aat	university
9irif, ya9rif	to know
ṭab9an	of course, certainly
usbuu9, asaabii9	week
shaghghaal(m), shaghghaala(f), shaghghaaliin(pl)	working
sikirteera	secretary
safaara, safaaraat	embassy
muwaẓẓaf, muwaẓẓafiin	civil servant, official (m)
muwaẓẓafa, muwaẓẓafaat	civil servant, official (f)
makaniiki, makaniikiiya	mechanic
wallaahi	my God!, really!
aṣlan	originally
mawluud(m), mawluuda(f), mawluudiin(pl)	born
sakan, yaskun	to live
9an iznak	excuse me
shughul	work
itlaaga, yitlaaga	to meet each other
wakit	time
allaa yisallimak	(see Drill 1)
leey	to me

7.4 Pronunciation drills: s, ṣ

Contrast drills

See Introduction, section 3 for instructions.
Lists (a) and (b) contrasting *s* and *ṣ* at the beginning of words.
Lists (c) and (d) contrasting *s* and *ṣ* in the middle of words.
Lists (e) and (f) contrasting *s* and *ṣ* at the end of words.

(a) s		(b) ṣ	
saahil	easy	ṣaaHib	friend
salaam	peace	ṣaghayyir	small
samak	fish	ṣafag	leaves
suug	market	ṣuura	picture
siniin	years	ṣifir	zero

مسك
جسم
اسامى
نسى
راسى

لبس
دروس
درس
راس
ناس

بصل
وصل
قصير
مصر
باصات

قميص
مخصوص
رُخص
رقص
خلاص

(c) s		(d) ṣ	
masak	he held	baṣal	onions
jisim	body	wiṣil	he arrived
asaami	names	giṣayyir	short
nisa	he forgot	maṣir	Egypt
raasi	my head	baaṣaat	busses

(e) s		(f) ṣ	
libis	he wore	gamiiṣ	shirt
duruus	lessons	ma<u>kh</u>ṣuuṣ	special
daris	lesson	ru<u>kh</u>aṣ	licences
raas	head	ragaṣ	he danced
naas	people	<u>kh</u>alaaṣ	finished

الدرس التامن

حوالر : فى المكتب

ل : ليلى م : منى ا : احمد

ل يا منى، ممكن تفتحى لى الكمبيوتر؟ دايرة اطبع جواب.

م طيب.

ل يا احمد، المراسلة استلم الجوابات من البسطة امبارح؟

ا لا، هو روّح مفتاح الصندوق. لكن ما فى مشكلة. فى مفتاح تانى هنا.

ل كويس. هو ماشى الليلة؟

ا بعد خمسة دقايق.

م يا ليلى، اطلّع الجواب دا فى ورقة؟

ل ايوه. شكرا. الطوابع وين؟

م فى درج الطربيزة هناك.

ل لازم ادخل الجواب فى ظرف واكتب العنوان. جيبى طابعة واحدة طوالى.

ا بسرعة. المراسلة ماشى هسع. اسمعى، المدير سافر لبنان. لازم ترسلى جواب إلكترونى له عن المؤتمر.

م المؤتمر متين؟

ا فى الاسبوع الجاى.

تمرين

٨,١,١

لازم تكتب جواب؟	اى، لازم اكتب جواب الليلة
لازم تشربى موية؟	اى، لازم اشرب موية طوالى
لازم تركبوا باص؟	اى، لازم نركب باص من السوق
لازم يفتح الصندوق؟	اى، لازم يفتح الصندوق للبت
لازم تغسل العدة؟	اى، لازم تغسل العدة كويس
لازم يسافروا؟	اى، لازم يسافروا الليلة
ممكن اساعد المكنيكى؟	لا، انت ما ممكن تساعد المكنيكى
ممكن اقطع اللحم؟	لا، انت ما ممكن تقطعى اللحم
ممكن تشرب اللبن؟	لا، انتوا ما ممكن تشربوا اللبن
ممكن هو يصلح المكنة؟	لا، ما ممكن يصلح المكنة الليلة
ممكن هى تعمل قهوة؟	لا، ما ممكن تعمل قهوة هنا
ممكن هم يدخلوا دقيق فى الكيس؟	لا، ما ممكن يدخلوا دقيق فى الكيس دا

ad daris at taamin	**Lesson 8**
Hiwaar: fi l maktab	**Dialogue: In the office**

l:	leela m: muna a: aHmad	L:	Leila M: Muna A: Ahmed
l:	ya muna, mumkin taftaHi leey al kombyuutar? daayra aṭba9 jawaab.	L:	Muna, can you switch on the computer for me? I want to type a letter.
m:	ṭaiyib.	M:	Okay.
l:	ya aHmad, al muraasla istalam aj jawaabaat min al busṭa umbaariH?	L:	Ahmed, did the messsenger collect the letters from the Post Office yesterday?
a:	la'. hu rawwaH muftaaH aṣ ṣanduug. laakin maa fii mushkila. fii muftaaH taani hina.	A:	No, he lost the key to the (post office) box. But there's no problem. There is another key here.
l:	kwaiyis. hu maashi alleela?	L:	Good. Is he going today?
a:	ba9d khamsa dagaayig.	A:	In five minutes.
m:	ya leela, aṭalli9 aj jawaab da fii waraga?	M:	Leela, shall I print out this letter?
l:	aiwa. shukran. aṭ ṭawaabi9 ween?	L:	Yes. Thank you. Where are the stamps?
m:	fii duruj aṭ ṭarabeeza hinaak.	M:	In the drawer of the desk over there.
l:	laazim adakhkhil aj jawaab fii ẓarif u aktib al 9unwaan. jiibi ṭaab9a waaHda ṭawwaali.	L:	I must put the letter into an envelope and write the address. Bring me one stamp quickly.
a:	bee sur9a. al muraasla maashi hassa9. asma9i, al mudiir saafar lubnaan. laazim tarassili jawaab iliktrooni leehu 9an al mu'tamar.	A:	Hurry. The messenger is going now. Listen, the director has gone to Lebanon. You must send him an email about the conference.
m:	al mu'tamar miteen?	M:	When is the conference?
a:	fi l usbuu9 aj jaay.	A:	Next week.

8.1 Drills: tamriin

8.1.1 *laazim* 'must' and *mumkin* 'may'

These are two very common words which can occur on their own. *laazim* means 'must, have to' and *mumkin* means 'possible, may'. They can also be used with the imperfect of the verb, e.g. *laazim aktib jawaab* 'I must write a letter'; *mumkin hu yiṣalliH al makana* 'it's possible for him to repair the engine'.

Repeat the following sentences:

laazim taktib jawaab?	ai, laazim aktib jawaab alleela
laazim tashrabi mooya ?	ai, laazim ashrab mooya ṭawwaali
laazim tarkabu baaṣ?	ai, laazim narkab baaṣ min as suug
laazim yaftaH aṣ ṣanduug?	ai, laazim yaftaH aṣ ṣanduug li l bitt
laazim taghassil al 9idda?	ai, laazim taghassil al 9idda kwaiyis
laazim yisaafru?	ai, laazim yisaafru alleela
mumkin asaa9id al makaniiki?	la', inta maa mumkin tasaa9id al makaniiki
mumkin agṭa9 al laHam?	la', inti maa mumkin tagṭa9i l laHam
mumkin nashrab al laban?	la', intu maa mumkin tashrabu l laban
mumkin hu yiṣalliH al makana?	la', maa mumkin yiṣalliH al makana alleela
mumkin hi ta9mil gahwa?	la', maa mumkin ta9mil gahwa hina
mumkin hum yidakhkhilu dagiig fi l kiis?	la', maa mumkin yidakhkhilu dagiig fi l kiis da

٨,١,٢

كان لازم تكتب جواب؟	اى، كان لازم اكتب جواب الليلة	(والى آخره)

٨,١,٣

داير ارسل جواب للمدير
ماشى ارسل جواب للمدير

دايرين نرسل جواب للمدير
ماشين نرسل جواب للمدير

دايرة افتح الكمبيوتر واطبع جواب
ماشة افتح الكمبيوتر واطبع جواب

عاوزين نفتح الكمبيوتر ونطبع جواب
ماشين نفتح الكمبيوتر ونطبع جواب

داير ادخل جواب فى ظرف واكتب العنوان
عاوزة ادخل جواب فى ظرف واكتب العنوان

ما دايرين ندخل جواب فى ظرف ونكتب العنوان
ما عاوزين ندخل جواب فى ظرف ونكتب العنوان

٨,١,٤

دا البيت	دا بيت احمد
دا الباب	دا باب البيت
دا الولد	دا ولد الضيف
دا الاكل	دا اكل الغنم
دا الكيس	دا كيس الزبونة
دا الراديو	دا راديو محمد

8.1.2 *laazim* and *mumkin* in the past

If you want to make a sentence using *laazim* or *mumkin* but referring to the past, you don't use the past tense of the verb. Instead you put the word *kaan* in front of *laazim* or *mumkin,* e.g. *kaan laazim aktib jawaab* 'I had to write a letter'; *kaan mumkin al makaniiki yiṣalliH al 9arabiiya* 'The mechanic was able to repair the car'.

Now repeat Drill 8.1.1 but this time insert *kaan* into every sentence, e.g. *kaan laazim taktib jawaab? ai, kaan laazim aktib jawaab alleela.*

8.1.3 *9aawz, daayir,* and *maashi* with the imperfect

These words can be used with the imperfect in the same way as *laazim,* e.g. *ana 9aawz arassil jawaab* 'I want to send a letter'.

Drill the following sentences. Try to keep a good speed and rhythm while pronouncing the words correctly.

daayir arassil jawaab li l mudiir
maashi arassil jawaab li l mudiir

daayriin narassil jawaab li l mudiir
maashiin narassil jawaab li l mudiir

daayra aftaH al kombyuutar u aṭba9 jawaab
maasha aftaH al kombyuutar u aṭba9 jawaab

9aawziin naftaH al kombyuutar u naṭba9 jawaab
maashiin naftaH al kombyuutar u naṭba9 jawaab

daayir adakhkhil jawaab fii ẓarif u aktib al 9unwaan.
9aawza adakhkhil jawaab fii ẓarif u aktib al 9unwaan.

maa daayriin nadakhkhil jawaab fii ẓarif u naktib al 9unwaan.
maa 9aawziin nadakhkhil jawaab fii ẓarif u naktib al 9unwaan.

8.1.4 Possessive noun phrases

In the dialogue there are two possessive phrases: *muftaaH aṣ ṣanduug* 'the key of the box', and *duruj aṭ ṭarabeeza* 'the drawer of the desk'. This is the usual way of showing possession in Arabic. The possessed noun stands first and the possessor second, e.g. *beet aHmad* 'Ahmed's house'. Note that there is no definite article before the first noun. It is *beet aHmad,* not *al beet aHmad.*

Feminine nouns ending in *a* add *t* when they occur in this type of phrase, e.g. *guffa* → *guffat al walad* ('the boy's basket'). This is why in the Arabic script they are written with a kind of *t*.

Repeat the following sentences:

da l beet	da beet aHmad
da l baab	da baab al beet
da l walad	da walad aḍ ḍeef
da l akil	da akl al ghanam
da l kiis	da kiis az zabuuna
da r raadyu	da raadyu muHammad

دا العيش	دا عيش البلد
دا السوق	دا سوق امدرمان
دى القفة	دى قفة البت
دى العربية	دى عربية حسن
دى السفارة	دى سفارة برطانيا
دى الجامعة	دى جامعة الخرطوم
دى الجوافة	دى جوافة منى
دى المرة	دى مرة امين
دى المدرسة	دى مدرسة البنات
دى الجبنة	دى جبنة الولد

كلمات

تامن
مكتب، مكاتب
كمبيوتر ، كمبيوترات
طبع، يطبع
جواب، جوابات
مراسلة، مراسلين
استلم، يستلم
مكتب البسطة
روّح، يروّح
مفتاح، مفاتيح
صندوق، صناديق
مشكلة، مشاكل
دقيقة، دقايق
طلّع، يطلّع فى ورقة
طابعة ، طوابع
درج، ادراج
طربيزة، طربيزات
هناك
دخّل ، يدخّل
عنوان، عناوين
طوالى
بسرعة
مدير ، مديرين
لبنان
رسل، يرسل
جواب إلكترونى
له
عن
مؤتمر ، مؤتمرات
متين
جاى
لازم

تمرين الاصوات

da l 9eesh	da 9eesh al balad
da s suug	da suug umdurmaan
di l guffa	di guffat al bitt
di l 9arabiiya	di 9arabiiyat Hassan
di s safaara	di safaarat bariṭaanya
di j jaam9a	di jaam9at al kharṭuum
di j jawaafa	di jawaafat muna
di l mara	di marat amiin (mara means *'wife'* as well as *'woman'*)
di l madrasa	di madrast al banaat
di j jibna	di jibnat al walad

Note that certain words lose a vowel in possessive noun phrases, e.g. *akil* → *akl* and *madrasa* → *madrast.* An explanation of this vowel loss will be given later in the course.

8.1.5 Conversation practice: the office

If you work in an office or have occasion to go to offices, make up a dialogue which you might have there and practise it with your teacher.

8.2 Role play

Act out the parts of some office workers discussing their work, using some of the terms from the dialogue and others you can ask your teacher for.

8.3 Vocabulary: kalmaat

taamin	eighth	duruj, adraaj	drawer (of desk)
maktab, makaatib	office	ṭarabeeza, ṭarabeezaat	desk, table
kombyuutar, kombyuutaraat	computer	hinaak	there
ṭaba9, yaṭba9	type, keyboard, print (in a press)	dakhkhal, yidakhkhil	to put into
jawaab, jawaabaat	letter	9unwaan, 9anaawiin	address
muraasla, muraasaliin	messenger	ṭawwaali	at once, immediately
istalam, yistalim	to collect	bee sur9a	quickly
(maktab) al busṭa	post office	mudiir, mudiiriin	director, boss
rawwaH, yirawwiH	to lose	lubnaan	Lebanon
muftaaH, mafaatiiH	key	rassal, yirassil	to send
ṣanduug, ṣanaadiig	box	jawaab iliktrooni	email
mushkila, mashaakil	problem, difficulty	leehu	to him
dagiiga, dagaayig	minute	9an	about, concerning
ṭalla9, yiṭalli9 fii waraga	to print out (from computer)	mu'tamar, mu'tamaraat	conference
ṭaab9a, ṭawaabi9	postage stamp	miteen	when?
		jaay	next, coming
		laazim	must

8.4 Pronunciation drills: t, ṭ, d, ḍ

Contrast Drills

Follow instructions in Introduction, section 3.

Lists (a) and (b) contrasting *t* and *ṭ* at the beginning of words.
Lists (c) and (d) contrasting *t* and *ṭ* at the end of words.
Lists (e) and (f) contrasting *d* and *ḍ* at the beginning of words.
Lists (g) and (h) contrasting *d* and *ḍ* in the middle of words.

تحت	طفل
تلاتة	طرق
تكسى	طلع
تقيل	طويل
تسعة	طابعة
بنات	بلاط
زيت	غلط
بيوت	مبسوط
تالت	شنط
وكت	شوط
دوا	ضاق
داك	ضرب
درس	ضيف
دقيقة	ضرورى
دهب	ضَهَر
قديم	يضوق
شديد	بضاعة
هدوم	بيضة
غدا	اوضة
مدن	فاضى

(a) t

tiHit	under
talaata	three
taksi	taxi
tagiil	heavy
tis9a	nine

(b) ṭ

ṭifil	baby
ṭurug	ways
ṭala9	he left
ṭawiil	long
ṭaab9a	stamp

(c) t

banaat	girls
zeet	oil
biyuut	houses
taalit	third
wakit	time

(d) ṭ

balaaṭ	tiles
ghalaṭ	wrong
mabsuuṭ	happy
shinaṭ	bags
shooṭ	a half (in football)

(e) d

dawa	medicine
daak	that
daris	lesson
dagiiga	minute
dahab	gold

(f) ḍ

ḍaag	he tasted
ḍarab	he hit
ḍeef	guest
ḍaruuri	necessary
ḍahar	back

(g) d

gadiim	old
shadiid	strong
hiduum	clothes
ghada	lunch
mudun	towns

(h) ḍ

yaḍuug	he tastes
buḍaa9a	goods
beeḍa	an egg
ooḍa	room
faaḍi	empty

الدرس التاسع

حوار : فى حصة العربى

م : مدرس ب : بول ج : جون إ : إليزابث س: سوزان

م صباح الخير.

الكل صباح النور.

م زاكرتوا درس امبارح؟

ب ايوه، نحن زاكرنا لكن ما فهمنا الكلمة دى.

م الكلمة شنو؟

ب طلع.

م طلع، يعنى مرق، زى هو مرق من البيت، ولا هو طلع من البيت، فى برضو معنى تانى، يعنى، ماشى فوق، مثلا هو طلع فوق الجبل. فهمت هسع؟

ب اى، شكرا.

م فى سؤال تانى؟

ج ايوه، ما عرفت 'paper' بالعربى.

م 'paper' يعنى ورق.

ج نعم؟

م ورق، بتقدر تكتب ورق فى السبورة؟

ج دا كدا صاح؟

م صاح. كتبت كويس. (لواحدة من النسوان) يا إليزابث، ممكن تتكلمى مع سوزان بالعربى؟

إ يا سوزان، ليكى كم سنة فى السودان؟

س حداشر سنة. متزوجة سودانى. يا إليزابث. انت بتدرّسى هنا فى السودان؟

إ اى، بدرّس انجليزى فى مدرسة البنات.

م شكرا. انتوا بتتكلموا عربى كويس.

ad daris at taasi9

Hiwaar: fii Hiṣṣat al 9arabi

m: mudarris P: Paul J: John E: Elizabeth S: Suzanne

m: ṣabaaH al kheer.
kull: ṣabaaH an nuur.
m: zaakartu daris umbaariH?
P: aiwa, niHna zaakarna laakin maa fihimna l kalma di.
m: al kalma shinuu?
P: 'ṭala9'.
m: 'ṭala9', ya9ni marag, zeey 'hu marag min al beet' walla 'hu ṭala9 min al beet.' fii barḍu ma9na taani, ya9ni, maashi foog, masalan, 'hu ṭala9 foog aj jabal.' fihimta hassa9?
P: ai, shukran.
m: fii su'aal taani?
J: aiwa. maa 9irifta *'paper'* bi l 9arabi.
m: *'paper'*, ya9ni 'warag'.
J: na9am?
m: 'warag'. bitagdar taktib 'warag' fi s sabbuura?
J: da kida ṣaaHH?
m: ṣaaHH. katabta kwaiyis.
(lee waaHda min an niswaan)
ya Elizabeth, mumkin titkallami ma9a Suzanne bi l 9arabi?
E: ya Suzanne, leeki kam sana fi s suudaan?
S: Hidaashar sana. mutzawwija suudaani. ya Elizabeth, inti bitdarrisi hina fi s suudaan?
E: ai, badarris ingliizi fii madrast al banaat.
m: shukran. intu bititkallamu 9arabi kwaiyis.

Lesson 9

Dialogue: In the Arabic class

t: teacher P: Paul J: John E: Elizabeth S: Suzanne

t: Good morning.
all: Good morning.
t: Have you learned yesterday's lesson?
P: Yes, we've learned it but we don't understand this word.
t: What's the word?
P: *'ṭala9'*
t: *'ṭala9'*, that's 'to go out', like 'he went out of the house' or *'hu ṭala9 min al beet'.* There is also another meaning, that is 'go up.' For example, *hu ṭala9 foog aj jabal* 'he went up the hill'. Do you understand now?
P: Yes, thank you.
t: Any more questions?
J: Yes. I don't know 'paper' in Arabic.
t: 'Paper', that's *'warag'*.
J: Please repeat.
t: *warag*. Can you write *'warag'* on the blackboard?
J: Is that correct?
t: Correct. You've written well.
(to one of the women)
Elizabeth, can you speak to Suzanne in Arabic?
E: Suzanne, how many years have you been in Sudan?
S: Eleven. I'm married to a Sudanese. Elizabeth, do you teach here in Sudan?
E: Yes, I teach English in the girls' school.
t: Thank you. You speak Arabic well.

Notes on the dialogue

1. *ṣabaaH al kheer,* literally 'morning of good', is another greeting frequently heard. The reply is *ṣabaaH an nuur,* 'morning of light'. There is an equivalent evening greeting, *misa al kheer,* with a reply *misa an nuur.* Note that the stress falls on the last syllable of *misa* when it is in these phrases.
2. *na9am*: this word, which is the literary Arabic for 'yes', is used by Sudanese in order to ask someone to repeat what they said, as one might say 'pardon' or 'excuse me' in English if one doesn't hear the other person said. It is also used on the telephone as a response to show that you are listening, much like 'yes....yes' in English.

تمرين

٩,١,١

اتكلم	نتكلم
تتكلم	تتكلموا
تتكلمى	
يتكلم	يتكلموا
تتكلم	

اشتغل، تشتغل (والى آخره)

استلم، اتعلم، انكسر، استعمل

Classroom drill

From now on the teacher should keep as far as possible to Arabic in class and avoid using English, if he is not already doing so. The students also should try to ask their questions in Arabic. Some phrases have been introduced in the dialogue for this lesson especially for that purpose. It's important to overcome the habit of always dropping back into English as soon as you find speaking Arabic a little bit difficult.

9.1 Drills: tamriin

9.1.1 Further variations in the verbs

In Lesson 4, section 4.1.1, it was pointed out that most Arabic verbs consist of three basic consonants but that some verbs may vary a little from the usual pattern. You learned two variations on the patterns of *ghassal* and *saafar.* Here are four more variations:

a) *i* before and *t* after the first consonant, e.g. *ishtaghal* 'to work' (like *shughul* 'work' and *shaghghaal* 'working man'); *istalam* 'to collect'.

b) *in* or *it* before the first consonant, e.g. *inkasar* 'to be broken'.

a) and b) both have vowels *a-a* in the past and *a-i* in the imperfect. Note that the stress falls on the *a* of the second syllable and not on the first syllable, i.e. it is an exception to the general rule given in section 3.4.

c) *it* before the first consonant and the middle consonant doubled, e.g. *itkallam* 'to speak'; *it9allam* 'to learn'.

d) *ista* before the first consonant, e.g. *ista9mal* 'to use'.

c) and d) have vowels *a-a* in the past *and* the imperfect.

The past tense of these verbs does not differ from that of *daras.* The imperfect has some slight differences in the person indicators like those of *ghassal* with *bi-* (see Lesson 7.1.3). Look at the table set out below. It serves as a pattern for all four variations, i.e. they all vary in the same way from the basic verb.

	Singular	**Plural**
1st	a-tkallam	n-itkallam
2nd m	t-itkallam	t-itkallam-u
2nd f	t-itkallam-i	
3rd m	y-itkallam	y-itkallam-u
3rd f	t-itkallam	

bi- is added to the above forms without any further changes except in the 3rd m sing. and 3rd pl., where the *yi* is dropped, e.g. *bitkallam* and *bitkallamu.*

Repeat the above table after the teacher until you know it, first with *itkallam* and then with the other verbs: *ishtaghal, yishtaghil*; *istalam, yistalim*; *it9allam, yit9allam*; *inkasar, yinkasir*; *ista9mal, yista9mal.*

(Note that *yishtaghil* and *yinkasir* lose the last *i* in the 2nd f sing. and 2nd and 3rd plur. in the same way as *yisaafir*, e.g. *tishtaghli*, etc.)

٩,١,٢

انا	امبارح
انتَ	دايما
انتِ	قاعد، قاعدة، قاعدين
هو	لازم
هى	ماشى، ماشة، ماشين
نحن	
انتوا	
هم	

هو، قاعد   هو قاعد يفطر   (والى آخره)

سافر، درّس، اشتغل، استعمل، اتكلم، فهم، عرف، ركب، رسم

٩,١,٣

انا قدرت افتح الباب

انا بقدر اصلح عربات

انا قدرت اركب القطر بدرى

البت   البت قدرت تفتح الباب

انتوا   انتوا قدرتوا تفتحوا الباب (والى آخره)

٩,١,٤

تلاطاشر
اربعطاشر
خمسطاشر
ستطاشر
سبعطاشر
تمنطاشر
تسعطاشر
عشرين

9.1.2 Revision of the past and imperfect of all verbs

Using the verb *faṭar, yafṭur* to start with, the teacher should say a pronoun from the column of pronouns below and an item from the second column, and the student respond with a whole sentence giving the appropriate form of the verb. This can be done several times until the student is able to answer promptly.

ana	umbaariH
inta	daayman *(always, often)*
inti	gaa9id, gaa9da, gaa9diin
hu	laazim
hi	maashi, maasha, maashiin
hum	
niHna	
intu	
hum	

For example, teacher says, *'hu,' 'gaa9id';* student responds, *'hu gaa9id yafṭur.'*

Follow the same procedure with these other verbs:

saafar, yisaafir; darras, yidarris; ishtaghal, yishtaghil; ista9mal, yista9mal; itkallam, yitkallam; fihim, yafham; 9irif, ya9rif; rikib, yarkab; rasam, yarsum.

9.1.3 *gidir* 'to be able'

gidir is a useful verb meaning 'to be able, to know how'. It can be used with the imperfect of another verb, e.g. *inta bitagdar taktib* 'you can write'; *al bitt gidrat tazaakir ad daris* 'the girl was able to learn the lesson'. Note that although *gidir* may occur in either the past or the imperfect, depending on the time referred to, the verb following it will always be in the imperfect.

Below are three sentences. The teacher should take one at a time and give the student a pronoun or noun subject in place of *ana*. The student should then say the whole sentence with the new subject and the appropriate forms of the verbs, e.g. teacher says, *'al bitt'* and the student replies, *'al bitt gidrat taftaH al baab.'* The reply could also be in the negative, e.g. *'al bitt maa gidrat taftaH al baab.'*

ana gidirta aftaH al baab.
ana bagdar aṣalliH 9arabaat.
ana gidirta arkab al gaṭar badri.

9.1.4 Numbers 10–20

In Arabic, the numbers from 3–10 are followed by plural nouns, but numbers over 10 are followed by the singular, e.g. *talaata shuhuur* but *Hidaashar shahar.* (See Lesson 11 for the number 2 and nouns.)

Revise numbers 1–12 (see Lesson 5) and memorize numbers 13–20 below:

13 talaṭṭaashar
14 arba9ṭaashar
15 khamuṣṭaashar
16 siṭṭaashar
17 saba9ṭaashar
18 tamanṭaashar
19 tisa9ṭaashar
20 9ishriin

كلمات

حصة، حصص

مدرس، مدرسين

مدرسة، مدرسات

صباح

صباح الخير

صباح النور

زاكر، يزاكر

فهم، يفهم

كلمة، كلمات

طلع، يطلع

معنى، معانى

مثلا

جبل، جبال

كدا

سؤال، اسئلة

يعنى

ورق

نعم

قدر، يقدر

سبورة، سبورات

صاح

نسوان

اتكلم، يتكلم

متزوج، متزوجة

اشتغل، يشتغل

انكسر، ينكسر

اتعلم، يتعلم

استعمل يستعمل

دايما

In pairs practice again the question you drilled in section 7.2, i.e. *leek kam sana fi s suudaan?* etc., but this time you can use any number from 1–20 in your answer, except 2.

9.1.5 Conversation practice: the meaning of words

Practise asking the teacher for the meaning of words and of listening to the explanation. The teacher needs to speak slowly and clearly and, as far as possible, should explain with words that the student already knows, just as in the dialogue the teacher explains the meaning of *ṭala9*. Listening with understanding is as important a language skill as speaking.

9.2 Role play

Now act out a classroom scene like in the dialogue with one of the students taking the role of teacher.

9.3 Vocabulary: kalmaat

Hiṣṣa, Hiṣaṣ	class period	warag	paper (collective)
mudarris, mudarrisiin	teacher (male)	na9am	excuse me, please
mudarrisa, mudarrisaat	teacher (female)		repeat
ṣabaaH	morning	gidir, yagdar	to be able
ṣabaaH al kheer	good morning!	sabbuura, sabbuuraat	blackboard
ṣabaaH an nuur	(reply to above)	ṣaaHH	correct, true
zaakar, yizaakir	to memorize	niswaan	women
fihim, yafham	to understand	itkallam, yitkallam	to speak, to talk
kalma, kalmaat	word	mutzawwij (m),	married
ṭala9, yaṭla9	to go out or up	mutzawwija (f)	
ma9na, ma9aani (m)	meaning	ishtaghal, yishtaghil	to work
masalan	for example	inkasar, yinkasir	to be broken
jabal, jibaal	hill, mountain	it9allam, yit9allam	to learn
kida	like that, and so on	ista9mal, yista9mal	to use
su'aal, as'ila	question	daayman	always, often
ya9ni	that's to say		

9.4 Pronunciation Drills: l , a , aa

l – this has two pronunciations. When the previous consonant or the next consonant in the word is *ṣ* or *ṭ* or *ḍ* then the *l* is pronounced as in English 'tell,' that is, with the back of the tongue raised; otherwise *l* is as in English 'let,' that is, without the back of the tongue raised, even at the end of words.

a – also has two pronunciations, a normal one and a slightly different one if it is preceded or followed by *ṣ* , *ṭ* or *ḍ*.

aa – has two pronunciations, a normal one and a slightly different one if it is preceded (but not if it is followed) by *ṣ* , *ṭ* or *ḍ*.

Contrast Drills

Follow the instructions in Introduction, section 3.

Lists (a) and (b) contrasting the two pronunciations of *l* at the end of words.
Lists (c) and (d) contrasting the two pronunciations of *a* in the first syllable of words.
Lists (e) and (f) contrasting the two pronunciations of *aa* in the second syllable of words.

تمرين الاصوات

طويل	اتفضل
عمل	رطل
انزل	وِصل
جمل	بصل
ولد	طلب
دهب	ضرب
مرة	مصر
وقع	بصل
شهر	صفق
تقيل	طويل
رجال	اصطاد
عنوان	بضاعة
كتار	مطار
طيارة	مطابخ
آثار	بطانة

(a) l normal

ṭawiil	long
9amal	he made
anzil	get off
jamal	camel

(b) l with ṭ, ṣ, ḍ

itfaḍḍal	please
raṭul	pound
wiṣil	he arrived
baṣal	onions

(c) a normal

walad	boy
dahab	bold
mara	woman
waga9	he fell
shahar	month
tagiil	heavy

(d) a with ṣ, ṭ, ḍ

ṭalab	he asked
ḍarab	he hit
maṣir	Egypt
baṣal	onions
ṣafag	leaves
ṭawiil	long

(e) aa normal

rujaal	men
9unwaan	address
kutaar	many
ṭayyaara	airplane
aasaar	ruins

(f) aa with ṣ, ṭ, ḍ

iṣṭaad	he hunted
buḍaa9a	goods
maṭaar	airport
maṭaabikh	kitchens
buṭaana	lining

Note: In some words such as *jabal* 'hill' and *laban* 'milk', *a* is pronounced by many people like the 'e' in English 'met.'

الدرس العاشر

حوار : الخياتة

آ : آمال   ق : قمر

آ شوفى القماش دا. اللون مش كويس؟

ق سمح، اخدتى من وين؟

آ حق ام زينب. هى اخدت القماش دا والقماش التقيل داك من مصر.

ق انت بتخيتى كتير؟

آ اى. اخدت مكنة قديمة قبل اربعة سنين وبخيت فساتين وملابس الاطفال.

ق خيتى القميص الكبير دا، انت؟

آ لا، دا من السوق. انا ما بخيت قمصان وبناطلين، هدوم النسوان والاطفال بس.

ق قاعدة تخيتى شنو هسع؟

آ الفستان الطويل دا.

ق الفستان حق منو؟

آ حق بت سارة. انت برضو بتخيتى؟

ق ما بعرف اخيت ملابس لكن بطرز صور.

آ انت شاطرة. ما بقدر اطرز ابدا. التطريز صعب.

ق ما صعب، ساهل.

آ ممكن تعملى لى صورة سمحة وانا اخيت ليكى فستان؟

ق كويس. خلاص، اتفقنا.

تمرين

١٠,١,١

ad daris al 9aashir — Lesson 10

Hiwaar: al khiyaata — Dialogue: Sewing

a:	aamaal g: gamar	A:	Amal G: Gamar
a:	shuufi l gumaash da. al loon mush kwaiyis?	A:	Look at this material. Isn't the color nice?
g:	samiH. akhatti min ween?	G:	Lovely. Where did you get it?
a:	Hagg umm zeenab. hi akhadat al gumaash da w al gumaash at tagiil daak min maṣir.	A:	It belongs to Zeinab's mother. She got this material and that thick material in Egypt.
g:	inti bitkhayyiti katiir?	G:	Do you sew a lot?
a:	ai. akhatta makana gadiima gabli arba9a siniin u bakhayyit fasaatiin u malaabis al aṭfaal.	A:	Yes. I got an old machine four years ago and I sew dresses and children's clothes.
g:	khayyatti l gamiiṣ al kabiir da, inti?	G:	Did you sew this big shirt?
a:	la', da min as suug. ana maa bakhayyit gumṣaan u banaaṭliin; hiduum an niswaan w al aṭfaal bass.	A:	No, that's from the market. I don't sew shirts and trousers; only women's and children's clothes.
g:	gaa9da takhayyiti shinuu hassa9?	G:	What are you sewing at the moment?
a:	al fustaan aṭ ṭawiil da.	A:	This long dress.
g:	al fustaan Hagg minuu?	G:	Who does the dress belong to?
a:	Hagg bitt saarra. inti barḍu bitkhayyiti?	A:	It belongs to Sara's daughter. Do you also sew?
g:	maa ba9rif akhayyit malaabis laakin baṭarriz ṣuwar.	G:	I don't know how to sew clothes but I embroider pictures.
a:	inti shaaṭra. maa bagdar aṭarriz abadan. at taṭriiz ṣa9ab.	A:	You're clever. I can't embroider at all. Embroidery is difficult.
g:	maa ṣa9ab; saahil.	G:	It's not difficult; it's easy.
a:	mumkin ta9mili leey ṣuura samHa u ana akhayyit leeki fustaan?	A:	Would you make me a nice picture and I'll sew you a dress?
g:	kwaiyis. khalaaṣ. ittafagna.	G:	Fine. That's agreed.

Notes on the dialogue

1. You may have noticed the sentence, *khayyatti l gamiiṣ al kabiir da inti?* The subject pronoun is sometimes put last like this for emphasis.
2. *akhad* 'to get, take': a final *d* changes to *t* when it is followed by one of the endings beginning in *t*, e.g. *akhad* plus *ti* becomes *akhatti.*
3. Don't try to use the imperfect of the verbs *akal*, *akhad*, or *wagaf*. A later lesson will deal with these verb forms.

10.1 Drills: tamriin

10.1.1 Adjectives

In Lesson 4.2 you practised masculine and feminine nouns with some adjectives, e.g. *kwaiyis, jaahiz,* and saw that these adjectives have a masculine form which goes with masculine nouns, and a feminine form ending in *-a* that goes with feminine nouns. That pattern is the same for all adjectives in Arabic.

Lists of nouns and adjectives are given below. The teacher should say one of the nouns and the student respond with a sentence containing that noun and one of the adjectives in agreement with it, e.g. teacher: *fustaan.* Student: *al fustaan ṭawiil* 'the dress is long'.

فستان	جاهز
قميص	صغير
جلابية	طويل
بنطلون	سمك
عربية	لحم
سمك	قديم
لحم	كويس
صابون	سمح
شوربة	لزيز
قفة	قريب

فستان ...... الفستان طويل (والى آخره)

١٠,١,٢

الدرس صعب	دا درس صعب
الخياتة صعبة	دى خياتة صعبة
الكيس فاضى	دا كيس فاضى
القفة فاضية	دى قفة فاضية
القماش تقيل	دا قماش تقيل
المكنة تقيلة	دى مكنة تقيلة
الموظف شاطر	دا موظف شاطر
السكرتيرة شاطرة	دى سكرتيرة شاطرة

١٠,١,٣

فى فسطان طويل وفى فسطان قصير	انت دايرة الفستان الطويل؟	لا، انا دايرة الفستان القصير
فى قماش تقيل وفى قماش خفيف	انت داير القماش التقيل؟	لا، انا داير القماش الخفيف
فى بيت كبير وفى بيت صغير	انتوا عاوزين البيت الكبير؟	لا، نحن عاوزين البيت الصغير
فى عربية جديدة وفى عربية قديمة	انت عاوز العربية القديمة؟	لا، انا عاوز العربية الجديدة

Nouns	**Adjectives**
fustaan	jaahiz
gamiiṣ	ṣaghayyir
jallaabiiya	ṭawiil
banṭaloon	kabiir
9arabiiya	tagiil
samak	gadiim
laHam	kwaiyis
ṣaabuun	samiH
shoorba	laziiz
guffa	gariib

Note that if the last vowel in the masculine form of the adjective is a short *i*, it is dropped when the feminine ending *-a* is added, e.g. *samiH* → *samHa*. The short *a* in *ṣa9ab* 'difficult' and *ka9ab* 'bad' is also dropped before the feminine ending, e.g. *ṣa9ba*.

10.1.2 Adjectives in different positions

The sentence *ad daris ṣa9ab* means 'the lesson is difficult'. The subject is *ad daris,* and *ṣa9ab* the predicate, the part of the sentence that tells something about the subject. Compare this with the phrase *daris ṣa9ab,* which means 'a difficult lesson'. In Arabic the adjective comes after the noun in both cases, but the presence or absence of the definite article is what makes a difference to the meaning. *daris ṣa9ab* can be put into a sentence, e.g. *da daris ṣa9ab* 'this is a difficult lesson'; now *da* is the subject and *daris ṣa9ab* the predicate.

Repeat the following sentences after the teacher:

ad daris ṣa9ab	da daris ṣa9ab
al khiyaata ṣa9ba	di khiyaata ṣa9ba
al kiis faaḍi	da kiis faaḍi
al guffa faaḍya	di guffa faaḍya
al gumaash tagiil	da gumaash tagiil
al makana tagiila	di makana tagiila
al muwaẓẓaf shaaṭir	da muwaẓẓaf shaaṭir
as sikirteera shaaṭra	di sikirteera shaaṭra

10.1.3 Adjectives with the definite article

Compare the phrase ad daris ṣa9ab 'the lesson is difficult' with ad daris aṣ ṣa9ab 'the difficult lesson'. In Arabic the definite article occurs twice in the latter phrase, before both noun and adjective.

Here are some pairs of adjectives: *ṭawiil* 'long'/*giṣayyir* 'short'; *tagiil* 'heavy'/*khafiif* 'light in weight'; *kabiir* 'big'/*ṣaghayyir* small'; *gadiim* 'old'/*jadiid* 'new'. First of all repeat the following sentences after the teacher:

fii fusṭaan ṭawiil u fii fusṭaan giṣayyir	inti daayra al fusṭaan aṭ ṭawiil?	la', ana daayra al fusṭaan al giṣayyir
fii gumaash tagiil u fii gumaash khafiif	inta daayir al gumaash at tagiil?	la', ana daayir al gumaash al khafiif
fii beet kabiir u fii beet ṣaghayyir	intu 9aawziin al beet al kabiir?	la', niHna 9aawziin al beet aṣ ṣaghayyir
fii 9arabiiya jadiida u fii 9arabiiya gadiima	inta 9aawz al 9arabiiya al gadiima?	la', ana 9aawz al 9arabiiya aj jadiida

١٠,١,٤

المفتاح .... منو؟ المفتاح حق منو؟ (والى آخره)

العربية .... ولد حسين

الكرسى ...... ابو سارة

القلم .... سيد الدكان

الطابعة .... البت

السبورة ...... المدرس

كلمات

عاشر
خياتة
قماش
لون، الوان
مش
اخد
حق
تقيل
مصر
خيّت، يخيت
مكنة، مكنات
قديم
فستان، فساتين
ملابس
طفل، اطفال
قميص، قمصان

كبير
بنطلون، بناطلين
هدوم
طويل
منو
صغير
برضو
طرّز، يطرز
صورة، صور
ابدا
تطريز
ساهل
اتفقنا
جلابية، جلاليب
كعب
قصير
خفيف
جديد

Now practise in pairs asking questions like those above, e.g. one person asks *intu 9aawziin al beet al kabiir* 'Do you (pl) want the big house?' and the other person replies, 'No we want the small house' or 'Yes, we want the big house.'

10.1.4 *Hagg* 'belongs to'

The word *Hagg* means 'belongs to', and has a masculine form *Hagg,* agreeing with masculine nouns, and a feminine form *Haggat,* agreeing with feminine nouns. It is thus something like an adjective but not exactly, e.g. *al gumaash Hagg aHmad* 'the material belongs to Ahmad', *aj jallaabiiya Haggat Hassan* 'the jelabiya belongs to Hassan',

Complete the sentences below by putting *Hagg* or *Haggat* in the gap:

al muftaaH	____________	minuu?
al 9arabiiya	____________	walad Husseen
al kursi	____________	abu saarra
al galam	____________	siid ad dukkaan
aṭ ṭaab9a	____________	al bitt
as sabbuura	____________	al mudarris

10.2 Role play

Act out the parts of people buying clothes from in the market or a shop. Among other things you could ask the price and bargain over it, and you could make comments on the clothes and say which you prefer.

10.3 Vocabulary: kalmaat

9aashir	tenth	kabiir	big
khiyaata	sewing	banṭaloon, banaaṭliin	trousers
gumaash	material	hiduum	clothes
loon, alwaan	color	ṭawiil	long, tall
mush	(an alternative to *maa* sometimes used with nouns and adjectives)	minuu?	who?
		ṣaghayyir	small
		barḍu	also
akhad	to get, obtain	ṭarraz, yiṭarriz	to embroider
Hagg	belonging to	ṣuura, ṣuwar	picture
tagiil	heavy, thick	abadan	not at all, never
maṣir	Egypt	taṭriiz	embroidery
khayyat, yikhayyit	to sew	saahil	easy
makana, makanaat	machine (sewing)	ittafagna	we've agreed
gadiim	old	jallaabiiya, jalaaliib	jelabiya
fustaan, fasaatiin	dress	ka9ab	bad
malaabis	clothes	giṣayyir	short
ṭifil, aṭfaal	child	khafiif	light in weight
gamiiṣ, gumṣaan	shirt	jadiid	new

تمرين الاصوات

مشيت	خشّيت
عشا	رشّيت
بشوف	قشّيت
ناشف	نشّف
جبل	شباك
قبيلة	ضبان
لبن	كباية
خبر	يحبوا
سكن	سكين
مكنة	ركاب
مكاتب	سكر
حكاية	دكان
سمع	عمة
شمال	عمى
سمك	امى
ليمون	محمر
قديم	خدام
جديد	بيدى
غدا	مدة
مدارس	جدا

10.4 Pronunciation drills

Doubled consonants

In the middle or at the end of words, consonants may be doubled, e.g. *bb, shsh*. These must be pronounced longer than the single form; compare the sound of sh in the English 'bishop' with the sound *sh sh* in the middle of 'fish shop.'

All consonants may be doubled; the drills give practice with only some of them.

Contrast drills.

See Introduction, section 3, for instructions.

Lists (a) and (b) contrast *sh* and *shsh*.
Lists (c) and (d) contrast *b* and *bb*.
Lists (e) and (f) contrast *k* and *kk*.
Lists (g) and (h) contrast *m* and *mm*.
Lists (i) and (j) contrast *d* and *dd*.

(a) sh		**(b) shsh**	
masheet	I went	khashsheet	I entered
9asha	supper	rashsheet	I sprayed
bashuuf	I look	gashsheet	I swept
naashif	dry	nashshaf	he dried (it)

(c) b		**(d) bb**	
jabal	hill	shubbaak	window
gabiila	tribe	ḍubbaan	flies
laban	milk	kubbaaya	a glass
khabar	news	yaHibbu	they love

(e) k		**(f) kk**	
sakan	he lived	sikkiin	knife
makana	machine	rukkaab	passengers
makaatib	offices	sukkar	sugar
Hikaaya	story	dukkaan	shop

(g) m		**(h) mm**	
simi9	he heard	9amma	aunt
shimaal	left	9ammi	my uncle
samak	fish	ummi	my mother
leemuun	limes	muHammar	fried

(i) d		**(j) dd**	
gadiim	old	khaddaam	servant
jadiid	new	biyaddi	he gives
ghada	lunch	mudda	period of time
madaaris	schools	jiddan	very much

اسئلة لمراجعة الدروس

من ٦ الى ١٠

١ ليك كم شهر فى السودان؟

٢ السكرتيرة بتشتغل فى دكان؟

٣ منو بغسل الهدوم؟

٤ ممكن الناس يستلموا جوابات من صندوق البسطة كل يوم؟

٥ البنات بيخيتوا فساتين فى المدرسة؟

٦ انت بتسافر كتير؟

٧ بتتكلموا عربى ولا انجليزى مع الجيران؟

٨ الكباية الصغيرة احسن ولا الكباية الكبيرة دى؟

٩ قدرت تفتح الابواب بالمفاتيح؟

١٠ جامعة الخرطوم جامعة قديمة؟

١١ عاوز ترسل جواب إلكترونى لمنو؟

١٢ العربى ساهل؟

١٣ النسوان فى السودان بيعرفوا انجليزى؟

١٤ انت متزوج؟

١٥ بتسمع الراديو فى الصباح؟

١٦ الاطفال قاعدين يلعبوا كويس؟

١٧ اخدت بيض امبارح؟

١٨ انت عاوز كيس كبير ولا كيس صغير؟

١٩ ضرورى تغير الزيت فى العربية كل اسبوع؟

٢٠ بتشرب الشاى بلبن؟

Revision questions for Lessons 6–10

Answer the following questions:

1. leek kam s̲h̲ahar fi s suudaan?

2. as sikirteera biti s̲h̲tag̲h̲il fii dukkaan?

3. minuu big̲h̲assil al hiduum?

4. mumkin an naas yistalmu jawaabaat min ṣanduug al busṭa kulli yoom?

5. al banaat bik̲h̲ayyitu fasaatiin fi l madrasa?

6. inta bitsaafir katiir?

7. bititkallamu 9arabi walla ingliizi ma9a j jeeraan?

8. al kubbaaya ṣ ṣag̲h̲ayra aHsan walla l kubbaaya l kabiira di?

9. gidirta taftaH al abwaab bi l mafaatiiH?

10. jaam9at al k̲h̲arṭuum jaam9a gadiima?

11. 9aawz tarassil jawaab iliktrooni lee minuu?

12. al 9arabi saahil?

13. an niswaan fi s suudaan bi9rifu ingliizi?

14. inta mutzawwij?

15. bitasma9 ar raadyu fi ṣ ṣabaaH?

16. al aṭfaal gaa9diin yal9abu kwaiyis?

17. ak̲h̲atta beeḍ umbaariH?

18. inta 9aawz kiis kabiir walla kiis ṣag̲h̲ayyir?

19. ḍaruuri tag̲h̲ayyir az zeet fi l 9arabiiya kulli usbuu9?

20. bita s̲h̲rab a s̲h̲ s̲h̲aay bee laban?

الدرس الحداشر

حوار : الفسحة

أ : احمد   ج : جماعة من الخواجات

أ   ازيكم.

ج   اهلا.

أ   انتو ماشين وين؟

ج   ماشين المقرن.

أ   ماشين تعملوا شنو هناك؟

ج   ماشين نصور النيلين ومجلس الشعب جنب الكبرى.

أ   ما ماشين توتى؟ توتى جزيرة حلوة.

ج   ما بنعرف الطريق.

أ   ممكن تركبوا البنطون من قدام قاعة الصداقة، وبعدين فى مواصلات لحدى الحلة .

ج   فى شنو فى توتى؟

أ   فى جناين كتيرة، يعنى جناين فواكه ... ليمون، منقه، برتقان وخدروات. حلوة خالص.

ج   ممكن نتفسح فى الجناين؟

أ   ايوه. ممكن تتفسحوا فى كل الجزيرة.

ج   شكرا.

أ   مع السلامة.

تمرين

١١,١,١

ad daris al Hidaashar — Lesson 11

Hiwaar: al fusHa — Dialogue: The outing

a:	aHmad j: jamaa9a min al khawaajaat	A:	Ahmad f: group of foreigners
a:	izzeeyyakum.	A:	How do you do?
j:	ahlan.	f:	Welcome.
a:	intu maashiin ween?	A:	Where are you going?
j:	maashiin al mugran.	f:	We are going to the Mogran.
a:	maashiin ta9milu shinuu hinaak?	A:	What are you going to do there?
j:	maashiin naṣawwir an niileen u majlis ash sha9b jamb al kubri.	f:	We're going to take photos of the two Niles and the People's Assembly beside the bridge.
a:	maa maashiin tuuti? tuuti jaziira Hilwa.	A:	Aren't you going to Tuti? Tuti's a lovely island.
j:	maa bina9rif aṭ ṭariig.	f:	We don't know the way.
a:	mumkin tarkabu l banṭoon min giddaam ghaa9at aṣ ṣadaagha, u ba9deen fi muwaaṣalaat liHaddi l Hilla.	A:	You can take the ferry from in front of Friendship Hall, and then there's public transport to the village.
j:	fii shinuu fii tuuti?	f:	What is there on Tuti?
a:	fii janaayin katiira, ya9ni janaayin fawaakih ... leemuun, manga, burtukaan u khudrawaat. Hilwa khaaliṣ.	A:	There are lots of gardens, fruit gardens... limes, mangoes, oranges and vegetables. It's beautiful.
j:	mumkin nitfassaH fi j janaayin?	f:	Can we go for a walk in the gardens?
a:	aiwa. mumkin titfassaHu fii kull aj jaziira.	A:	Yes. You can walk about in the whole of the island.
j:	shukran.	f:	Thank you.
a:	ma9a s salaama.	A:	Good-bye.

11.1 Drills: tamriin

11.1.1 Nouns in the dual

In Arabic the number 2 does NOT occur with a noun following it, e.g. you can't say *itneen shuhuur* to mean 'two months.' So how can one talk about two of anything? The answer is, by adding an ending *-een* to the singular of the noun, e.g. *beet* 'house' → *beeteen* 'two houses'; *an niil* 'the Nile' → *an niileen* 'the two Niles' (i.e. the White Nile and the Blue Nile).

Note that:

a) Nouns with a short i or u in the last syllable, the i or u is lost when -een is added unless there is more than one consonant before them, e.g. *ẓarif* → *ẓarfeen; rijil* → *rijleen, ukhut* → *ukhteen.*

b) Nouns ending in *-a* which add *-t* (see Lesson 8.4) in a possessive phrase, also add *-t* before *-een* and usually lose the *-a* provided it is proceeded by a single consonant and not two, e.g. *madrasa* → *madrasteen, kubbaaya* → *kubbaayteen;* but *marra* → *marrateen, guffa* → *guffateen.*

The teacher should ask the students to form duals for the following words. This would also be a good opportunity to test them on the plurals of these words.

حصة، جواب، دقيقة، صندوق، مفتاح، طابعة، اسبوع، جامعة، بحر، قلم، بت، كرسى، عربية، كبرى، ولد، خدام، راجل، شهر، سنة، ساعة، زول

فستان ...... فستانين فساتين (والى آخره)

١١,١,٢

المرة موجودة	النسوان موجودين
المدرس شاطر	المدرسين شاطرين
البت حلوة	البنات حلوين
السواق عيان	السواقين عيانين
الزول كويس	الناس كويسين
الولد صغير	الاولاد صغار
الراجل كبير	الرجال كبار
الضيف طويل	الضيوف طوال
الموظف قصير	الموظفين قصار

الصورة سمحة	الصور سمحة
الجزيرة حلوة	الجزر حلوة
القلم بيظ	الاقلام بايظة
الدرس صعب	الدروس صعبة
القميص خفيف	القمصان خفيفة
الفستان طويل	الفساتين طويلة
المفتاح جديد	المفاتيح جديدة
الصندوق تقيل	الصناديق تقيلة
الباب كبير	الابواب كبيرة

١١,١,٣

fustaan, ṣuura, Hiṣṣa, jawaab, dagiiga, ṣanduug, muftaaH, ṭaab9a, usbuu9, jaam9a, baHar, galam, bitt, kursi, 9arabiiya, kubri, walad, khaddaam, raajil, shahar, sana, saa9a, zool.

Note that a few words, mainly of foreign origin, do not have a dual, e.g. *kiilu.* One says *itneen kiilu.*

11.1.2 Plural nouns with adjectives

In section 10.1 you practiced the difference between masculine and feminine nouns and adjectives. Now we come to adjectives with plural nouns. Most adjectives have a plural form, which from now on will be given after the singular in the vocabularies for each lesson. Some of the plurals are formed by changing the vowels, e.g. *kabiir, kubaar.* Some are formed by adding the ending *-iin,* e.g. *moojuud, moojuudiin.*

Note that:

a) Plural nouns referring to human beings take plural adjectives, e.g. *ar rujaal ash shaaṭriin* 'the clever men', *awlaad ṣughaar* 'small children', *banaat kwaiysiin* 'good girls'.
b) All other plural nouns take adjectives in the feminine singular, e.g. *duruus ṣa9ba* 'difficult lessons', *juzur kabiira* 'big islands', *aglaam baayẓa* 'pens that don't work'.

It should be added, however, that not all Sudanese follow the above rules. There are considerable dialectal and personal variations where plural nouns and their adjectives are concerned, so don't be surprised to hear alternative usages.

Repeat the following sentences after the teacher. On the left are phrases in the singular of the pattern *al mara moojuuda* 'the woman is present', and on the right are equivalent phrases in the plural, such as *an niswaan moojuudiin* 'the women are present'.

al mara moojuuda	an niswaan moojuudiin
al mudarris shaaṭir	al mudarrisiin shaaṭriin
al bitt Hilwa	al banaat Hilwiin
as sawwaag 9ayyaan	as sawwaagiin 9ayyaaniin
az zool kwaiyis	an naas kwaiysiin
al walad ṣaghayyir	al awlaad ṣughaar
ar raajil kabiir	ar rujaal kubaar
aḍ ḍeef ṭawiil	aḍ ḍuyuuf ṭuwaal
al muwaẓẓaf giṣayyir	al muwaẓẓafiin guṣaar

The following are some sentences with nouns which do not refer to human beings:

aṣ ṣuura samHa	aṣ ṣuwar samHa
aj jaziira Hilwa	aj juzur Hilwa
al galam baayiẓ	al aglaam baayẓa
ad daris ṣa9ab	ad duruus ṣa9ba
al gamiiṣ khafiif	al gumṣaan khafiifa
al fustaan ṭawiil	al fasaatiin ṭawiila
al muftaaH jadiid	al mafaatiiH jadiida
aṣ ṣanduug tagiil	aṣ ṣanaadiig tagiila
al baab kabiir	al abwaab kabiira

Note: Adjectives with dual nouns will not be taught until Lesson 24.

11.1.3 More practice on nouns with adjectives

Lists of nouns and adjectives referring to things you could buy are given below. Practise making sentences containing a noun with an adjective on the pattern of: *ana akhatta (ṭarabeeza kabiira) min as suug* 'I got/bought a (big table) from the market'. Use plurals as well as singulars.

طربيزة، كيس، بنطلون، كباية، ظرف، بطارية، كرسى، راديو، صندوق، فواكه، فستان، قلم، ورق، قميص، منقة، سكر، شاى

كبير، طويل، قصير، صغير، حلو، سمح، جاهز، كويس، قديم، جديد، تقيل، خفيف

انا اخدت ... من السوق   انا اخدت طربيزة كبيرة من السوق (والى آخره)

ولد، بت، مرة، راجل، سواق ، خدام، خدامة، موظف، مدرس، مدرّسة، مكنيكى، سودانى، سودانية، خواجة، خواجية

صغير، طويل، قصير، شاطر، كبير، حلو، سمح، كويس، متزوج

... ماشى البيت   الولد الصغير ماشى البيت   (والى آخره)

١١,١,٤

دا درس صعب ...... دى دروس صعبة (والى آخره)

كلمات

فسحة، فسح	اتفسح، يتفسح
المقرن	اخت، اخوات
صوّر، يصور	مرّة، مرات
النيل	كيلو
مجلس الشعب	طيب، طيبين
توتى	سمح، سمحين
جزيرة، جزر	متزوج، متزوجين
حلو، حلوة، حلوين	قديم، قدام
طريق، طرق	صغير، صغار
بنطون، بنطونات	كتير، كتار، كتيرين
قاعة الصداقة	قريب، قريبين
مواصلات	شغال، شغالين
لحدى	تقيل، تقال
حلة، حلال	طويل، طوال
جنينه، جناين	جديد، جداد
فواكه	قصير، قصار
منقة	خفيف، خفيفين
خدروات	كبير، كبار
خالص	

Nouns: *ṭarabeeza, kiis, banṭaloon, kubbaaya, ẓarif, baṭṭaariiya, kursi, raadyu, ṣanduug, fawaakih, fustaan, galam, warag, gamiiṣ, manga, sukkar, shaay*

Adjectives: *kabiir, ṭawiil, giṣayyir, ṣaghayyir, Hilu, samiH, jaahiz, kwaiyis, gadiim, jadiid, tagiil, khafiif.*

Lists of nouns and adjectives referring to people are given here. Practise making sentences containing a noun with an adjective on the pattern of: *(al walad aṣ ṣaghayyir) maashi l beet* '(the small boy) is going home.'

Nouns: *walad, bitt, mara, raajil, sawwaag, khaddaam, khaddaama, muwaẓẓaf, mudarris, mudarrisa, makaniiki, suudaani, suudaaniiya, khawwaaja, khawwaajiiya.*
Adjectives: *ṣaghayyir, ṭawiil, gisayyir, shaaṭir, kabiir, Hilu, samiH, kwaiyis, mutzawwij.*

11.1.4 Plurals of 'this' and 'that'

The plural of *da, di* 'this' is *deel* 'these', and the plural of *daak, diik* 'that' is *deelaak* 'those'. However, as with adjectives, the plural forms are used mainly with nouns referring to people while nouns referring to things take the feminine singular. So you will most probably hear *an naas deel* 'these people' but *al gumṣaan di* 'these shirts', or *ar rujaal deelaak* 'those men' but *al buyuut diik* 'those houses'.

Practise making sentences, using any noun and adjective that you like, on the pattern of *da (daris ṣa9ab), di (duruus ṣa9ba)* 'this is (a difficult lesson)', 'these are (difficult lessons).'

11.1.5 Conversation practice: 'Where are you going?'

Practise asking each other *inta maashi ween?* or *inti maasha ween?* 'Where are you going?' and giving a reply. Then ask, *maashi ta9mil shinuu hinaak?* or *maasha ta9mili shinuu hinaak?* 'What are you going to do there?' and reply.

11.2 Role play

Act out the parts of people explaining to their friends that they are going on an outing. You can talk about how you will get there—by car or train or bus—and what you will do there. The teacher can supply names of places and other vocabulary that you may need.

11.3 Vocabulary: kalmaat

fusHa, fusaH	outing, walk	itfassaH, yitfassaH	to go for a walk
al mugran	the Mogran (in Khartoum)	ukhut, ukhwaat	sister
		marra, marraat	time (e.g. two times, twice)
ṣawwar, yiṣawwir	to photograph	kiilu	kilogram
an niil	the Nile	ṭaiyib, ṭaiybiin	good, alright
majlis ash sha9b	the National Assembly	samiH, samHiin	beautiful
tuuti	Tuti Island	mutzawwij, mutzawwijiin	married
jaziira, juzur	island		
Hilu (m), Hilwa (f), Hilwiin (pl)	pleasant, nice, sweet	gadiim, gudaam	old
		ṣaghayyir, ṣughaar	small
ṭariig, ṭurug	way	katiir, kutaar *or* katiiriin	many
banṭoon, banṭoonaat	ferry		
ghaa9at aṣ ṣadaagha	Friendship Hall	gariib, gariibiin	near
muwaaṣalaat	(public) transport	shaghghaal, shaghghaaliin	working
liHaddi	to, until		
Hilla, Hilaal	village	tagiil, tugaal	heavy
jineena, janaayin	garden	ṭawiil, ṭuwaal	long, tall
fawaakih	fruit	jadiid, judaad	new
manga	mango, mangoes	giṣayyir, guṣaar	short
khudrawaat	vegetables	khafiif, khafiifiin	light in weight
khaaliṣ	very	kabiir, kubaar	big

تمرين الاصوات

سجوك	نجّض
حاجة	سجل
ايجار	اجر
راجل	حاجّة

اخوى	دخّل
اخد	بخيت
اخيرا	اتاخر
اخت	سخّن

فاضى	وضّح
بضاعة	اتفضل
بيضة	نضارة
اوضة	نضف

بصل	وصّل
يوصل	قصيت
قصير	قصة
مصر	نصّه

11.4 Pronunciation drills: More doubled consonants

Contrast Drills

Lists (a) and (b) contrasting *j* and *jj*.
Lists (c) and (d) contrasting *kh* and *khkh*.
Lists (e) and (f) contrasting *ḍ* and *ḍḍ*.
Lists (g) and (h) contrasting *ṣ* and *ṣṣ*.

(a) j

sujuuk	sausages
Haaja	thing
iijaar	rent
raajil	man

(b) jj

najjaḍ	he cooked
sajjal	he registered
ajjar	he rented
Haajja	pilgrim (woman)

(c) kh

akhuuy	my brother
akhad	he took
akhiiran	finally
ukhut	sister

(d) khkh

dakhkhal	he put in
bakhkheet	I spat
it'akhkhar	he was late
sakhkhan	he heated

(e) ḍ

faaḍi	empty
buḍaa9a	goods
beeḍa	egg
ooḍa	room

(f) ḍḍ

waḍḍaH	he explained
itfaḍḍal	please
naḍḍaara	spectacles
naḍḍaf	he cleaned

(g) ṣ

baṣal	onions
yooṣal	he arrives
giṣayyir	short
maṣir	Egypt

(h) ṣṣ

waṣṣal	he connected
gaṣṣeet	I cut
giṣṣa	story
nuṣṣu	half of it

الدرس الاطناشر

حوار : الاسرة

م : مصطفى   ج : جعفر

م   ازى الحال.

ج   مرحبا.

م   ان شاء الله كويسين.

ج   الحمد لله. الصحة كيف؟

م   بخير، الحمد لله، مشتاقين.

ج   بالاكتر، طولت ما شفتك، وين المدة دى كلّها؟

م   عمى الحاج كيف؟   ان شاء الله كويس.

ج   كويس.

م   اخبار اخوك كيف؟

ج   هو برضو كويس جدا، اتزوج السنة دى.

م   اتزوج من وين؟

ج   اتزوج بت خالى. انت، ابوك كويس؟

م   ايوه، كويس، لكن حبوبتى عيانة.

خ   سلامتها.

م   الله يسلمك.

خ   عيانة بشنو؟

م   عيانة بوجع ضهر.

خ   ربنا يشفيها.

تمرين

ad daris al iṭnaashar — Lesson 12

Hiwaar: al usra — Dialogue: The family

m: muṣṭafa j: ja9far	M: Mustafa J: Jafar
m: izzeey al Haal.	M: How are you?
j: marHaba.	J: Welcome.
m: in shaa' allaa kwaiysiin.	M: You're well, I hope.
j: al Hamdu lillaa. aṣ ṣaHHa keef?	J: Thank God. How's your health?
m: bee kheer, al Hamdu lillaa. mushtaagiin.	M: Fine thank God. We've missed you.
j: bi l aktar. ṭawwalta maa shuftak; ween al mudda di kullaha?	J: The same here. I haven't seen you for a long time. Where've you been all this time?
m: 9ammi l Haajj keef? in shaa' allaa kwaiyis.	M: How is my uncle the hajji? Well, I hope.
j: kwaiyis.	J: Fine.
m: akhbaar akhuuk keef?	M: What's the news of your brother?
j: hu barḍu kwaiyis jiddan. itzawwaj as sana di.	J: He's also very well. He's got married this year.
m: itzawwaj min ween?	M: Who did he marry?
j: itzawwaj bitt khaali. inta, abuuk kwaiyis?	J: He married my uncle's daughter. And you, is your father well?
m: aiwa, kwaiyis, laakin Habboobti 9ayyaana.	M: Yes, he's well, but my grandmother is ill.
j: salaamata.	J: I hope she'll be well soon.
m: allaa yisallimak.	M: Thank you.
j: 9ayyaana bee shinuu?	J: What is she ill of?
m: 9ayyaana be waja9 ḍahar.	M: She's got a pain in her back.
j: rabbana yishfiiha.	J: God heal her!

Notes on the dialogue

1. *marHaba* is another word for 'welcome' and is a common expression in many Arabic-speaking countries.
2. *mushtaag* means literally 'eager, longing'. In the context of greeting someone it implies that you have been looking forward to seeing them.
3. *9ammi l Haajj*: In the dialogue Mustafa uses this phrase of Jafar's father even though he is not his uncle and may not actually have been to Mecca. It is simply a sign of respect. Older people, even foreigners, are often addressed as *Haajj* or *Haajja*.
4. Aunts and uncles: In Arabic there is a distinction between the brother and sister of a person's father, *9amm* and *9amma*, and the brother and sister of his or her mother, *khaal* and *khaala*. No single word exists equivalent to the English 'cousin.' Cousins are the sons and daughters of your uncles and aunts, e.g. *bitt khaali, bitt 9ammati, walad khaalti*, etc.
5. Notice that Jafar says that his brother married their uncle's daughter, that is, a cousin on their father's side of the family. It is very common for Sudanese from so-called 'Arab' tribes to marry within their clan or extended family. However, Sudanese from African tribes, in contrast, are not permitted by tribal custom to marry anyone related to them.

12.1 Drills: tamriin

12.1.1 Possessive pronouns

In English the possessive pronouns are separate words that come before the noun, e.g. 'my father,' 'your father,' 'her father,' etc. In Arabic they come after the noun and are attached to it. See table (1) below.

١٢,١,١

ولدى	ولدنا
ولدَك	ولدكم
ولدِك	
ولده	ولدهم
ولدها	

خالى خالك (والى آخره) هدومى، مدرسى، جوابى

اختى (والى آخره) صاحبى

خالتى (والى آخره) عمتى

امى	امنا
امَك	امكم
امِك	
امه	امهم
امها	

جدى (والى آخره) بتى، عمى

١٢,١,٢

اختك كيف؟ ...... اختى كويسة

دى هدومه؟ (والى آخره)

مدرسكم سافر امبارح؟

اختك قاعدة تدرس شنو؟

قفتها وين؟

انت روحت ساعتك؟

ولدنا عيان بشنو؟

منو صلح عربيتى؟

امهم بتغسل الهدوم؟

رسلتى جواب لامك؟

ضيفه بيشرب شاى؟

مدرستها فى الخرطوم ولا فى امدرمان؟

(1) Nouns ending in one consonant:

	Singular		Plural	
1st	walad-i	my son	walad-na	our son
2nd m	walad-ak	your son	walad-kum	your son
2nd f	walad-ik	your son		
3rd m	walad-u	his son	walad-um	their son
3rd f	walad-a	her son		

Repeat the above table after the teacher. Then try replacing *walad* with the following words: *khaal, hiduum, mudarris, jawaab.*

Note the following:

a) Nouns with a short *i* or *u* in the last syllable lose the *i* or *u* when followed by the pronouns *-i, -ak, -ik, -u,* e.g. *ukhut* → *ukhti.* But notice that when these nouns are followed by the 3rd feminine singular *-a*, the *i* or *u* is not lost because there is a stress shift in the word, e.g. *ukhuta* 'her sister'.

Drill all the pronouns with *ukhut* and *ṣaaHib.*

b) Nouns ending in *a* that add *t* in possessive noun phrases (see Lesson 8.4) also add it before pronouns, and are therefore counted as ending in a consonant, e.g. *mara* → *maratu* 'wife' → 'his wife'; *khaala* → *khaalti* 'aunt' → 'my aunt.' In many words the *a* drops out if it is preceded by a single consonant and followed by one of the pronouns *-i, -ak, -ik, -u,* e.g. *khaala* → *khaalti* → *khaalata*; *9amma* → *9ammati* → *9ammata.*

Drill *khaala* and *9amma* with all the pronouns.

(2) Nouns ending in two consonants:

	Singular		Plural	
1st	umm-i	my mother	umma-na	our mother
2nd m	umm-ak	your mother	umma-kum	your mother
2nd f	umm-ik	your mother		
3rd m	umm-u	his mother	umma-hum	their mother
3rd f	umma-ha	her mother		

Note that for nouns ending in two consonants the differences are:

a. The 3rd fem. sg. and the 3rd pl. pronouns have an *h* at the beginning, i.e. *ha* and *hum* instead of *a* and *um.*
b. An extra *a* is added to the stem before pronouns beginning with a consonant, e.g. *umma-na.* This is to prevent three consonants coming together, a combination Arabic does not allow.

Drill all pronouns with: *umm, jidd, bitt, 9amm. kull* 'all' is also like *umm*, e.g. *kullaha* 'all of it'.

12.1.2 Question and answer drill on possessive pronouns

Now the teacher can ask the students the following questions, and let them supply the correct answers, e.g. teacher: '*ukhtak keef?*' student: '*ukhti kwaiysa.*'

di hiduumu?
mudarriskum saafar umbaariH?
ukhtik gaa9da tadrus shinuu?
guffata ween?
inta rawwaHta saa9tak?
waladna 9ayyaan bee shinuu?

minuu ṣallaH 9arabiiyti?
ummahum bitghassil al hiduum?
rassalti jawaab lee ummik?
ḍeefu bishrab shaay?
madrasata fi l kharṭuum walla fi umdurmaan?

١٢,١,٣

ابوى	ابونا
ابوك	ابوكم
ابوكِ	
ابوه	ابوهم
ابوها	

اخوى (والى آخره)

١٢,١,٥

ابو

ام

اخو

اخت

ولد

بت

The teacher can make up more questions of the same kind if the class is larger or the students need more practice.

12.1.3 More on possessives

A few masculine nouns end in a vowel, and as a result take a slightly different set of pronoun endings. Also the final vowel of the noun is lengthened, e.g. *abu l awlaad* 'the boys' father' but *abuuhum* 'their father'. See the table below.

Nouns ending in a vowel:

	Singular		Plural	
1st	abuu-y	my father	abuu-na	our father
2nd m	abuu-k	your father	abuu-kum	your father
2nd f	abuu-ki	your father		
3rd m	abuu-hu	his father	abuu-hum	their father
3rd f	abuu-ha	her father		

Repeat the above table after the teacher and then replace *abu* with: *akhu.*

Note: *abu* and *akhu* are unusual words in that they lose the final *u* when preceded by the definite article, e.g. *al ab, al akh*. Their duals are *abuyeen, akhuyeen.*

12.1.4 Polite expressions

In the dialogue for this lesson are included a number of polite expressions you may find it useful to know:

(a) *ṭawwalta maa shuftak*: 'I haven't seen you for a long time' is a common expression. If you are addressing a woman the correct form is *ṭawwalta maa shuftik*. (See Lesson 13 for the verb *shaaf, yashuuf*, and Lesson 18 for object pronouns.)

(b) *salaamata*: This is the usual polite thing to say when you hear that someone is ill. The *a* at the end is the 3rd f. sg. pronoun and changes according to the situation. You say *salaamtak* to a man who is ill, *salaamtik* to a woman, *salaamtu* for a sick man who is not present. The proper reply is *allaa yisallimak/ik.*

(c) *rabbana yishfiiha*: This expressions is another way of wishing health to a sick person. It means literally 'our Lord heal her!' For a man you would say *rabbana yishfiihu. rabbana* is a name given to God by both Muslims and Christians.

Practise these expressions as they would be said to a man or a woman or to a group of people.

12.1.5 Conversation practice: friends and family

With your teacher's help write some sentences about your family which you could tell to friends who ask you about them. Record the teacher saying these sentences and then listen and memorize them. It will also help you to carry round with you some photos of your family to show to people, as the family is always a good conversation topic in Sudan. Below is a list of relatives to assist you in composing your sentences:

abu	father
umm	mother
akhu	brother
ukhut	sister
walad	son
bitt	daughter

جد

حبوبة

عم

عمة

خال

خالة

كلمات

اسرة، اسر	خبر، اخبار
مرحبا	اتزوج، يتزوج
صحة	خال، خيلان
بخير	حبوبة، حبوبات
مشتاق، مشتاقين	سلامة
بالاكتر	وجع، اوجاع
طوّل، يطوّل	ضهر
ما شفتك	ربنا يشفيها
مدة، مدد	جد، جدود
عم، اعمام	صاحب، اصحاب
حاج، حجاج	صاحبة، صاحبات
ابو، ابهات	خالة، خالات
حاجة، حاجات	عمة، عمات

تمرين الاصوات

طابعة	قطع	فطر
جامعة	اسمع	يقدر
سبعة	وقع	كسر
تسعة	هسع	سكر

ماشى	يعمل	غربى
شافوا	شعرى	شربات
راجل	بعدين	وردة
حاجة	معلقة	اركب

jidd	grandfather
Habbooba	grandmother
9amm	paternal uncle
9amma	paternal aunt
khaal	maternal uncle
khaala	maternal aunt

12.2 Role play

Act out the parts of two or three people meeting each other after some time and exchanging news about the members of their families.

12.3 Vocabulary: kalmaat

usra, usar	family	khabar, akhbaar	news
marHaba	welcome	itzawwaj, yitzawwaj	to get married
ṣaHHa	health	khaal, kheelaan	maternal uncle
bee kheer	well	Habbooba, Habboobaat	grandmother
mushtaag, mushtaagiin	eager, longing	salaamat	(see 12.1.4)
bi l aktar	more so	waja9, awjaa9	pain
ṭawwal, yiṭawwil	to be a long time	ḍahar	back
maa shuftak	(see 12.1.4)	rabbana yishfiiha	God heal her!
mudda, mudad	period of time	jidd, juduud	grandfather
9amm, a9maam	paternal uncle	ṣaaHib, aṣHaab	friend (m)
Haajj, Hujjaaj	a man who has made the pilgrimage to Mecca	ṣaaHba, ṣaaHbaat	friend (f)
		khaala, khaalaat	maternal aunt
abu, ubbahaat	father	9amma, 9ammaat	paternal aunt
Haajja, Haajjaat	woman who has made the pilgrimage to Mecca		

12.4 Pronunciation drills: Further practice on *9*

Contrast drills

Lists (a) and (b) contrasting *9a* and *a9* at the end of words.
Lists (b) and (c) contrasting *a9* and *ar* at the end of words.
Lists (d) and (e) contrasting *aa* and *a9* in the middle of words.
Lists (e) and (f) contrasting *a9* and *ar* in the middle of words.

(a) 9a		(b) a9		(c) ar	
ṭaab9a	stamp	gaṭa9	he cut	faṭar	he breakfasted
jaam9a	university	asma9	listen	yagdar	he can
sab9a	seven	waga9	he fell	kasar	he broke
tis9a	nine	hassa9	now	sukkar	sugar

(d) aa		(e) a9		(f) ar	
maashi	going	ya9mil	he does	gharbi	western
shaafu	they saw	sha9ri	my hair	sharbaat	fruit drink
raajil	man	ba9deen	afterwards	warda	rose
Haaja	thing	ma9laga	spoon	arkab	get on

9 alters the sound of *i* when it occurs before or after it. Listen and imitate the difference.

Lists (g) and (h) contrast *i* before other consonants and *i* before *9*.
Lists (i) and (j) contrast *i* after other consonants and *i* after *9*.

صفر	جامع
ساكن	شارع
لبس	سمع
راجل	تاسع

سكة	عندك
ملح	عيون
جبنة	علبة
لبس	عرس

(g) iC

ṣifir	zero
saakin	dwelling
libis	he wore
raajil	man

(h) i9

jaami9	mosque
shaari9	street
simi9	he heard
taasi9	ninth

(i) Ci

sikka	way
miliH	salt
jibna	cheese
libis	he wore

(j) 9i

9indak	with you
9iyuun	eyes
9ilba	packet
9iris	wedding

الدرس التلاطاشر

حوار : البكا

ج : جميلة   س : سعاد

ج يا صعاد، شفت صيوان جنب بيتكم. حق منو؟

س داك حق ناس محمود. فى بكا. اخوه الكبير اتوفى اول امبارح.

ج والله، ما سمعت. اخوه المحامى؟

س ايوه. هو كان عيان، رقد فى المستشفى اسبوعين ومات يوم السبت. الليلة آخر يوم.

ج الله يصبرهم. لازم امشى اقول البركة فيكم لناس البيت. مرة المحامى كانت صحبتى لكن هى ماتت قبل سنتين. انا متأسرة شديد.

س تعالى. نمشى سوا. انا جايبة كسرة هسع لمرة محمود.

تمرين

١٣,١,١

شفت	اشوف	بشوف
شفت	تشوف	بتشوف
شفتى	تشوفى	بتشوفى
شاف	يشوف	بيشوف
شافت	تشوف	بتشوف

ad daris at talaaṭṭaashar — Lesson 13

Hiwaar: al bika — Dialogue: The funeral

j:	jamiila s: su9aad	J:	Jamila S: Suad
j:	ya su9aad, shufta ṣeewaan jamb beetkum. Hagg minuu?	J:	Suad, I saw a canopy next to your house. Whose is it?
s:	daak Hagg naas maHmuud. fii bika. akhuuhu al kabiir itwaffa awwal umbaariH.	S:	That belongs to Mahmood's people. There's a funeral. His elder brother died the day before yesterday.
j:	wallaahi, maa simi9ta. akhuuhu al muHaami?	J:	Goodness, I hadn't heard. Is that his brother the lawyer?
s:	aiwa. hu kaan 9ayyaan, ragad fi l mustashfa usbuu9een u maat yoom as sabit. alleela aakhir yoom.	S:	Yes. He was ill, spent two weeks in hospital and died on Saturday. Today is the last day of the funeral.
j:	allaa yiṣabbirum. laazim amshi aguul al baraka fiikum lee naas al beet. marat al muHaami kaanat ṣaaHbati laakin hi maatat gabli sanateen. ana mut'assira shadiid.	J:	May God comfort them! I must go and say *al baraka fiikum* to the people of the house. The lawyer's wife was my friend but she died two years ago. I am very sorry indeed.
s:	ta9aali. namshi sawa. ana jaayba kisra hassa9 lee marat maHmuud.	S:	Come! Let's go together. I am just taking some kisra to Mahmood's wife.

Notes on the dialogue

1. Loyalty to the family or clan and respect for older people are two very important values in Sudanese society, no matter from which part of the country people come. For this reason funerals are extremely significant occasions. Customs in different parts of Sudan vary as to the exact number of days a funeral lasts and the nature of the rites performed. In all cases it is expected that friends and neighbours will go to the house where the funeral is being held to express their sympathy and possibly make some contribution to funeral expenses.
2. In Khartoum you will normally find that a funeral lasts three days. You can go on any of these days to say *al baraka fiikum* to the family. Other Sudanese, however, do not always use this expression and say instead *kaffaara.* Men generally go to the canopy erected in the street outside the person's house, but women go inside the house. Once you have said one of the above phrases you just sit for about quarter of an hour, or longer if you wish. You may be brought a drink of some kind but you do not have to wait for it. Many other people will be coming and going.

13.1 Drills: tamriin

13.1.1 Verbs like *shaaf (shufta), yashuuf*

Revise the verb *ghassal* in the past tense (Lesson 4.1.1), the imperfect (Lesson 6.1.3), and the imperfect with *bi-* (Lesson 7.1.3).

Now look at the table below for the verb *shaaf, (shufta), yashuuf* 'to see'.

		Past	Imperfect	Imperfect with *bi-*
Sing.	1	shufta	ashuuf	bashuuf
	2 m	shufta	tashuuf	bitshuuf
	2 f	shufti	tashuufi	bitshuufi
	3 m	shaaf	yashuuf	bishuuf
	3 f	shaafat	tashuuf	bitshuuf

شفنا	نشوف	بنشوف
شفتوا	تشوفوا	بتشوفوا
شافوا	يشوفوا	بيشوفوا

كنت (والى آخره)، قلت، شلت، جبت، خفت

١) شفت صيوان جنب بيتكم

٢) شلت منقة من القفة

٣) جبت شوية اكل للاولاد

٤) خفت من الاسد

امبارح، كل يوم

نحن، كل يوم ...... كل يوم بنشوف صيوان جنب بيتكم (والى آخره)

١٣,١,٢

الولد فى البيت	الولد كان فى البيت
البت فى الدكان	البت كانت فى الدكان
انت عيان؟	انت كنت عيان؟
انت شغالة؟	انت كنتى شغالة؟
انا فى البكا	انا كنت فى البكا
نحن مع ناس البلد	نحن كننا مع ناس البلد
هو مكنيكى	هو كان مكنيكى
هى مدرسة	هى كانت مدرسة

كنت وين امبارح؟ ...... كنت فى الخرطوم (والى آخره)

Plur.	1	shufna	nashuuf	binshuuf
	2	shuftu	tashuufu	bitshuufu
	3	shaafu	yashuufu	bishuufu

You will see that these forms are very similar to the tables for *ghassal* with these differences:
1. There are only two basic consonants instead of three, the middle one having dropped out.
2. The past tense has one long vowel in the 3rd person singular and plural, e.g. *shaaf, shaafu,* and a different vowel in the other persons, e.g. *shufta, shufti,* etc.

There are quite a number of verbs like *shaaf* including some very common ones. Some of them have an *u* in the imperfect, e.g. *kaan, (kunta), yakuun* 'to be', *gaal, (gulta), yaguul* 'to say'; some have an *i*, e.g. *shaal, (shilta), yashiil* 'to take', *jaab, (jibta), yajiib* 'to bring'; and an odd one is *khaaf, (khufta), yakhaaf* 'to fear' with an *a*.

Drill the tables for *shaaf* and then for these other verbs till you know them by heart.

Below are some sentences in the past tense. The teacher should say one of the sentences, and a subject pronoun, and one of the two expressions *umbaariH* or *kulli yoom*. The student should repeat the sentence, making the necessary substitutions, e.g.:

teacher: *shufta ṣeewaan jamb beetkum, niHna, kulli yoom*;
student: *kulli yoom binshuuf ṣeewaan jamb beetkum.*

(a) *shufta ṣeewaan jamb beetkum.* 'I saw a canopy next to your house'.
(b) *shilta manga min al guffa.* 'I took a mango from the basket'.
(c) *jibta shwaiyat akil li l awlaad.* 'I have brought a little food to the children'.
(d) *khufta min al asad.* 'I was afraid of the lion'.

13.1.2 How to use *kaan* 'to be'

The verb *kaan (kunta), yakuun* does not occur on its own in the present tense, only in the past or future or as an auxiliary verb. Compare *al walad fi l beet* 'the boy is in the house' with *al walad kaan fi l beet* 'the boy was in the house'.

Repeat the following sentences after the teacher. The left-hand column has sentences in the present tense and the right-hand column has sentences in the past tense.

al walad fi l beet	al walad kaan fi l beet
al bitt fi d dukkaan	al bitt kaanat fi d dukkaan
inta 9ayyaan?	inta kunta 9ayyaan?
inti shaghghaala?	inti kunti shaghghaala?
ana fi l bika	ana kunta fi l bika
niHna ma9a naas al balad	niHna kunna ma9a naas al balad
hu makaniiki	hu kaan makaniiki
hi mudarrisa	hi kaanat mudarrisa

Now let the teacher and students take turns to ask each other questions using the verb *kaan*. For example, the teacher could ask, *kunta ween umbaariH?* 'Where were you yesterday'? Student replies, *(ana) kunta fi l kharṭuum* 'I was in Khartoum'.

In Lesson 23 you will learn how to use *kaan* as an auxiliary verb with another verb in order to form the past continuous tense.

١٣,١,٣

اخترت	اختار
اخترت	تختار
اخترتى	تختارى
اختار	يختار
اختارت	تختار
اخترنا	نختار
اخترتوا	تختاروا
اختاروا	يختاروا

ارتحت (والى آخره)

١٣,١,٤

عشرين
واحد وعشرين
اتنين وعشرين
تلاتة وعشرين
اربعة وعشرين
خمسة وعشرين
ستة وعشرين
سبعة وعشرين
تمنية وعشرين
تسعة وعشرين
تلاتين
اربعين
خمسين
ستين
سبعين
تمنين
تسعين
مية

13.1.3 Verbs like *ikhtaar (ikhtirta), yikhtaar*

Revise variations of the verb in Lessons 9.1.1 and 9.1.2. *ikhtaar, (ikhtirta), yikhtaar* 'to choose', *irtaaH, (irtiHta), yirtaaH* 'to rest', and *iHtaaj, (iHtijta), yiHtaaj* 'to need' are three fairly common verbs of the same pattern as *ishtaghal.* They have *i* before and *t* after the first basic consonant, but like *shaaf* they have only two basic consonants, not three. You may meet other verbs like *shaaf* but showing some of the other variations. A table is given here for *ikhtaar.*

		Past	Imperfect
Sing.	1	ikhtirta	akhtaar
	2 m	ikhtirta	tikhtaar
	2 f	ikhtirti	tikhtaari
	3 m	ikhtaar	yikhtaar
	3 f	ikhtaarat	tikhtaar
Plur.	1	ikhtirna	nikhtaar
	2	ikhtirtu	tikhtaaru
	3	ikhtaaru	yikhtaaru

bi- is added to the imperfect without changes.

Drill *ikhtaar* and *irtaaH* in the past and the imperfect.

13.1.4 Numbers 20–100

Revise numbers 13–20 (see Lesson 9.1.4) and memorise the numbers below:

20	9ishriin
21	waaHid u 9ishriin
22	itneen u 9ishriin
23	talaata u 9ishriin
24	arba9a u 9ishriin
25	khamsa u 9ishriin
26	sitta u 9ishriin
27	sab9a u 9ishriin
28	tamanya u 9ishriin
29	tis9a u 9ishriin
30	talaatiin
40	arba9iin
50	khamsiin
60	sittiin
70	sab9iin
80	tamaniin
90	tis9iin
100	miiya

For practice in using the numbers go through the following steps:

(a) The teacher picks a number between 1 and 100 and writes it in figures and the students shout out the Arabic for it. This can be done with 10 or 15 different numbers.

(b) The teacher writes a figure between 1 and 100 and asks the students in turn whether it is such-and-such a number. The students have to reply 'yes' or 'no.' If the answer is 'no' the student should say the correct number, e.g. 72 – *waaHid u talaatiin? – la', itneen u sab9iin.*

Playing Bingo in Arabic is also good practice in learning numbers.

كلمات

بكا
شاف (شفت)، يشوف
صيوان، صيوانات
اتوفى، يتوفى
اول امبارح
محامى، محاميين
رقد ، يرقد
مستشفى، مستشفيات
مات، يموت
آخر
البركة فيكم
متأسر ، متأسرين

كان (كنت)، يكون
نمشى
سوا
كسرة
كفارة
قال (قلت)، يقول
خاف (خفت)، يحاف
شال (شلت)، يشيل
جاب (جبت)، يجيب
اسد، اسود
اختار (اخترت) يختار
ارتاح (ارتحت)، يرتاح

13.1.5 Conversation practice: funeral greetings

Practise with the teacher the proper greetings and words of condolence to use at a funeral.

13.2 Role play

Act out the parts of people discussing the death of someone—how the person died, where and when— and their intention of going to condole with the family.

13.3 Vocabulary: kalmaat

bika	funeral, mourning	kaan, (kunta), yakuun	to be (not used in present tense)
shaaf, (shufta), yashuuf	to see	namshi	let's go
ṣeewaan, ṣeewaanaat	canopy, awning	sawa	together
itwaffa, yitwaffa	to die (formal word)	kisra	Sudanese pancakes
awwal umbaariH	the day before yesterday	kaffaara	word of condolence (see Notes on the dialogue)
muHaami, muHaamiyiin	lawyer	gaal, (gutta), yaguul (*l* plus *t* becomes *tt*)	to say
ragad, yargud	lie, lie down	khaaf, (khufta), yakhaaf	to be afraid
mustashfa, mustashfayaat	hospital	shaal, (shilta), yashiil	to take, carry
maat, yamuut	die	jaab, (jibta), yajiib	to bring
aakhir	last	asad, usuud	lion
al baraka fiikum	word of condolence (see Notes on the dialogue)	ikhtaar, (ikhtirta), yikhtaar	to choose
mut'assir, mut'assiriin	very sorry	irtaaH, (irtiHta), yirtaaH	to rest

الدرس الاربعطاشر

حوار: شغل البيت

ج : جميلة   ي : يوسف

ج   يا يوسف.

ي   حاضر.

ج   نضف الصالون واوضة النوم وغسل البلاط كويس.

ي   طيب. ضرورى انضف العفش؟

ج   اى، نضف العفش كمان. كان فى تراب كتير امبارح. بعدين غسل الهدوم دى.

ي   يوم الاتنين الصابون ما كان كفاية.

ج   فى هسع. محجوب جاب علبة كبيرة من الدكان. اهى.

ي   المكوة وين، يا جميلة؟

ج   شوف فى الدولاب فى المطبخ.

ي   ايوه، فى.

ج   كويس. انت مسافر بكرة؟

ي   ايوه. ممكن اشيل قروشى الليلة؟

ج   ممكن، بعد الغدا. انا ماشة السوق. ما تفتح الشبابيك، عشان الحر.

ي   طيب.

تمرين

ad daris al arba9ṭaashar — Lesson 14

Hiwaar: shughl al beet — Dialogue: Housework

j:	jamiila y: yuusif	J:	Jamila Y: Yusif
j:	ya yuusif.	J:	Yusif.
y:	Haaḍir.	Y:	Here.
j:	naḍḍif aṣ ṣaaluun u ooṭṭ an noom u ghassil al balaaṭ kwaiyis.	J:	Clean the living room and the bedroom and wash the floors well.
y:	ṭaiyib. ḍaruuri anaḍḍif al 9afash?	Y:	Okay. Do I need to clean the furniture?
j:	ai, naḍḍif al 9afash kamaan. kaan fii turaab katiir umbaariH. ba9deen ghassil al hiduum di.	J:	Yes, clean the furniture too. It was very dusty yesterday. And then wash these clothes.
y:	yoom al itneen aṣ ṣaabuun maa kaan kifaaya.	Y:	On Monday there wasn't enough soap.
j:	fii hassa9. maHjuub jaab 9ilba kabiira min ad dukkaan. ahii!	J:	There is now. Mahjoub brought a large packet from the shop. Here it is!
y:	al makwa ween, ya jamiila?	Y:	Where's the iron, Jamila?
j:	shuuf fi d doolaab fi l maṭbakh.	J:	Look in the cupboard in the kitchen.
y:	aiwa, fii.	Y:	Yes, it's here.
j:	kwaiyis. inta musaafir bukra?	J:	Good. Are you going away tomorrow?
y:	aiwa. mumkin ashiil guruushi alleela?	Y:	Yes. May I take my money today?
j:	mumkin, ba9d al ghada. ana maasha s suug. maa taftaH ash shabaabiik, 9ashaan al Harr.	J:	Yes, after lunch. I'm going to market. Don't open the windows, because it's hot.
y:	ṭaiyib.	Y:	Okay.

Notes on the dialogue

1. The Mahjoub referred to in the dialogue is presumed to be the woman's husband. Sudanese generally refer to their husbands by name in speaking to servants or other adults. Children often refer to their parents by name too. With the exception of a few families Sudanese do not have a surname or family name in the European sense. There are different naming customs in different ethnic groups of Sudan, but a common pattern is for each person to have one given name and after it to add the name of his (or her) father and then his grandfather in order to distinguish himself from other individuals with the same given name, e.g. Mohammed Hassan Ali, Jamila Ahmed Taj-ed-Din. Women do not adopt their husband's name when they marry.
2. 'Here it is' is expressed by *ahuu* or *ahuu da* (m), *ahii* or *ahii di* (f) depending on the gender of the object referred to.

14.1 Drills: tamriin

14.1.1 The imperative

The imperative is that form of the verb used for giving orders, e.g. in English 'fetch me a spoon.' In Arabic it is used when in English we would have a polite request, e.g. 'Please would you fetch me a spoon.' No word corresponding to 'please' is normally used in this sort of request. In Sudanese Arabic there are three forms of the imperative—masculine, feminine, and plural—which you already know from *shuuf, shuufi, shuufu* and *asma9, asma9i, asma9u.*

It is easy to learn the imperative:

(a) For verbs like *daras* the masculine singular imperative is the same as the first person singular of the imperfect, and the *i* and *u* are added to this form to form the feminine and plural, e.g. *adrus, adrusi, adrusu; ashrab, ashrabi, ashrabu; agfil, agfili, agfilu.*

١٤,١,١

افتح الباب	اكتب حاجة بالانجليزى	استعمل القلم
اقفل الشباك	ادفع لى خمسة الف	جيب ساعة
اشرب موية	دخل القلم فى كيس	شيل كباية من الطربيزة
ارسم صورة	اتكلم مع المدرس	

١٤,١,٢

ما تفتح الشباك ما تغسلى الهدوم

اشربوا موية ...... ما تشربوا موية (والى آخره)

١٤,١,٣

مية
مية وواحد
مية خمسة وعشريت
(والى آخره)
ميتين
تلتمية
اربعمية
خمسمية
ستمية
سبعمية
تمنمية
تسعمية
الف
الفين
تلاتة الف
(والى آخره)

(b) For other verbs that you have learned, the masculine singular imperative is the same as the imperfect stem without the *a* in front, and the same endings are added to form the feminine and plural, e.g. *ghassil, ghassili, ghassilu; itkallam, itkallami, itkallamu; ishtaghil, ishtaghli, ishtaghlu; shuuf, shuufi, shuufu.*

Repeat the following orders after your teacher:

aftaH al baab	aktib Haaja bi l ingliizi	ista9mil al galam
agfil ash shubbaak	adfa9 leey khamsa alf	jiib saa9a
ashrab mooya	dakhkhil al galam fi kiis	shiil kubbaaya min aṭ ṭarabeeza
arsum ṣuura	itkallam ma9a l mudarris	

Now the teacher should give the first student one of these orders or a similar one, using known vocabulary, and the student should obey it, e.g. teacher says, *ya Mary, aftaHi l baab,* so Mary gets up and opens the door. Then Mary gives a different order to one of the other students or several together and so on round the class. If the class consists of only one or two people, perhaps the teacher can take the part of a man and a woman alternately in order to give the students practice with both masculine and feminine. Keep up a good pace in this drill.

14.1.2 The negative imperative

In English if we want to tell someone *not* to do something we say 'Don't...', or 'Please don't....' In Sudanese Arabic *maa* is used with the second person of the imperfect, e.g. 'don't open the window' (to a man) *maa taftaH ash shubbaak;* 'don't wash the clothes' (to a woman) *maa taghassili l hiduum.*

For practice in the negative imperative the teacher should give the students orders like those in Drill 14.1.1 above, and have them respond with the negative, e.g. teacher says *ashrabu mooya;* and student replies *maa tashrabu mooya.*

14.1.3 Numbers over 100

Revise the numbers from 20–100 (see Lesson 13.1.4). Then memorise the numbers listed below:

100	miiya
101	miiya u waaHid
125	miiya khamsa u 9ishriin
etc.	
200	miiyteen
300	tultumiiya
400	urbu9umiiya
500	khumsumiiya
600	suttumiiya
700	sub9umiiya
800	tumnumiiya
900	tus9umiiya
1000	alf
2000	alfeen
3000	talaata alf
etc.	

Give the Arabic for the following numbers: 65, 82, 133, 496, 218, 909, 54, 1620, 5112, 47, 71, 823, 4700.

14.1.4 Conversation practice: giving instructions

With your teacher's help prepare some sentences giving orders which you might personally have to use with people in your employment or working under you, e.g. 'Put the medicine in the fridge,'

كلمات

نضف، ينضف
اوضة، اوض
اوضة النوم
نوم
عفش
تراب
يوم الاتنين
كفاية
اهو دا، اهى دى
علبة، علب

مكوة
دولاب، دواليب
مطبخ، مطابخ
مسافر، مسافرة، مسافرين
غدا
شباك، شبابيك
عشان
حر
دفع، يدفع

‘Lift up that box,’ ‘Type this letter.’ Have your teacher record the sentences so that you can listen and memorise them.

Also, if people regularly give orders to you and you want to be sure of understanding and reacting correctly, you could do the same thing with those orders

14.2 Role play

Act out the parts of a woman giving directions to her servant about the day’s work.

14.3 Vocabulary: kalmaat

naḍḍaf, yinaḍḍif	to clean	makwa (m)	ironing, iron
ooḍa, uwaḍ	room	doolaab, dawaaliib	cupboard
ooṭṭ an noom	bedroom (*ḍ* plus *t* = *ṭṭ*)	maṭbakh, maṭaabikh	kitchen
noom	sleep	musaafir (m), musaafra (f), musaafriin (pl)	travelling, going or gone away
9afash	furniture, luggage	ghada (m)	lunch
turaab	dust, duststorm	shubbaak, shabaabiik	window
yoom al itneen	Monday	9ashaan	on account of, so that
kifaaya	enough	Harr	heat
ahuu da (m), ahii di (f)	here it is	dafa9, yadfa9	to pay
9ilba, 9ilab	packet, tin can		

الدرس الخمسطاشر

حوار : لعبة الكورة

ح : حسين ك : كمال (وصاحبه)

ح شفتوا المباراة بين المريخ والهلال يوم السبت الفات؟

ك ايوة، شفنا.

ح الغلب منو؟

ك المريخ غلب اتنين صفر. القون التانى كان قبل نهاية المباراة بدقيقتين.

ح مستوى المباراة كان كيف؟

ك كان كدا كدا. فى الشوط التانى لعبوا أحسن عشان سخنوا.

ح السجل القونين منو؟

ك الجناح اليمين سجل الاول والسنتر فرود سجل التانى.

ح هو لاعب جديد، مش كدا؟

ك ايوه، كان ممتاز.

ح الاسبوع الجاى المباراة مع منو؟

ك مع الموردة فى استاد الهلال.

ح خلاص. نتقابل هناك. مع السلامة.

تمرين

ad daris al khamusṭaashar — Lesson 15

Hiwaar: la9bat al kuura — Dialogue: The football game

H:	Husseen k: kamaal (u ṣaaHbu)	H:	Hussein K: Kamaal (and his friend)
H:	shuftu l mubaara been al marriikh w al hilaal yoom as sabit al faat?	H:	Did you see the match between Marrikh and Hilaal last Saturday?
k:	aiwa, shufna.	K:	Yes, we saw it.
H:	al ghalab minuu?	H:	Who won?
k:	al marriikh ghalab itneen ṣifir. al goon at taani kaan gabli nihaayat al mubaara bee dagiigteen.	K:	Marriikh won two nil. The second goal came two minutes before the end of the match.
H:	mustawa l mubaara kaan keef?	H:	What sort of match was it?
k:	kaan kida kida. fi sh shooṭ at taani li9bu aHsan 9ashaan sakhkhanu.	K:	So-so. They played better in the second half because they'd warmed up.
H:	as sajjal al gooneen minuu?	H:	Who scored the two goals?
k:	aj janaaH al yamiin sajjal al awwal w as sintir firwid sajjal at taani.	K:	The right wing scored the first goal, and the center forward the second one.
H:	huwa laa9ib jadiid, mush kida?	H:	He's a new player, isn't he?
k:	aiwa, kaan mumtaaz.	K:	Yes, he was excellent.
H:	al usbuu9 aj jaay al mubaara ma9a minuu?	H:	Who's the match against next week?
k:	ma9a l moorada fii istaad al hilaal.	K:	Against Morada at the Hilaal stadium.
H:	khalaaṣ. nitgaabal hinaak. ma9a s salaama.	H:	Okay. Let's meet there. Good-bye.

Notes on the dialogue

1. In Arabic a sentence such as 'Who won?' can be either *minuu ghalab?* or *al ghalab minuu?* with the definite article preceding the verb.
2. Football (soccer) is the most popular sport in Sudan. The most celebrated teams are al-Hilal and al-Merrikh, both of whose grounds are in Omdurman not far from the main market. The emblem of al-Hilal is the crescent moon, and that of al-Merrikh is a star. Football supporters may often be seen driving around the city waving the flag of their team out of a car window or from the back of a pickup.

Notes on grammar

1. Note on another use of the imperfect: The 1st person singular and plural of the imperfect alone can be used to express 'let me' or 'let us' sentences, e.g. in the dialogue Hussein says *nitgaabal hinaak* 'let's meet there'. A person might say *aftaH al baab* 'let me open the door/ I'll open the door'; or *narkab al baaṣ da* 'let's get on this bus'.

2. Useful time expressions: Two useful words to know are *faat* 'last' and *jaay* 'next, coming' referring to a day or month or year, etc., e.g. *yoom as sabit al faat* 'last Saturday'; *al usbuu9 aj jaay* 'next week'.

Since *faat* and *jaay* are parts of verbs they have masculine and feminine forms. So 'last month' is *ash shahar al faat,* but 'last year' is *as sana l faatat.* 'Next month' is *ash shahar aj jaay,* but 'next year' is *as sana j jaaya.*

15.1 Drills: tamriin

15.1.1 The active participle

You have already learned, *maashi, maasha, maashiin*; *gaa9id, gaa9da, gaa9diin* and *saakin, saakna,*

١٥,١,١

قاعد	قاعدة	قاعدين
واقف	واقفة	واقفين
راقد	راقدة	راقدين
نايم	نايمة	نايمين
ساكن	ساكنة	ساكنين
ماسك	ماسكة	ماسكين
شايف	شايفة	شايفين
خايف	خايفة	خايفين
عارف	عارفة	عارفين
ماشى	ماشة	ماشين
جاى	جاية	جايين
جايب	جايبة	جايبين
شايل	شايلة	شايلين
فاهم	فاهمة	فاهمين
نازل	نازلة	نازلين
قايل	قايلة	قايلين
مارق	مارقة	مارقين

١٥,١,٢

يوم الاحد
يوم الاتنين
يوم التلاتا
يوم الاربعا
يوم الخميس
يوم الجمعة
يوم السبت

١٥,١,٣

saakniin. These are the active participles of the verbs *masha, ga9ad,* and *sakan,* and you can see that they all follow the same pattern. Nearly all verbs like *daras, shaaf,* and *masha* (see Lesson 17) have participles formed on this pattern. Some of these participles are in very common use, so much so that they tend to be used for the present continuous of their verbs instead of *gaa9id* with the imperfect, e.g. *ana maaska galam* 'I'm holding a pen' rather than *gaa9da amsik galam.* These commonly used participles are the ones taught here. More on active participles will be taught in a later lesson.

Most of the participles in common use describe either (a) a state as compared to an action, or (b) an action involving movement. See the list below.

gaa9id, gaa9da, gaa9diin	sitting
waagif, waagfa, waagfiin	standing
raagid, raagda, raagdiin	lying
naayim, naayma, naaymiin	sleeping
saakin, saakna, saakniin	living
maasik, maaska, maaskiin	holding
shaayif, shaayfa, shaayfiin	seeing, looking
khaayif, khaayfa, khaayfiin	afraid
9aarif, 9aarfa, 9aarfiin	knowing
maashi, maasha, maashiin	going
jaay, jaaya, jaayiin	coming (see Lesson 24 for the verb 'to come')
jaayib, jaayba, jaaybiin	bringing
shaayil, shaayla, shaayliin	taking, carrying
faahim, faahma, faahmiin	understanding
naazil, naazla, naazliin	getting off/down
gaayil, gaayla, gaayliin	saying, thinking
maarig, maarga, maargiin	going out

Repeat the list after the teacher, paying attention to correct pronunciation.

Now the teacher should perform an action, and ask the student a question about it, e.g. teacher stands up and asks the student, *ana gaa9id?*; student replies *la', inta maa gaa9id, inta waagif.* The students can also practice with each other.

15.1.2 Days of the week

Once you know the numbers in Arabic it is easy to learn the names of the days of the week and the months, because most of them are derived from numbers. Memorise this list of the days of the week:

Sunday	yoom al aHad
Monday	yoom al itneen
Tuesday	yoom at talaata
Wednesday	yoom al arbi9a
Thursday	yoom al khamiis
Friday	yoom aj jum9a
Saturday	yoom as sabit

Practise the days of the week by saying what you did on the various days of the past week, e.g. *yoom al itneen ana katabta jawaab, yoom at talaata akhatta fustaan jadiid, yoom al arbi9a shufta la9bat al kuura,* etc.

15.1.3 What is the date?

Usually in Sudan the months of the year are referred to by their number, e.g. January is *shahri waaHid,* February *shahri itneen* etc. Note that in this context it is *shahri,* not *shahar.*

شهرى واحد

شهرى التنين

(والى آخره)

كلمات

لعبة، لعبات
كورة، كور
مباراة، مباريات
بين
الفات
غلب، يغلب
قون، اقوان
نهاية
مستوى
جاى
استاد، استادات

كدا كدا
شوط
سخّن، يسخن
سجّل، يسجل
جناح، جنحين
سنتر فرور
لاعب، لاعبين
اتقابل، يتقابل
ممتاز ، ممتازة، ممتازين
نام (نمت)، ينوم
نزل، ينزل
تاريخ، تواريخ

Below is a list of the months of the year:

January	shahri waaHid
February	shahri itneen
March	shahri talaata
April	shahri arba9a
May	shahri khamsa
June	shahri sitta
July	shahri sab9a
August	shahri tamanya
September	shahri tis9a
October	shahri 9ashara
November	shahri Hidaashar
December	shahri iṭnaashar

In Arabic you ask the date by saying *at tariikh kam?* (literally 'The date is how much?'). You can reply along the lines of 'day one, month three'—*yoom waaHid, shahri talaata*—that is, March 1st.

Once you have memorised the months, fetch a calendar and the teacher can point to a date and ask a student what the date is in Arabic. Go on doing this until students are all reasonably fluent in their answers.

15.1.4 Conversation practice: talking about sport

If there is a sport you are interested in, ask the teacher for the Arabic terms connected with that sport and record them so that you can talk about it.

Commentaries on football games in Sudan are broadcast on Radio Omdurman in Sudanese Arabic. If you are interested in football you could listen to these commentaries for listening practice. You will not understand everything but you will begin to pick up some frequently repeated expressions.

It is a cultural experience to watch a game of football with a Sudanese crowd, or to join in a local match.

15.2 Role play

Act out the parts of people discussing a football match or some other sport they are interested in. You can also bring in other matches you have seen in the past on other dates in other places.

15.3 Vocabulary: kalmaat

la9ba, la9baat	a game	kida kida	so-so
kuura, kuwar	ball, football	shooṭ	a half (in a football match)
mubaara, mubaarayaat	match (football)		
been	between	sakhkhan, yisakhkhin	to warm up
al faat	(see Notes on the Grammar)	sajjal, yisajjil	to score, record
		janaaH, jinHeen	wing
ghalab, yaghlib	to win	sintir firwid	center forward
goon, agwaan	goal	laa9ib, laa9biin	player
nihaaya	end	itgaabal, yitgaabal	to meet each other
mustawa(m)	performance, standard	mumtaaz (m), mumtaaza (f), mumtaaziin (pl)	excellent
jaay	(see Notes on the Grammar)	naam, (numta), yanuum	to sleep
		nazal, yanzil	to get off, get down
istaad, istaadaat	stadium	taariikh, tawaariikh	date (of month, etc.)

اسئلة لمراجعة الدروس

من ١١ الى ١٥

١ بتجيب قلم وورق لحصة العربى؟

٢ لازم السنتر فرود يسجل الاقوان فى الكورة؟

٣ منو بينضف العفش فى بيتكم؟

٤ فى بلدك الناس بيستعملوا صيوانات للبكا؟

٥ شفت جناين فواكه فى جزيرة توتى؟

٦ اخو جعفر اتزوج منو؟

٧ السودانيين بيدرسوا عربى ولا انجليزى فى المدرسة؟

٨ شعرك طويل ولا قصير؟

٩ فى السنة فى كم يوم؟

١٠ الموظفين السودانيين بيشتغلوا يوم الجمعة؟

١١ جيرانكم بيسمعوا الاخبار من راديو امدرمان؟

١٢ انت عارف تطبع فى الكمبيوتر؟

١٣ ولدك الصغير ما نام لسع؟

١٤ يوم الاتنين الفات التاريخ كان كم؟

١٥ كان فى حاجة انكسرت فى المطبخ أول امبارح؟

١٦ مدرس العربى بيستعمل سبورة؟

١٧ بتدفع كم للخدروات كل اسبوع؟

١٨ البرتقان فى السودان حلو؟

١٩ اصحابك مسافرين؟

٢٠ صورت شنو فى الخرطوم؟

Revision questions for Lessons 11–15

Answer the following questions:

1. bitjiib galam u warag lee Hiṣṣat al 9arabi?
2. laazim as sintir firwid yisajjil al agwaan fi l kuura?
3. minuu binaḍḍif al 9afash fii beetkum?
4. fii baladak an naas bista9milu ṣeewaanaat li l bika?
5. shufta janaayin fawaakih fii jaziira tuuti?
6. akhu ja9far itzawwaj minuu?
7. as suudaaniiyiin biyadrusu 9arabi walla ingliizi fi l madrasa?
8. sha9rak ṭawiil walla giṣayyir?
9. fi s sana fii kam yoom?
10. al muwaẓẓafiin as suudaaniiyiin bishtaghlu yoom aj jum9a?
11. jeeraankum biyasma9u l akhbaar min raadyu umdurmaan?
12. inta 9aarif taṭba9 fi l kombyuutar?
13. waladak aṣ ṣaghayyir maa naam lissa9?
14. yoom al itneen al faat at taariikh kaan kam?
15. kaan fii Haaja inkasarat fi l maṭbakh awwal umbaariH?
16. mudarris al 9arabi bista9mil sabbuura?
17. bitadfa9 kam li l khudrawaat kulli usbuu9?
18. al burtukaan fi s suudaan Hilu?
19. aṣHaabak musaafriin?
20. ṣawwarta shinuu fi l kharṭuum?

الدرس السطاشر

حوار : حفلة الشاى

ف : فاطمة   س : سامية   م : مارى

س   يا خالتى، دى صاحبتى من فرنسا. ليها سنة فى السودان. ساكنة قريب مننا.

ف   اتفضلى.

س   ودى خالتى، فاطمة.

ف   اسمك منو؟

م   اسمى مارى.

ف   نعم؟

م   مارى.

ف   انت متزوجة؟

م   ايوه، راجلى مهندس فى الشركة الفرنسية السودانية.

ف   عندك أولاد؟

م   ايوه، تلاتة، ولدين وبت. عندك أولاد، انت؟

ف   ايوه، خمسة. واحد فى الجيش، واحد قاعد مع جده فى عطبرة، والتانيين هنا معاى.

م   انت محمولة. فى ولد بيشتغل معاك؟

ف   لا، بشتغل براى، ودا صعب عشان عندى شغل برّا.

س   (بتجيب شاى) اتفضلوا.

ف   اشربى. السكر كفاية؟

م   شكرا. فى سكر كفاية.

تمرين

ad daris as siṭṭaashar — Lesson 16

Hiwaar: Haflat ash shaay — Dialogue: The tea party

f:	faaṭna M: Marie s: saamya	F:	Fatna M: Marie S: Saamya
s:	ya khaalti, di ṣaaHbati min faransa. leeha sana fi s suudaan. saakna gariib minnana.	S:	Aunt, this is my friend from France. She has been a year in Sudan. She lives near us.
f:	itfaḍḍali.	F:	Please sit down.
s:	u di khaalti, faaṭna.	S:	And this is my aunt, Fatna.
f:	ismik minuu?	F:	What is your name?
M:	ismi Marie.	M:	My name is Marie.
f:	na9am?	F:	Pardon me?
M:	Marie.	M:	Marie.
f:	inti mutzawwija?	F:	Are you married?
M:	aiwa, raajli muhandis fi sh sharika l faransiiya s suudaaniiya.	M:	Yes, my husband is an engineer with the Franco-Sudanese company.
f:	9indik awlaad?	F:	Have you any children?
M:	aiwa, talaata. waladeen u bitt. 9indik awlaad, inti?	M:	Yes, three. Two boys and a girl. Have you any?
f:	aiwa, khamsa. waaHid fi j jeesh, waaHid gaa9id ma9a jiddu fii 9aṭbara, w at taanyiin hina ma9aay.	F:	Yes, five. One's in the army, one's living with his grandfather in Atbara, and the others are here with me.
M:	inti maHmuula. fii walad bishtaghil ma9aaki?	M:	You must be busy. Do you have a househelp?
f:	la', bashtaghil baraay, u da ṣa9ab 9ashaan 9indi shughul barra.	F:	No, I do my own housework, and that's hard because I go out to work.
s:	(bitjiib shaay) itfaḍḍalu.	S:	(Brings tea) Please drink.
f:	ashrabi! as sukkar kifaaya?	F:	Drink up! Is the sugar enough?
M:	shukran. fii sukkar kifaaya.	M:	Thank you. There's enough sugar.

Notes on the dialogue

1. In Arabic if you ask a person's name you say *ismak/ismik minuu?,* not *ismak/ismik shinuu?*
2. *walad* is often used with the meaning of 'servant' instead of *khaddaam.*
3. It is polite to encourage one's guests to drink by saying *ashrab* and to press people to eat and drink more. You should also note that you should not ask guests whether they want a drink. Just bring them one without asking. If you ask whether they want something Sudanese will think that you do not really want to give them anything or that you don't have anything to offer them. However, you can give your guests a choice, such as asking if they prefer tea or coffee or something cold. In hot weather it is good to bring a visitor a glass of water as soon as they arrive and then juice or tea or coffee later.

If you are visiting Sudanese you must accept anything brought you to eat or drink, but if you don't like it just take a few sips and leave the rest. If there is some medical reason why you can't drink something, let the drink stand, and then when they tell you to drink it you can explain that you are unable to take this particular thing.

16.1 Drills: tamriin

16.1.1 Prepositions with pronouns

Revise the possessive pronouns (Lesson 12.1.1 and 12.1.2). These pronouns are also the ones used after prepositions, e.g. *giddaam-u* ('in front of him'); *lee-k* ('to you'). There are the same

١٦,١,١

قدامى	جنبى	لى
قدامَك	جنبَك	ليك
قدامِك	جنبِك	ليكِ
قدامه	جنبه	ليه
قدامها	جنبها	ليها
قدامنا	جنبنا	لينا
قدامكم	جنبكم	ليكم
قدامهم	جنبهم	ليهم

منى (والى آخره) معاى، فى (والى آخره)

١٦,١,٢

عندك عربية؟	لا، ما عندى عربية
عندِك أولاد؟	ايوه، عندى اولاد
عنده راديو جديد؟	لا، عنده راديو قديم
عندها مكنة خياتة؟	ايوه، عندها مكنة خياتة
عندكم ضيوف الليلة؟	ايوه، عندنا ضيوف الليلة
عندهم بيت فى الخرطوم؟	لا، عندهم بيت فى امدرمان

١٦,١,٣

هو ماشى معاك؟ ...... لا، انا ماشى براى

variations in the pronouns, depending on whether the preposition ends in one consonant or two or a vowel. Below are tables showing the pronouns with *giddaam* 'in front of', *jamb* 'beside', and *lee* 'to'.

giddaam-i	jamb-i	lee-y
giddaam-ak	jamb-ak	lee-k
giddaam-ik	jamb-ik	lee-ki
giddaam-u	jamb-u	lee-hu
giddaam-a	jamba-ha	lee-ha
giddaam-na	jamba-na	lee-na
giddaam-kum	jamba-kum	lee-kum
giddaam-um	jamba-hum	lee-hum

Repeat the tables after the teacher.

Note the following points about other prepositions:

(a) *been* 'between', *foog* 'on', and *Hawl* 'round' add the pronouns without change, like *giddaam*; *bee* 'by' also adds the pronouns without change like *lee*.

(b) *ba9ad* 'after' and *tiHit* 'under' become *ba9d-* and *tiHt-* and then follow the same pattern as *jamb*, e.g. *ba9dana*.

(c) *min* 'from' and *zeey* 'like' double the last consonant and then follow the same pattern as *jamb*, e.g. *minnik, zeeyyana*.

(d) *ma9a* 'with', *wara* 'behind', *gabli* 'before', and any other prepositions ending in a short vowel lengthen it before adding the pronouns, e.g. *ma9aay, gabliihu*. *9ala* 'on, to' changes to *9alee*, e.g. *9aleek*.

Now drill all the pronouns with these prepositions: *min, ma9a, fii*.

As a drill on the prepositions with pronouns the teacher should take some object and place it somewhere in relation to himself or one of the students. For example, he can take a pen and put it in front of one student and ask him, *al galam ween?* The student replies *al galam giddaami*, and so on. The same thing can be done with two objects; for example, the teacher holds a pen above the table and asks *al galam foog aṭ ṭarabeeza?* Student replies *aiwa, al galam fooga*.

16.1.2 *9ind* 'have'

9ind, though a preposition, is equivalent in Arabic to the verb 'to have' in English. *9indi* means 'I have', *9indak* means 'you (m) have', *9indu* means 'he has', etc. For example, *9indi fustaan jadiid* 'I have a new dress'. It follows the same pattern in adding pronouns as *jamb*.

Repeat the following questions and answers after the teacher. Make sure you understand what they mean.

9indak 9arabiiya?	la', maa 9indi 9arabiiya.
9indik awlaad?	aiwa, 9indi awlaad.
9indu raadyu jadiid?	la', 9indu raadyu gadiim.
9indaha makanat khiyaata?	aiwa, 9indaha makanat khiyaata.
9indakum ḍuyuuf alleela?	aiwa, 9indana ḍuyuuf alleela.
9indahum beet fi l kharṭuum?	la', 9indahum beet fii umdurmaan.

Now in pairs practice using *9ind* by asking each other similar questions and giving answers.

16.1.3 *bara* 'by oneself'

bara means 'alone, on one's own', e.g. *bashtaghil baraay* means 'I work on my own' (i.e. do my own work); *hi saakna baraaha* 'she lives alone'. It follows the same pattern as *ma9a*.

Below is a set of questions for the teacher to ask the students. The students should reply using *bara*, e.g. Teacher: *hu maashi ma9aak?* Student: *la', ana maashi baraay*.

هم ماشين معاكم؟   (والى آخره)

البت بتشتغل معاكِ؟

الولد كتب الجواب مع اخته؟

انت ماشة مع امك؟

فى خدامين بيشتغلوا معاكم؟

١٦,١,٤

سمح، جاهز، كويس، شاطر، بايظ، طيب، ساهل

دا، دى، ديل

كويس، دى ...... دى كويسة (والى آخره)

شرب، قدر، لعب، سمع، ركب، عرف

هو، هى، هم

شرب، هى ...... هى شربت ليمون (والى آخره)

اخت، شغل، صاحب، راحل، شارع، ظرف، درس، قرد، اسم

انا، انتَ، انتِ، هو، اتنين

اسم، انا ...... اسمى (والى آخره)

كلمات

حفلة، حفلات

فرنسا

اسم، اسامى

راجل، رجال

مهندس، مهندسين

عند

محمول، محمولة، محمولين

برا

فوق

hum maa<u>sh</u>iin ma9aakum?
al bitt biti<u>sh</u>ta<u>gh</u>il ma9aaki?
al walad katab aj jawaab ma9a u<u>kh</u>tu?
inti maa<u>sh</u>a ma9a ummik?
fii <u>kh</u>addaamiin bi<u>sh</u>ta<u>gh</u>lu ma9aakum?

16.1.4 The *i* and *u* that drop out

In a number of contexts in this course it has been pointed out that short *i* and *u* drop out when an additional syllable is added to a word. (See Lessons 3.1.1, 6.1.2, 8.1.4, 10.1.1, 11.1.1, and 12.1.1). For reference sake a rule is given here which covers all these instances and others you will come across as you go on in Arabic. Here it is:

> When the last syllable of a word contains a short *i* or *u* preceded and followed by a single consonant, e.g. *kwaiyis, daris, u<u>kh</u>ut,* the *i* or *u* is lost if an ending is added that begins with a vowel (for this purpose the 3rd person pronouns *-a* and *-um* have to be treated as beginning with a consonant) or if it is followed by the definite article *al.*

You may not want to spend much time on the rule but the drill below will help you get it right when speaking. There are three parts to the drill:

1. Below is a list of adjectives. The teacher should say one of the adjectives and then *da, di,* or *deel,* e.g. *kwaiyis, di.* Student replies with a sentence, e.g. *di kwaiysa.*
samiH, jaahiz, kwaiyis, <u>sh</u>aaṭir, baayiẓ, ṭaiyib, saahil.

2. Below is a list of verbs. The teacher should say one of the verbs and then *hu, hi,* or *hum,* e.g. *<u>sh</u>irib, hi.* The student replies with a full sentence in the past tense, e.g. *hi <u>sh</u>irbat leemuun.*
<u>sh</u>irib, gidir, li9ib, simi9, rikib, 9irif.

3. Lastly, here is a list of nouns:
u<u>kh</u>ut, <u>sh</u>ughul, ṣaaHib, raajil, <u>sh</u>aari9, ẓarif, daris, girid, isim.

There are five endings that affect the nouns: *-i* (my), *-ak* (your, masc.), *-ik* (your, fem.), *-u* (his), *-een* (dual). The teacher should say a noun first and then one of the following: *ana, inta, inti, hu,* or *itneen.* The student supplies the appropriate form of the noun, e.g. Teacher: *isim, ana.* Student: *ismi.*

16.1.5 Conversation practice: 'What's your name?' 'Are you married?'

ismak/ismik minuu? 'What is your name?', *inta mutzawwij/inti mutzawwija* 'Are you married?', *9indak/9indik awlaad?* 'Have you got children?' These are three questions you will constantly be asked, especially if you are a woman and mix with Sudanese women. Learn these questions so that you recognise them when you hear them and so that you can ask them of other people. Then prepare answers which apply to yourself and practise them with your teacher.

16.2 Role play

You are introduced to the relative of a friend. Have a conversation about yourself and the others present, asking as many things about each other as you are able.

16.3 Vocabulary: kalmaat

Hafla, Haflaat	party	9ind	to have (see 16.1.2)
faransa	France	maHmuul (m), maHmuula (f),	overloaded
isim, asaami	name	maHmuuliin (pl)	
raajil, rujaal	husband	bara	alone (see 16.1.3)
muhandis, muhandisiin	engineer	foog	over, above

شركة، شركات	حول
فرنسي، فرنسية، فرنسيين	زى
جيش، جيوش	على
قعد، يقعد	ورا
تحت	قرد، قرود

sharika, sharikaat	company	Hawl	around, surrounding
faransi (m), faransiiya (f), faransiiyiin (pl)	French	zeey	like
jeesh, jiyuush	army	9ala	on, over
ga9ad, yag9ud	to stay, live, sit	wara	behind
tiHit	under, below	girid, guruud	monkey

الدرس السبعطاشر

حوار : ملى اورنيك

خ : خواجة   س : سودانى

خ   يا اخى، لازم املى الاورنيك دا، لكن ما بعرف اقرا عربى. ممكن تملى لى؟
س   عملت دمغة؟
خ   ايوه، عملت دمغة.
س   كويس. اسمك منو؟
خ   فولفغانق بيرنس.
س   تانى، جنسك شنو؟
خ   المانى
س   صاحبك هناك، هو من المانيا؟
خ   لا، هو من كوريا.
س   من كوريا الشمالية ولا الجنوبية؟
خ   من الجنوبية.
س   كويس. وظيفتك، يعنى شغلك شنو؟
خ   مستشار زراعى.
س   تاريخ الميلاد؟
خ   يوم اطناشر، شهرى تمنية، الف تسعمية وسبعين.
س   نمرة جوازك كم؟
خ   مكتوب هنا فى نوتى وعنوانى برضو.
س   اخيرا، تاريخ وصولك فى السودان متين؟
خ   وصلت شهرى اربعة يوم تلاتين فى السنة دى.
س   تمام. خلاص.
خ   شكرا جزيلا.

تمرين

١٧,١,١

ad daris as saba9ṭaashar

Hiwaar: mali urneek

Lesson 17

Dialogue: Filling in a form

k: <u>kh</u>awaaja s: suudaani

f: foreigner S: Sudanese

k: ya a<u>kh</u>i, laazim amla l urneek da, laakin maa ba9rif agra 9arabi. mumkin tamla leey?

f: Friend, I have to fill in this form, but I can't read Arabic. Could you fill it in for me?

s: 9amalta dam<u>gh</u>a?

S: Have you put a revenue stamp on it?

k: aiwa, 9amalta dam<u>gh</u>a.

f: Yes, I've put a stamp on it.

s: kwaiyis. ismak minuu?

S: Good. What's your name?

k: Wolfgang Behrens.

f: Wolfgang Behrens.

s: taani, jinsak <u>sh</u>inuu?

S: Next, what's your nationality?

k: almaani.

f: German.

s: ṣaaHbak hinaak, hu min almaanya?

S: Your friend over there, is he from Germany?

k: la', hu min kuuriiya.

f: No, he's from Korea.

s: min kuuriiya <u>sh</u> <u>sh</u>imaaliiya walla j januubiiya?

S: From North or South Korea?

k: min aj januubiiya.

f: From South Korea.

s: kwaiyis. waẓiiftak, ya9ni <u>sh</u>u<u>gh</u>lak <u>sh</u>inuu?

S: Good. What is your occupation, that's to say, your work?

k: musta<u>sh</u>aar ziraa9i.

f: Agriculturalist.

s: taarii<u>kh</u> al miilaad?

S: Date of birth?

k: yoom iṭnaa<u>sh</u>ar, <u>sh</u>ahri tamanya, alf tus9umiiya u sab9iin

f: 12th of August 1970

s: nimrat jawaazak kam?

S: What's the number of your passport?

k: maktuub hina fii nootti wa 9unwaani barḍu.

f: It's written here in my notebook, and my address too.

s: a<u>kh</u>iiran, taarii<u>kh</u> wuṣuulak fi s suudaan miteen?

S: Lastly, what was the date of your arrival in Sudan?

k: wiṣilta <u>sh</u>ahri arba9a, yoom talaatiin, fi s sana di.

f: I arrived on the 30th of April this year.

s: tamaam. <u>kh</u>alaaṣ.

S: Fine. That's all.

k: <u>sh</u>ukran jaziilan.

f: Many thanks.

Note on dialogue

ya a<u>kh</u>i, translated here as 'friend' is a rather casual style of addressing a man. It is often used by one man to another of the same or lower social standing but should not be used to people of higher status than the speaker.

17.1 Drills: tamriin

17.1.1 Verbs like *ma<u>sh</u>a, (ma<u>sh</u>eet), yam<u>sh</u>i* and *gara, (gareet), yagra*

In Lesson 13 you learned verbs like *shaaf* which have only two basic consonants because the middle one has dropped out. In this lesson we introduce verbs which have lost their final basic consonant. As a result they take a slightly different set of endings in the past tense and show a few other differences from verbs like *daras*. Most of these verbs are like *masha* with an *i* in the imperfect, but a few are like *gara* with an *a*. The past tense of *gara* is like that of *masha* so only the one verb is given below in the past.

مشيت	امشى	اقرا
مشيت	تمشى	تقرا
مشيتى	تمشى	تقرى
مشى	يمشى	يقرا
مشت	تمشى	تقرا
مشينا	نمشى	نقرا
مشيتوا	تمشوا	تقروا
مشوا	يمشوا	يقروا

امشى، امشوا   اقرا، اقرى، اقروا

ماشى، ماشة، ماشين   قارى، قارية قارين

رمى، يرمى   كوى، يكوى   بنى، يبنى

ملا، يملا   بدا، يبدا

انا، كوى ...... انا كويت   (والى آخره)

١٧,١,٢

خلّى، سوّى
خليت خليتى خلى (والى آخره)
اخلى تخلى يخلى (والى آخره)
خلِى خلوا

نادى
ناديت ناديتى نادى (والى آخره)
انادى تنادى ينادى (والى آخره)
نادى نادوا

اشترى
اشتريت اشتريتى اشترى (والى آخره)
اشترى تشترى يشترى (والى آخره)
اشترى اشتروا

اتغدى
اتغديت اتغديتى اتغدى (والى آخره)
أتغدى تتغدَى تتغدِى يتغدى (والى آخره)
اتغدَى اتغدِى اتغدوا

		Past		Imperfect	
Singular	1	ma<u>sh</u>-eet	a-m<u>sh</u>i	a-gra	
	2 m	ma<u>sh</u>-eet	ta-m<u>sh</u>i	ta-gra	
	2 f	ma<u>sh</u>-eeti	ta-m<u>sh</u>i	ta-gr-i	
	3 m	ma<u>sh</u>-a	ya-m<u>sh</u>i	ya-gra	
	3 f	ma<u>sh</u>-at	ta-m<u>sh</u>i	ta-gra	
Plural	1	ma<u>sh</u>-eena	na-m<u>sh</u>i	na-gra	
	2	ma<u>sh</u>-eetu	ta-m<u>sh</u>-u	ta-gr-u	
	3	ma<u>sh</u>-u	ya-m<u>sh</u>-u	ya-gr-u	

Notes:

(a) *bi-* is added to the imperfect without change, e.g. *bitam<u>sh</u>i, binagra*.

(b) Imperative: *am<u>sh</u>i* (m. and f.), *am<u>sh</u>u* (pl); *agra* (m), *agri* (f), *agru* (pl).

(c) Active participle: *maa<u>sh</u>i* (m), *maa<u>sh</u>a* (f), *maa<u>sh</u>iin* (pl); *gaari* (m), *gaarya* (f), *gaariin* (pl)

Drill *ma<u>sh</u>a* and *gara* until you know them by heart. Then drill other verbs of the same kind. See below:

(a) like *ma<u>sh</u>a: rama, yarmi* 'to throw'; *kawa, yakwi* 'to iron'; *bana, yabni* 'to build'

(b) like *gara: mala, yamla* 'to fill'; *bada, yabda* 'to begin'

As a third step the teacher can name a pronoun and a verb and let the student give the correct form of that verb in the past tense, e.g. Teacher: *ana, kawa*. Student: *kaweet*. Then do the same for the imperfect.

17.1.2 Some variations on verbs like *masha* and *gara*

You are familiar now with variations on the basic verb, such as *<u>gh</u>assal, saafar, i<u>sh</u>ta<u>gh</u>al*, etc. It is possible to have the same kinds of variations on verbs like *ma<u>sh</u>a* and *gara* which have lost their final consonant. Below are some common verbs of this kind:

a) *<u>kh</u>alla* 'to leave, let'; *sawwa* 'to make': these differ from *ma<u>sh</u>a* in the same way as *<u>gh</u>assal* differs from *daras*.

Past tense:	<u>kh</u>alleet, <u>kh</u>alleeti, <u>kh</u>alla, etc.
Imperfect:	a<u>kh</u>alli, ta<u>kh</u>alli, yi<u>kh</u>alli, etc.
Imperative:	<u>kh</u>alli (m. and f.), <u>kh</u>allu (pl).

b) *naada* 'to call': this corresponds to *saafar*.

Past tense:	naadeet, naadeeti, naada, etc.
Imperfect:	anaadi, tanaadi, yinaadi, etc.
Imperative:	naadi (m. and f.), naadu (pl).

c) *i<u>sh</u>tara* 'to buy': this corresponds to *i<u>sh</u>ta<u>gh</u>al*.

Past tense:	i<u>sh</u>tareet, i<u>sh</u>tareeti, i<u>sh</u>tara, etc.
Imperfect:	a<u>sh</u>tari, ti<u>sh</u>tari, yi<u>sh</u>tari, etc.
Imperative:	i<u>sh</u>tari (m. and f.), i<u>sh</u>taru.

d) *it<u>gh</u>adda* 'to eat lunch': this follows the pattern of *gara* and differs from it as *itkallam* does from *daras*.

Past tense:	it<u>gh</u>addeet, it<u>gh</u>addeeti, it<u>gh</u>adda, etc.
Imperfect:	at<u>gh</u>adda, tit<u>gh</u>adda, tit<u>gh</u>addi, yit<u>gh</u>adda, etc.
Imperative:	it<u>gh</u>adda (m), it<u>gh</u>addi (f), it<u>gh</u>addu (pl).

اتلاقوا
اتلاقينا اتلاقيتوا اتلاقوا
نتلاقى تتلاقوا يتلاقوا

ادى
اديت اديتى ادى (والى آخره)
ادى تدى يدى (والى آخره)
ادى ادوا

١٧,١,٣

هى اشترت ملابس جاهزة
منو اشترت ملابس جاهزة؟
اختى الصغيرة اشترت ملابس جاهزة
اختى الصغيرة اشترت ملابس جاهزة من وين؟
اختى الصغيرة اشترت ملابس جاهزة من الدكان القريب
اختى الصغيرة اشترت ملابس جاهزة من الدكان القريب متين؟
اختى الصغيرة اشترت ملابس جاهزة من الدكان القريب يوم الاحد

هم مشوا بلدهم
منو مشوا بلدهم؟
اخوان حسين مشوا بلدهم
اخوان حسين مشوا بلدهم مع منو؟
اخوان حسين مشوا بلدهم مع جدهم
اخوان حسين مشوا بلدهم مع جدهم متين؟
اخوان حسين مشوا بلدهم مع جدهم قبل شهرين

هو دايما بيلعب كورة
منو دايما بيلعب كورة؟
ولد خالى دايما بيلعب كورة
ولد خالى دايما بيلعب كورة مع منو؟
ولد خالى دايما بيلعب كورة مع اصحابه
ولد خالى دايما بيلعب كورة مع اصحابه وين؟
ولد خالى دايما بيلعب كورة مع اصحابه فى الشارع قدام بيتهم

هم شربوا قهوة سودانية
منو شربوا قهوة سودانية؟
الخواجات شربوا قهوة سودانية
الخواجات شربوا قهوة سودانية كم مرة؟
الخواجات شربوا قهوة سودانية مرة واحدة بس
الخواجات شربوا قهوة سودانية مرة واحدة بس وين؟
الخواجات شربوا قهوة سودانية مرة واحدة بس فى بيت جيرانهم

e) *itlaagu* 'to meet each other': this also follows the pattern of *itghadda* as to endings but has a long vowel instead of a double consonant. (Note that this particular verb can only take a plural subject because of its meaning.)

Past tense:	itlaageena, itlaageetu, itlaagu
Imperfect:	nitlaaga, titlaagu, yitlaagu.
No Imperative	

f) *adda* 'to give': this is like *khalla* but has lost the first as well as the last basic consonant.

Past tense:	addeet, addeeti, adda, etc.
Imperfect:	addi, taddi, yaddi, etc. (Note that the *a* of the stem and the *a* of the person indicator have been fused.)
Imperative:	addi (m. and f.), addu (pl).

Drill one verb from each of these six groups in the same way as you drilled *masha* and *gara*.

17.1.3 Expansion drill

The purpose of this drill is to help the student gain control over longer stretches of speech. The teacher should say the sentences below at normal speed, and the students repeat them after him.

hi ishtarat malaabis jaahza.
minuu ishtarat malaabis jaahza?
ukhti ṣ ṣaghayra ishtarat malaabis jaahza.
ukhti ṣ ṣaghayra ishtarat malaabis jaahza min ween?
ukhti ṣ ṣaghayra ishtarat malaabis jaahza min ad dukkaan al gariib.
ukhti ṣ ṣaghayra ishtarat malaabis jaahza min ad dukkaan al gariib miteen?
ukhti ṣ ṣaghayra ishtarat malaabis jaahza min ad dukkaan al gariib yoom al aHad.

hum mashu baladum.
minuu mashu baladum?
akhwaan Husseen mashu baladum.
akhwaan Husseen mashu baladum ma9a minuu?
akhwaan Husseen mashu baladum ma9a jiddahum.
akhwaan Husseen mashu baladum ma9a jiddahum miteen?
akhwaan Husseen mashu baladum ma9a jiddahum gabli shahreen.

hu daayman biyal9ab kuura.
minuu daayman biyal9ab kuura?
walad khaali daayman biyal9ab kuura.
walad khaali daayman biyal9ab kuura ma9a minuu?
walad khaali daayman biyal9ab kuura ma9a aṣHaabu.
walad khaali daayman biyal9ab kuura ma9a aṣHaabu ween?
walad khaali daayman biyal9ab kuura ma9a aṣHaabu fi sh shaari9 giddaam beetum.

hum shirbu gahwa suudaaniiya.
minuu shirbu gahwa suudaaniiya?
al khawaajaat shirbu gahwa suudaaniiya.
al khawaajaat shirbu gahwa suudaaniiya kam marra?
al khawaajaat shirbu gahwa suudaaniiya marra waaHda bass.
al khawaajaat shirbu gahwa suudaaniiya marra waaHda bass ween?
al khawaajaat shirbu gahwa suudaaniiya marra waaHda bass fii beet jeeraanum.

كلمات

ملى
اورنيك، ارانيك
ملا (مليت)، يملا
قرا (قريت)، يقرا
دمغة، دمغات
عمل دمغة
جنس، اجناس
المانى، المانية، المانيين
المانيا
كوريا
شمال
شمالى
جنوب
شمالى
جنوب
جنوبى
وظيفة
مستشار
زراعى، زراعية، زراعيين
ميلاد
نمرة، نمر
جواز ، جوازات

مكتوب
نوتة، نوت
اخيرا
وصول
وصل
تمام
شكرا جزيلا
مشى (مشيت)، يمشى
رمى (رميت)، يرمى
كوى (كويت)، يكوى
بنى (بنيت)، يبنى
بدا (بديت)، يبدا
خلى (خليت)، يخلى
سوى (سويت)، يسوى
نادى (ناديت)، ينادى
اشترى (اشتريت)، يشترى
اتغدى (اتغديت)، يتغدى
اتلاقوا (اتلاقينا)، يتلاقوا
ادى (اديت)، يدى

17.1.4 Practice with form-filling

With the teacher's help go through the questions in the dialogue, and any others you have been asked by officials, and provide answers relevant to yourself. Have your teacher record them with the questions so that you can listen and memorise them.

17.2 Role play

Act out the parts of people filling in forms at an office and discussing what they should put down.

17.3 Vocabulary: kalmaat

mali	filling (in)	maktuub (m)	written
urneek, araaniik	official form	noota, nuwat	notebook
mala (maleet), yamla	to fill (in)	akhiiran	lastly, recently
gara (gareet), yagra	to read	wuṣuul	arrival
damgha, damghaat	revenue stamp	wiṣil (for imperfect, see Lesson 25.1.1)	to arrive
9amal damgha	to affix a revenue stamp		
		tamaam	fine, splendid!
jinis, ajnaas	nationality	shukran jaziilan	many thanks
almaani (m), almaaniiya (f), almaaniiyiin (pl)	German	masha (masheet), yamshi	to go
		rama (rameet), yarmi	to throw
almaanya	Germany	kawa (kaweet), yakwi	to iron
kuuriiya	Korea	bana (baneet), yabni	to build
shimaal	north, left (side)	bada (badeet), yabda	to begin
shimaali	northern	khalla (khalleet), yikhalli	to leave (something), let
januub	south		
januubi	southern	sawwa (sawweet), yisawwi	to make
waẓiifa	occupation	naada (naadeet), yinaadi	to call
mustashaar	consultant, specialist	ishtara (ishtareet), yishtari	to buy
ziraa9i (m), ziraa9iiya (f), ziraa9iiyiin (pl)	agricultural	itghadda (itghaddeet), yitghadda	to have lunch
miilaad	birth, birthday	itlaagu (itlaageena), yitlaagu	to meet each other
nimra, nimar	number		
jawaaz, jawaazaat	passport	adda (addeet), yaddi	to give

الدرس التمنطاشر

حوار : محل الهدايا

ز : زبون　　س : سيد الدكان　　م : مرة الزبون

ز　السلام عليكم.

س　وعليكم السلام. اتفضلوا.

ز　شايف عندك شنط جلد. انت بتسوى شنط جلد؟

س　بنسويها. داير كم شنطة؟

ز　حسب السعر.

س　اديك اتنين زى ديل بسبعين الف.

ز　كويس. نستلمهم متين.

س　تعالوا يوم الاربعة الجاى.

م　عندك جمل من خشب؟

س　ما فى هنا لكن فى زول حيجيب لكى واحد من المخزن.

م　الحيوانات دي بكم.

س　يعنى، الفيل بعشرين. الزرافة بخمسطاشر والاسد بعشرين برضو.

م　دا غالى خلاص. والتمساح هناك فى الرف؟

س　دا بخمسطاشر لكن اديكى له باربعطاشر. شفتى، يا ست، دا خشب بابانوس اصلى.

ز　(لمرته) قايلة اخوكى بيحب الاسد دا؟

م　دا مكسور. الافيال دى كيف؟

ز　ما من العاج؟ ما نشترى عاج.

م　لا، دا ما عاج. بيسووا الحاجات دى من عضم.

ز　(لسيد الدكان) اسمع، ادينا الاسد دا والافيال والزرافة الصغيرة بتلاتين كله.

س　والله، حاكون خسران. السعر خمسين.

ز　دا كتير. خفض شوية.

س　شيلها باربعين وازيدك السكين السمحة دى فوق.

ز　طيب. شكرا. لو سمحت، عاوز وصل.

ad daris at tamanṭaashar

Lesson 18

Hiwaar: maHall al hadaaya

Dialogue: The gift shop

z:	zabuun s: siid ad dukkaan m: marat az zabuun	c:	customer s: shopkeeper w: wife of the customer
z:	as salaamu 9aleekum.	c:	Good evening.
s:	wa 9aleekum as salaam. itfaḍḍalu.	s:	Good evening. Please come in.
z:	shaayif 9indak shinaṭ jilid. inta bitsawwi shinaṭ jilid?	c:	I see you have leather bags. Do you make leather bags?
s:	binsawwiha. daayir kam shanṭa?	s:	We make them. How many bags do you want?
z:	Hasab as si9ir.	c:	That depends on the price.
s:	addiik itneen zeey deel bee sab9iin alif.	s:	I'll give you two like these for seventy thousand.
z:	kwaiyis. nastalimum miteen?	c:	Okay. When can we collect them?
s:	ta9aalu yoom al arbi9a j jaay.	s:	Come next Wednesday.
m:	9indak jamal min khashab?	w:	Do you have a wooden camel?
s:	maa fii hina laakin fii zool Hayajiib leeki waaHid min al makhzan.	s:	There are none here but someone will bring you one from the storeroom.
m:	al Hayawaanaat di bee kam?	w:	How much are these animals?
s:	ya9ni, al fiil bee 9ishriin, az zaraafa bee khamusṭaashar wa l asad bee 9ishriin barḍu.	s:	The elephant is twenty thousand, the giraffe fifteen and the lion also twenty.
m:	da ghaali khalaaṣ. wa t tumsaaH hinaak fi r raff?	w:	That's very expensive. And the crocodile on the shelf?
s:	da bee khamusṭaashar laakin addiiki leehu bee arba9ṭaashar. shufti, ya sitt, da khashab baabaanuus aṣli.	s:	That's fifteen but I'll give it to you for fourteen. You see, Madam, this is real ebony wood.
z:	(li maratu) gaayla akhuuki biHibb al asad da?	c:	(To his wife) Do you think your brother will like this lion?
m:	da maksuur. al afyaal di keef?	w:	That one's damaged. How about these elephants?
z:	maa min al 9aaj? maa nashtari 9aaj.	c:	Aren't they from ivory? Don't let's buy ivory.
m:	la', da maa 9aaj. bisawwu l Haajaat di min 9aḍum.	w:	No, this isn't ivory. They make these things from bone.
z:	(lee siid ad dukkaan) asma9, addiina al asad da wa l afyaal wa z zaraafa aṣ ṣaghayyira bee talaatiin kullu.	c:	(To the shopkeeper) Listen, give us this lion and the elephants and the small giraffe for thirty altogether.
s:	wallaahi, Haakuun khasraan. as si9ir khamsiin.	s:	Goodness, I should be making a loss. The price is fifty.
z	da katiir. khaffiḍ shwaiya.	c:	That's too much. Come down a bit.
s:	shiila bee arba9iin u aziidak as sikkiin as samHa di foog.	s:	Take them for forty and I'll add this pretty knife for you.
z:	ṭaiyib. shukran. law samaHta, 9aawiz waṣil.	c:	Okay. Thank you. Please, I want a receipt.

Note on the dialogue

The shopkeeper says *addiiki leehu* 'I'll give it to you'. This type of construction will be explained in Lesson 22.1.2.

تمرين

١٨,١,١

بيضربنى	نادانى
بيضربَك	ناداك
بيضربِك	ناداكِ
بيضربه	ناداه
بيضربها	ناداها
بيضربنا	نادانا
بيضربكم	ناداكم
بيضربهم	ناداهم

ضربتنى
ضربتَك
ضربتِك
ضربته
ضربتها
ضربتنا
ضربتكم
ضربتهم

١٨,١,٢

انتَ ضربتنى؟

انتِ	صوّر
هو	ساعد
هى	شاف
هم	نادى

هو شافنى؟ ...... ايوه، هو شافك (والى آخره)

18.1 Drills: tamriin

18.1.1 Object pronouns

In English there is a set of pronouns used as objects of a verb or after prepositions, i.e. 'me, you, him, her.' In Arabic too, the same pronouns that are used after prepositions are used as objects of verbs, except the 1st pers. sg. is *-ni* instead of *-i, -y*. The tables below show object pronouns after a verb ending in a consonant, and after a verb ending in a vowel:

Sing.	1	biyaḍrub-ni	he hits me	naadaa-ni	he called me
	2 m	biyaḍrub-ak	he hits you	naadaa-k	he called you
	2 f	biyaḍrub-ik	he hits you	naadaa-ki	he called you
	3 m	biyaḍrub-u	he hits him/it	naadaa-hu	he called him
	3 f	biyaḍrub-a	he hits her/it	naadaa-ha	he called her
Plur.	1	biyaḍrub-na	he hits us	naadaa-na	he called us
	2	biyaḍrub-kum	he hits you	naadaa-kum	he called you
	3	biyaḍrub-um	he hits them	naadaa-hum	he called them

Note that:

(a) the final vowel of verbs is lengthened before adding the pronouns, e.g. *naada* becomes *naadaa-*.

(b) in the 3rd pers. pl. of the past tense the *u* changes to *oo,* not *uu*, e.g. *ḍarabu* plus *-ha* becomes *ḍarabooha.*

(c) the ending *-ta* of the past tense (i.e. 1st sing. and 2nd sing. masc. of most verbs) behaves differently with the pronouns as follows:

ḍarabtani	you (m) hit me
ḍarabtak	I hit you (m)
ḍarabtik	I hit you (f)
ḍarabtu	I hit him
ḍarabtaha	I hit her
ḍarabtana	you (m) hit us
ḍarabtakum	I hit you (pl)
ḍarabtahum	I hit them

Repeat the above tables after your teacher, paying attention to good pronunciation.

18.1.2 Substitution drill for object pronouns

There are three questions below consisting of a subject pronoun, a verb, and an object pronoun. Underneath the subject and verb are lists of words that can be substituted for them. The teacher should ask the students questions using a variety of subjects and verbs, but keeping the same object pronoun. The student replies with a correct answer, e.g. Teacher: *hu shaafni?* Student: *aiwa, hu shaafak* or *la', hu maa shaafak.*

(a) inta ḍarabtani? 'Did you hit me?'

inti	ṣawwar
hu	saa9ad
hi	shaaf
hum	naada

انت ضربتها؟

انتِ	صوّر
نحن	ساعد
هى	شاف
هم	نادى

هم ساعدوها؟ ...... ايوه، هم ساعدوها (والى آخره)

هو ضربكم؟

هى	صوّر
هم	ساعد
	شاف
	نادى

هى صورتكم؟ ...... ايوه، هى صورتنا (والى آخره)

١٨,١,٣

شفت القلم؟ ...... اى، شفته (والى آخره)

بتشربى الشاى؟

بتسوى شنط جلد؟

البت خيتت الجلابية دى؟

اكلتوا الجبنة السودانية؟

الاولاد قاعدين يكتبوا الجوابات؟

هم غسلوا البلاط؟

قريت الاورنيك؟

بيشوف عربية ابوه؟

انت عاوز تشترى اللحم دا؟

خلينا مفتاحنا معاكم؟

بتسمع الراديو كل يوم؟

الخدام قاعد يستعمل المكوة هسع؟

لسع ما شربت اللبن؟

(b) inta ḍarabtaha? 'Did you hit her?'

inti	ṣawwar
niHna	saa9ad
hi	shaaf
hum	naada

(c) hu ḍarabkum? 'Did he hit you?'

hi	ṣawwar
hum	saa9ad
	shaaf
	naada

The students can also drill each other in this way.

18.1.3 Changing noun objects to pronouns

It is important to realize that the 3rd pers. object pronouns, *-u/-hu, -a/-ha, -um/-hum,* can refer to things as well as people. (This is not true of subject pronouns, *hu, hi, hum,* which usually refer to people only. *da, di* and *deel* are used for things.) The singular object pronouns must agree in gender with the nouns they refer to.

Below are questions with noun objects. The teacher can ask these, and the students supply an answer using a pronoun in place of the noun, e.g. Teacher: *shufta l galam?* Student: *ai, shuftu.*

bitashrabi sh shaay?
bitsawwi shinaṭ jilid?
al bitt khayyatat aj jallaabiiya di?
akaltu j jibna s suudaaniiya?
al awlaad gaa9diin yaktibu j jawaabaat?
hum ghassalu l balaaṭ?
gareet al urneek?
bishuuf 9arabiiyt abuuhu?
inta 9aawz tishtari l laHam da?
khalleena muftaaHna ma9aakum?
bitasma9 ar raadyu kulli yoom?
al walad gaa9id yista9mil al makwa hassa9?
lissa9 maa shiribta l laban?

18.1.4 Conversation practice: 'Where have you been in Sudan?'

Now that you know the verb *masha* 'to go' (See Lesson 17), prepare some questions and answers about where you have been in Sudan or other countries, and what you saw there. Have the teacher record the sentences so that you can listen and memorize. You could also add some sentences about places which you would like to visit. The words for 'east' and 'west' have been added to the vocabulary for this lesson to help you with describing locations. You will find 'north' and 'south' in Lesson 17.

18.2 Role play

Act out the parts of people who are buying things or ordering things in a shop. Now that you know more Arabic you can bargain more convincingly than at the beginning. Remember that the shopkeeper will expect you to bargain.

Afterwards, make a visit to a gift shop or some other type of shop to practise the same thing in real life.

كلمات

هدية، هدايا
شنطة، شنط
جلد، جلود
حسب
سعر
استلم، يستلم
جمل، جمال
خشب
مخزن
حيوان، حيوانات
فيل، افيال
زراف
زرافة
غالى، غاليين
تمساح، تماسيح

ست، ستات
بابانوس
اصلى
عاج
عضم
خسران
خفّض، يخفض
سكين، سكاكين
جملة، جمل
وصل، وصولات
ضرب، يضرب
غرب
غربى
شرق
شرقى

18.3 Vocabulary: kalmaat

hadiiya, hadaaya	gift	sitt, sittaat	Madam, lady
shanṭa, shinaṭ	bag, suitcase	baabaanuus	ebony
jilid, juluud	skin, leather	aṣli	real, genuine, original
Hasab	according to, depending on	9aaj	ivory
		9aḍum	bone
si9ir	price	khasraan	at a loss (in price)
istalam, yistalim	to collect	khaffaḍ, yikhaffiḍ	to reduce the price
jamal, jimaal	camel	sikkiin, sakaakiin (f)	knife
khashab	wood	jumla, jumal	total
makhzan	storeroom	waṣil, waṣuulaat	receipt
Hayawaan, -aat	animal	ḍarab, yaḍrub	to beat, hit
fiil, afyaal	elephant	gharib	west
zaraaf	giraffe	gharbi	western
zaraafa	a giraffe	sharig	east
ghaali, ghaaliyiin	expensive	shargi	eastern
tumsaaH, tamaasiiH	crocodile		

الدرس التسعطاشر

حوار : كلام بالتلفون

ل : ليلى   ي : يوسف   ح : حسن   س : سكرتيرة

ل   يا يوسف، حسن من وزارة المالية ضرب ليك تلفون قبل عشرة دقايق.

ي   هو قال شنو؟

ل   قال، انت تضرب له هسع. هو مسافر بكرة.

ي   (بيضرب التلفون) ما فى حرارة.

ل   اضرب تانى. يمكن التلفون مشغول.

(يوسف بيضرب مرة تانية)

س   هلو، وزارة المالية.

ي   هلو، حسن موجود؟ لو سمحتي داير اكلمه.

س   دقيقة. انا اديه لك.

ح   هلو. حسن معاك.

ي   كيف الحال؟ انا يوسف. ان شاء الله انت شديد.

ح   الله يبارك فيك. ان شاء الله خير؟

ي   ليلى قالت انت ضربت لى قبل شوية.

ح   ايوه. حامشى الابيض بكرة. ممكن تجيب الاوراق حقة المشروع الزراعى قبل الساعة حداشر الية؟

ي   نعم؟ الخط دا ما كويس.

ح   قلت، جيب الاوراق ديلاك قبل الساعة حداشر.

ي   كويس. سمعت. حاجيبهم ليك طوالى.

تمرين

١٩،١،١

حادرس	حاغسل
حتدرس	حتغسل
حتدرسى	حتغسلى
حيدرس	حيغسل
حتدرس	حتغسل
حندرس	حنغسل
حتدرسوا	حتغسلوا
حيدرسوا	حيغسلوا

ad daris at tisa9ṭaashar — Lesson 19

Hiwaar: kalaam bi t talafoon — Dialogue: A telephone conversation

l:	leela y: yuusif H: Hassan s: sikirteera	L:	Leila Y: Yusif H: Hassan s: secretary
l:	ya yuusif, Hassan min wizaarat al maaliiya ḍarab leek talafoon gabli 9ashara dagaayig.	L:	Yusif, Hassan from the Ministry of Finance phoned you ten minutes ago.
y:	hu gaal shinuu?	Y:	What did he say?
l:	gaal, inta taḍrub leehu hassa9. hu musaafir bukra.	L:	He said you should phone him now. He is going away tomorrow.
y:	(biḍrub at talafoon) maa fii Haraara.	Y:	(dialling) There's no dialling tone.
l:	aḍrub taani. yimkin at talafoon mashghuul.	L:	Dial again. Perhaps the number is engaged/busy.
	(yuusif biyaḍrub marra taanya)		(Yusif dials again)
s:	hallo, wizaarat al maaliiya.	s:	Hallo, Ministry of Finance.
y:	hallo, Hassan moojuud? law samaHti daayir akallimu.	Y:	Hallo, is Hassan there? I want to speak to him, please.
s:	dagiiga. ana addiihu leek.	s:	One minute. I'll get him for you.
H:	hallo. Hassan ma9aak.	H:	Hallo, this is Hassan speaking.
y:	keef al Haal. ana yuusif. in shaa' alla inta shadiid.	Y:	How are you? This is Yusif. I hope you are well.
H:	alla yibaarik fiik. in shaa'alla kheer?	H:	May God bless you. I trust all is well.
y:	leela gaalat inta ḍarabta leey gabli shwaiya.	Y:	Leila said you phoned me a short while ago.
H:	aiwa. Haamshi l ubeeyiḍ bukra. mumkin tajiib al awraag Haggat al mashruu9 az ziraa9i gabli s saa9a Hidaashar alleela?	H:	Yes. I am going to El Obeid tomorrow. Can you bring the papers about the agricultural scheme before 11 o'clock today?
y:	na9am? al khaṭṭ da maa kwaiyis.	Y:	Pardon? This line is not good.
H:	gulta, jiib al awraag deelaak gabli s saa9a Hidaashar.	H:	I said, bring those papers before 11 o'clock.
y:	kwaiyis. simi9ta. Hajiibum leek ṭawwaali.	Y:	Okay. I heard. I will bring them to you at once.

Note on dialogue

keef al Haal 'How are you?' is another common Sudanese greeting, similar to *izzeey al Haal* and *izzeeyak.*

19.1 Drills: tamriin

19.1.1 The future tense

The future tense in Khartoum Arabic is formed by adding *Ha-* to the imperfect, e.g. *Haadrus* 'I will study'. Complete tables for *daras* and *ghassal* are set out below. Note that the future tense with *Ha-* is a feature of the city dialect. In rural areas you will hear the *bi-* form used for the future.

Sing.	1	Ha-adrus	Ha-aghassil
	2 m	Ha-tadrus	Ha-tghassil
	2 f	Ha-tadrusi	Ha-tghassili
	3 m	Ha-yadrus	Ha-yghassil
	3 f	Ha-tadrus	Ha-tghassil
Plur.	1	Ha-nadrus	Ha-nghassil
	2	Ha-tadrusu	Ha-tghassilu
	3	Ha-yadrusu	Ha-yghassilu

١٩,١,٢

الموظف كتب العنوان فى الظرف ...... الموظف حيكتب العنوان فى الظرف
عمتى مشت غرب السودان يوم الخميس ...... (والى آخره)
ركبنا القطر لحدى كوستى ورجعنا بعربية
المستشار الزراعى كان فى الخرطوم شهرى ستة
انا مسكت سمك من النيل
نضفتى البلاط فى اوضة النوم كويس؟
جبتوا منقا ولا برتقان من محل الفواكه؟
الكباية انكسرت
قفلت الباب قبل الساعة عشرة انت؟
اخوى استلم الشنطتين من السوق

١٩,١,٣

اشرب القهوة ...... اشربها، اشربيها (والى آخره)

شوف الصورة دى	ساعد المرة الكبيرة
خلى الولد	رسل الجوابات الليلة
اكوى بنطلونى	استعمل القلم دا
اركب العربية	اقطع كل البطاطس

ساعد ...... ساعدنى ساعدينى ساعدونى ساعدنا ساعدينا (والى آخره)
صوّر ...... صوّرنى (والى آخره)
نادى، شوف، خلى

١٩,١,٤

كبير	اكبر
طويل	اطول
ساهل	اسهل
صغير	اصغر

Note that:

(a) the first vowel in *taghassil, yighassil,* etc. is lost when *Ha-* is added. This is the same change as when *bi-* is added.

(b) verbs like *masha, itkallam, ishtaghal, inkasar, ista9mal,* and *itgaabal* behave like *daras,* that is, they don't lose a vowel after *Ha-*. Verbs like *saafar, shaaf* behave like *ghassal* and lose their vowel.

Repeat the above tables after the teacher until you know them by heart. Then drill all the verbs mentioned under (b) in the same way, e.g. *masha, itkallam,* etc.

19.1.2 Putting sentences into the future tense

Below are sentences in the past tense. The teacher should read them out and the students change them into the future tense.

al muwaẓẓaf katab al 9unwaan fi ẓ ẓarif.
9ammati mashat gharb as suudaan yoom al khamiis.
rikibna l gaṭar liHaddi koosti u raja9na bee 9arabiiya.
al mustashaar az ziraa9i kaan fi l kharṭuum shahri sitta.
ana masakta samak min an niil.
naḍḍafti l balaaṭ fii ooṭṭ an noom kwaiyis?
jibtu manga walla burtukaan min maHall al fawaakih?
al kubbaaya inkasarat.
gafalta l baab gabli s saa9a 9ashara, inta?
akhuuy istalam ash shanṭateen min as suug.

19.1.3 Imperatives with object pronouns

The same rules apply to imperatives followed by object pronouns as apply to the past and imperfect followed by them (see 18.1.1), e.g. *aktibu* 'write it!' (m); *aktibiihu* 'write it!' (f).

Below are some masculine imperatives with noun objects. The teacher should say them one by one, and the students repeat them in both masculine and feminine with the noun replaced by a pronoun, e.g. teacher: *ashrab al gahwa*; student: *ashraba, ashrabiiha.*

shuuf aṣ ṣuura di	saa9id al mara l kabiira
khalli l walad	rassil aj jawaabaat alleela
akwi banṭalooni	ista9mil al galam da
arkab al 9arabiiya	agṭa9 kull al baṭaaṭis

Now try the following imperatives in masculine, feminine, and plural with the object pronouns *-ni* and *-na*:

saa9id, ṣawwir, naadi, shuuf, khalli (meaning 'let, allow').

19.1.4 The comparative of adjectives

The usual way of making the comparative form of an adjective is on the following pattern:

kabiir	big	akbar	bigger
ṭawiil	long	aṭwal	longer
saahil	easy	ashal	easier
ṣaghayyir	small	aṣghar	smaller

حلو	احلى
غالى	اغلى

خفيف	اخف
شديد	اشد

اخوى اكبر منى   اختى اكبر منى

كبير، صغير، طويل، قصير، تقيل، خفيف، سمح، قديم

القلم دا اطول من داك؟   اى، القلم دا اطول من داك

القلم دا ما اطول من داك. دا اقصر (والى آخره)

كلمات

كلام
تلفون، تلفونات
وزارة، وزارات
وزارة المالية
ضرب، يضرب لواحد تلفون
حرارة
مشغول

كلم، يكلم
كيف الحال
ورقة، اوراق
مشروع، مشاريع
وصّل، يوصّل
النمرة غلط
خط، خطوط
منزل
نفصول

Adjectives with only two basic consonants behave as follows:

Hilu	sweet	aHla	sweeter
ghaali	expensive	aghla	more expensive

And those with the 2nd and 3rd consonants the same:

khafiif	light	akhaff	lighter
shadiid	severe	ashadd	more severe

Masculine, feminine, and plural all have the same form, e.g. *akhuuy akbar minni* 'my brother is bigger (older) than me,' *ukhti akbar minni* 'my sister is older than me'. Note that in Arabic *min* is the equivalent of the English 'than' in these sentences.

Now take two pens and two books or any other objects readily available. Make sentences comparing the two, using some of the following adjectives or any other adjective you know:

kabiir, ṣaghayyir, ṭawiil, giṣayyir, tagiil, khafiif, samiH, gadiim

This drill could be done in pairs, using a question and answer method, e.g. Teacher: *al galam da aṭwal min daak?* Student: *ai, al galam da aṭwal min daak.* and so on. It can be varied with the negative, e.g. *al galam da maa aṭwal min daak. da agṣar.*

19.2 Role play

Act out the parts of people having a telephone conversation. You can first try phoning someone at their house. Then try phoning an office where you have to go through an operator and ask to speak to someone. In the dialogue you will find expressions often used on the telephone, and some extra ones have been added in the vocabulary, such as *al nimra ghalaṭ* 'it's the wrong number', *mafṣuul* 'cut off' and manzil 'residence'. This last word is often used instead of beet 'house' when people answer the phone and say 'This is so-and-so's house.'

19.3 Vocabulary: kalmaat

kalaam	talk	kallam, yikallim	to talk to, tell
talafoon, talafoonaat	telephone	keef al Haal	how are you?
wizaara, wizaaraat	ministry	waraga, awraag	a paper, document
wizaarat al maaliiya	the Ministry of Finance	mashruu9, mashaarii9	scheme, project
ḍarab, yaḍrub lee waaHid talafoon	to phone someone	waṣṣal, yiwaṣṣil	to connect
Haraara	dialling tone	al nimra ghalaṭ	wrong number
mashghuul	busy/engaged	khaṭṭ, khuṭuuṭ	line
		manzil	residence (private house)
		mafṣuul	cut off

الدرس العشرين

حوار : المشتل

ز : زبونة　　　س : سيد المشتل

ز　　عندكم زهور للبيع؟

س　　ايوه، كل الزهور تحت الشجرة للبيع. عاوزة شنو؟

ز　　عاوزة زهرة صغيرة حمرة. عندك حاجة منها؟

س　　فى جهنمية صغيرة هنا. كان فى وردة سمحة لكن فى زول اشتراها امبارح.

ز　　عندى وردة لونها احمر. بيضة ما فى؟

س　　فى. ما شفتيها؟ بين الصفرا والبمبية.

ز　　اى، شفتها. لذيذة. حاشيلها وكمان الجهنمية الحمرا.

س　　تانى شنو؟

ز　　كان عندى شتلات كتيرة زى الشتلات ديل لكن الصفق نشف. دا من شنو؟

س　　نشف ساكت؟

ز　　اى، نشف ساكت.

س　　يمكن ما سقيتيهم كفاية.

تمرين

٢٠,١,١

اسود	سودا	سود
ابيض	بيضا	بيض
احمر	حمرا	حمر
اخدر	خدرا	خدر
ازرق	زرقا	زرق
اصفر	صفرا	صفر
اسمر	سمرا	سمر

القلم احمر؟ ...... ايوه، القلم احمر (والى آخره)

ad daris al 9ishriin

Hiwaar: al mashtal

s: siid al mashtal z: zabuuna

z: 9indakum zuhuur li l bee9?
s: aiwa, kull az zuhuur tiHt ash shajara li l bee9. 9aawza shinuu?
z: 9aawza zahra ṣaghayra Hamra. 9indak Haaja minnaha?
s: fii jahannamiiya ṣaghayra hina. kaan fii warda samHa laakin fii zool ishtaraaha umbaariH.
z: 9indi warda loona aHmar. beeḍa maa fii?
s: fii. maa shuftiiha, been aṣ ṣafra w al bambiiya?
z: ai, shuftaha. laziiza. Haashiila u kamaan aj jahannamiiya l Hamra.
s: taani shinuu?
z: kaan 9indi shatlaat katiira zeey ash shatlaat deel laakin aṣ ṣafag nishif. da min shinuu?
s: nishif saakit?
z: ai, nishif saakit.
s: yimkin maa sageetiihum kifaaya.

Lesson 20

Dialogue: The plant nursery

n: nurseryman c: customer

c: Do you have flowering plants for sale?
n: Yes, all the flowers under the tree are for sale. What would you like?
c: I want a small red flower. Do you have anything of that kind?
n: There is a small bougainvillea here. There was a lovely rose but someone bought it yesterday.
c: I have a red rose. Isn't there a white one?
n: There is. Didn't you see it, between the yellow one and the pink one?
c: Yes, I see it. It's beautiful. I'll take it and also the red bougainvillea.
n: What else?
c: I had a lot of plants like those plants but the leaves withered. What would that be from?
n: They just withered?
c: Yes, just withered.
n: Maybe you didn't water them enough.

20.1 Drills: tamriin

20.1.1 Color adjectives

There is a group of adjectives in Arabic, mainly colors and physical handicaps (blind, deaf, etc.) which form their masculine, feminine, and plural on a different pattern from the usual one. Below are set out the common words of this kind:

Masculine	Feminine	Plural	
aswad	soda	suud	black
abyaḍ	beeḍa	buyuḍ	white
aHmar	Hamra	Humur	red
akhdar	khadra	khudur	green
azrag	zarga	zurug	blue
aṣfar	ṣafra	ṣufur	yellow
asmar	samra	sumur	brown-skinned

Other color adjectives follow the usual pattern, e.g. *bambi, bambiiya, bambiiyiin* 'pink'.

The teacher should first read through the list of color adjectives above, with the students repeating after him. Then assemble objects of different colors. Using these, the teacher can drill the students, e.g. teacher shows a red pen and asks, *al galam aHmar?* Student replies, *aiwa, al galam aHmar*, and so on.

٢٠,١,٢

كان عندى جبنة بيضا لكن اكلتها
كان عندِك وردة حمرا لكن نشفت
كان عندَك شتلات كويسة لكن الغنم اكلهم
كان عندنا كورة زرقا لكن روّحناها
كان عندكم تلفون فى بيتكم لكن هسع ما شغال
كان عنده قميص اخدر لكن اداه لولد اخته
كان عندها فستان اصفر لكن خلته فى بيت عمتها
كان عندهم صندوق اسود لكن انكسر

٢٠,١,٣

زيت، سكر، دقيق، بيرة، بيض، شاى، صابون، ملح، عيش، جبنة

امبارح، بكرة

زيت، امبارح ...... امبارح كان فى زيت (والى آخره)

٢٠,١,٤

مدرسة، عربية، خالة، قفة، جامعة، سفارة، كورة، نمرة، جنينة، اسرة، ورقة

بنات، بت، ولد، الخرطوم، السودان، نسوان، مرة، راجل، مدرس، موظف، جواز، حيوانات

20.1.2 *kaan* and *Haykuun* with *9ind* 'I had' and 'I will have'

To make a sentence with *9ind* refer to the past, you put *kaan* before it, e.g. *kaan 9indi saa9a laakin rawwaHtaha* 'I had a watch but I lost it'.

To make a sentence refer to the future use *Haykuun*, e.g. *Haykuun 9indana ḍeef yoom as sabit* 'We will have a guest on Saturday'.

To drill *kaan 9ind* repeat the following sentences after the teacher, making sure you understand them.

kaan 9indi jibna beeḍa laakin akaltaha.
kaan 9indik warda Hamra laakin nishfat.
kaan 9indak shatlaat kwaiysa laakin al ghanam akalum.
kaan 9indana kuura zarga laakin rawwaHnaaha.
kaan 9indakum talafoon fii beetkum laakin hassa9 maa shaghghaal.
kaan 9indu gamiiṣ akhdar laakin addaahu lee walad ukhtu.
kaan 9indaha fustaan aṣfar laakin khallatu fii beet 9ammata.
kaan 9indahum ṣanduug aswad laakin inkasar.

20.1.3 *kaan* and *Haykuun* with *fii* 'there was' and 'there will be'

To make a sentence with *fii* refer to the past you do the same as with *9ind*, and put *kaan* before it, e.g. *kaan fii Hafla umbaariH* 'there was a party yesterday'. To make *fii* refer to the future, you put *Haykuun* before it, e.g. *Haykuun fii Hafla bukra* 'there will be a party tomorrow'.

Here is a drill on *kaan* and *Haykuun* with *fii*. The teacher should say one word from the list of nouns below and then either *umbaariH* or *bukra*, e.g. *zeet, umbaariH*. The student responds with a complete sentence, e.g. *umbaariH kaan fii zeet*.

zeet, sukkar, dagiig, biira, beeḍ, shaay, ṣaabuun, miliH, 9eesh, jibna

20.1.4 The *a* that drops out

In Lesson 16.1.4 a rule is given for the *i* and *u* that drop out under certain conditions. You have seen that *a* also drops out sometimes (sections 8.1.4, 10.1.1, 11.1.1, 12.1.1). Again for reference sake some rules are given to explain the loss of *a*, but you need not spend a lot of time on them if you are not interested. Concentrate on the drills that follow.

1. Words ending in *a* that add *t* in the dual and the possessive, e.g. *saa9a*, *madrasa*, etc.:

If the *a* is preceded by a single consonant only, it is lost when an ending is added beginning with a vowel (except the pronouns *-a* and *-um*), or when it is followed by the definite article *al*, e.g. *saa9ti* ('my watch'); *dagiigteen* ('two minutes'); *madrast al banaat* ('the girls' school'); but *guffati, guffateen, guffat al bitt*.

Exceptions to the above rule are: *mara* 'woman' and *sana* 'year', perhaps because they are short words. In them the *a* is not lost, e.g. *maratu* 'his wife', *sanateen* '2 years'.

Below are two lists of nouns; list (a) words end in *a*. The teacher should say one of the words from the first list and the student supply a complete possessive phrase, using a noun from the list (b) or any other appropriate noun as the possessor, e.g. Teacher: *madrasa*. Student: *madrast al banaat*.

(a) madrasa, 9arabiiya, khaala, guffa, jaam9a, safaara, kuura, nimra, jineena, usra, waraga
(b) banaat, bitt, walad, al kharṭuum, as suudaan, niswaan, mara, raajil, mudarris, muwaẓẓaf, jawaaz, Hayawaanaat

2. Words of the pattern *shahar*:

There are a number of words having in common an *a-a* vowel pattern and a middle consonant of the group *h, H, 9*. These words lose the second *a* when an ending is added beginning with a vowel (except the pronouns *-a* and *-um*), or when followed by the definite article, e.g. *ka9ba* 'bad (fem.)'; *baHreen* 'two rivers/seas'; *shahri talaata* 'March', Words with other middle consonants, however, do not lose the second *a*, e.g. *walad - waladeen, laban - laban al ghanam*.

بحر، شهر، شعر، ضهر، لحم، نحل، اهل

انا، انتَ، انتِ، هو، اتنين

بحر، اتنين ...... بحرين

انا، اهل ...... اهلى (والى آخره)

كلمات

مشتل، مشاتل
زهرة، زهور
للبيع
شجرة، شجر
احمر
جهنمية
وردة، ورد
ابيض
اصفر
بمبى، بمبية، بمبيين
شتلة، شتلات

صفق
نشف، ينشف
ساكت
سقى (سقيت)، يسقى
اسود
اخدر
ازرق
اسمر
شعر
نحل
اهل

Here is a list of words of the *shahar* pattern:

baHar, shahar, sha9ar, ḍahar, laHam, naHal *'bee',* ahal *'family'.*

The teacher should say one of these words and then one of the following: *ana, inta, inti, hu, itneen.* The student supplies the appropriate form of the word, e.g. teacher: *baHar, itneen.* Student: *baHreen.* Or, teacher: *ana, ahal.* Student: *ahli.*

20.2 Role play

Act out the parts of people who are buying plants from a plant nursery and asking the nurseryman's advice. You could be planning to put your plants in pots on the verandah or make an outside garden.

20.3 Vocabulary: kalmaat

mashtal, mashaatil	nursery (plants)	ṣafag	leaves
zahra, zuhuur	plant, flower	nishif, yanshaf	to become dry
li l bee9	for sale	saakit	just, only
shajara, shajar	tree	saga, (sageet), yasgi	to water
aHmar	red (see 20.1.1)	aswad	black
jahannamiiya	bougainvillea	akhdar	green
warda, warid	rose	azrag	blue
abyaḍ	white (see 20.1.1)	asmar	brown-skinned
aṣfar	yellow (see 20.1.1)	sha9ar	hair
bambi(m), bambiiya(f),	pink	naHal	bees
bambiiyin(pl)		ahal	family, relatives
shatla, shatlaat	seedling, plant		

اسئلة لمراجعة الدروس
من ١٦ الى ٢٠

١ عندك اخوان واخوات؟

٢ بتعرف تقرى عربى؟

٣ بتشترى لحم من وين؟

٤ حتمشى المكتب بعد بكرة ولا حتقعد فى البيت؟

٥ الوان النيلين شنو؟

٦ اول مرة مشيت سوق امدرمان كان متين؟

٧ المرة اخدت الوردة من وين؟

٨ منو ضرب ليوسف تلفون؟

٩ الناس لازم يملوا ازانيك كتيرة فى الايام دى؟

١٠ فى حاجة تحت الطربيزة؟

١١ خالة سامية بتشتغل براها ولا عندها ولد؟

١٢ انت عاوز تمشى جنوب السودان؟

١٣ اختك اطول من راجلها ولا اقصر؟

١٤ الوزارة روحت جوازك؟

١٥ الاولاد الصغار شافوا تماسيح فى البحر؟

١٦ فى شجرات قدام بيتكم وبتسقيهم كل يوم؟

١٧ الضيوف الفرنسيين اتغدوا معاكم؟

١٨ شهرى شنو حيكون فى تراب كتير هنا؟

١٩ طولت فى السودان؟

٢٠ ضرورى تتعلم كل الكلمات فى الدروس ديل؟

Revision questions for Lessons 16–20

Answer the following questions:

1. 9indak akhwaan u ukhwaat?
2. bita9rif tagra 9arabi?
3. bitashtari laHam min ween?
4. Hatamshi l maktab ba9ad bukra walla Hatag9ud fi l beet?
5. alwaan an niileen shinuu?
6. awwal marra masheet suug umdurmaan kaan miteen?
7. al mara akhadat al warda min ween?
8. minuu ḍarab lee yuusif talafoon?
9. an naas laazim yamlu araaniik katiira fi l ayyaam di?
10. fii Haaja tiHt aṭ ṭarabeeza?
11. khaalat saamya bitishtaghil baraaha walla 9indaha walad?
12. inta 9aawz tamshi januub al kharṭuum?
13. ukhtak aṭwal min raajila walla agṣar?
14. al wizaara rawwaHat jawaazak?
15. al awlaad aṣ ṣughaar shaafu tamaasiiH fi l baHar?
16. fii shajaraat giddaam beetkum u bitasgiihum kulli yoom?
17. aḍ ḍuyuuf al faransiiyiin itghaddu ma9aakum?
18. shahri shinuu Haykuun fii turaab katiir hina?
19. ṭawwalta fi s suudaan?
20. ḍaruuri tit9allam kull al kalmaat fi d duruus deel?

الدرس الواحد وعشرين

حوار : فى البيت

ع : عواطف ن : نادية ف : فتحية س : سامية

ع (فى المطبخ) قاعدة تعملى شنو؟

ن قاعدة انجض محشى. ما لك؟

ع المقص وين؟ دايرة اقص شعر فتحية.

ن ختيته فى فرشك. ما شفتيه؟

ع لا. ماشة اشوفه هسع. (بتمرق)

ن (لفتحية) ادينى السكين والمعلقة واضوق الرز.

ف هاكى. منى قاعدة تقش فى الحوش لسع؟ قالت قبل نص ساعة هى ماشة تستحم.

ن هى كسلانة. خلت المقشاشة وقاعدة تقرى الجريدة.

ف اتذكرت. فى زول ادانى كتاب ليها لكن لسع ما اديته ليها. (بتمرق)

س (بتخش) الكهربة قطعت. ما بقدر اكوى قستانى.

ن الكهربة قطعت؟ اقفلى التلاجة. دى فرصة انضفها.

س طيب، ممكن اساعدك؟

تمرين

ad daris al waaHid u 9ishriin

Hiwaar: fi l beet (2)

9: 9awaaṭif n: naadya
f: fatHiiya s: saamya

9: (fi l maṭba<u>kh</u>) gaa9da ta9mili <u>sh</u>inuu?
n: gaa9da anajjiḍ maH<u>sh</u>i. maalik?

9: al maga<u>ṣ</u><u>ṣ</u> ween? daayra agu<u>ṣ</u><u>ṣ</u> <u>sh</u>a9ar fatHiiya.
n: <u>kh</u>atteetu fii far<u>sh</u>ik. maa <u>sh</u>uftiihu?
9: la'. maa<u>sh</u>a a<u>sh</u>uufu hassa9.

(bitamrug)
n: (lee fatHiiya) addiini s sikkiin w al ma9laga u aḍuug ar ruzz.
f: haaki. muna gaa9da tagu<u>sh</u>sh fi l Hoo<u>sh</u> lissa9? gaalat gabli nuṣṣ saa9a hi maa<u>sh</u>a tistaHamm.
n: hi kaslaana. <u>kh</u>allat al mug<u>sh</u>aa<u>sh</u>a u gaa9da tagra j jariida.
f: itzakkarta. fii zool addaani kitaab leeha laakin lissa9 maa addeetu leeha.

(bitamrug)
s: (bit<u>kh</u>u<u>sh</u>sh) al kahraba gaṭa9at. maa bagdar akwi fustaani.
n: al kahraba gaṭa9at? agfili t tallaaja. di furṣa anaḍḍifa.
s: ṭaiyib, mumkin asaa9dik?

Lesson 21

Dialogue: At home (2)

A: Awaatif N: Naadya
F: Fathiiya S: Saamya

A: (in the kitchen) What are you doing?
N: I'm cooking stuffed vegetables. What's the matter?

A: Where are the scissors? I want to cut Fathiiya's hair.
N: I put them on your bed. Didn't you see them?
A: No. I'll go and look for them now.

(She goes out.)
N: (To Fathiiya) Give me the knife and spoon and I'll taste the rice.
F: Here you are. Is Muna still sweeping the yard? She said half an hour ago that she was going to take a bath.
N: She's lazy. She left off sweeping and is reading the newspaper.
F: I've remembered. Someone gave me a book for her but I still haven't given it to her.

(She goes out.)
S: (Entering) The electricity has gone off. I can't iron my dress.
N: Has the electricity gone off? Switch off the fridge. This is my chance to clean it.
S: Okay. Can I help you?

Notes on the dialogue

1. *maalik?*: In the dialogue one girl asks the other, *maalik?* 'What's the matter?' This expression consists of *maal-*, and a pronoun, in this case *-ik*. So 'what's the matter with him?' would be *maalu?*; 'what's the matter with her?' would be *maala?*, and so on.
2. *haaki*: In the dialogue this is used when one girl hands another a knife and spoon. It is a way of saying, 'Here you are.' There are three forms—*haak* (m), *haaki* (f), and *haakum* (pl)—consisting of a stem *haa-* which has no meaning apart from this phrase, and the 2nd person pronoun endings. It is not the imperative of a verb.
3. Note that in Arabic the idiom for 'the electricity has gone off' is *al kahraba gaṭa9at.*

21.1 Drills: tamriin

21.1.1 Verbs like <u>kh</u>atta (<u>kh</u>atteet), ya<u>kh</u>utt

The characteristic of these verbs is that the second and third basic consonants are the same, and the vowel between them has dropped out. In the past tense their vowel is always *a* and they take the same set of endings as *masha* (see Lesson 17.1.1). In the imperfect their vowel may be *u, i,* or *a.* Look at the tables below for <u>kh</u>atta 'to put'.

٢١,١,١

ختيت	اخت	حاخت
ختيت	تخت	حتخت
ختيتى	تختى	حتختى
خت	يخت	حيخت
ختت	تخت	حتخت
ختينا	نخت	حنخت
ختيتوا	تختوا	حتختوا
ختوا	يختوا	حيختوا

خت ختى ختوا
خات خاتة خاتين

قصيت (والى آخره)، قشيت، لفيت، خشيت، حبيت

استحميت (والى آخره)

انا انتَ انتِ هو هى نحن انتو هم
انا، قص ...... انا قصيت (والى آخره)

٢١,١,٢

الولد قص الورق بمقص صغير، وانا قصيت الورق بمقص كبير.
البت ختت الكبابى فى الطربيزة، وانا ختيت الكبابى فى الدولاب.
الخدام قش الحوش بمقشاشة طويلة، وانا قشيت البيت بمقشاشة قصيرة.
المرة لفت الملابس بسرعة، وانا لفيت الفساتين بالراحة.
الراجل استحم فى البحر، وانا استحميت فى الحمام.

٢١,١,٣

انا	لف البنطلون	امبارح
انتَ	خش البيت	بكرة
انتِ	خت المقص فى الفرش	دايما
هو	قص القماش	هسع
هى	استحم فى البحر	
نحن		
انتوا		
هم		

نحن، قص القماش، هسع ...... قاعدين نقص القماش هسع (والى آخره)

		Past	Imperfect	Future
Sing.	1	khatt-eet	a-khutt	Ha-akhutt
	2 m	khatt-eet	ta-khutt	Hat-khutt
	2 f	khatt-eeti	ta-khutt-i	Hat-khutt-i
	3 m	khatt-a	ya-khutt	Hay-khutt
	3 f	khatt-at	ta-khutt	Hat-khutt
Plur.	1	khatt-eena	na-khutt	Han-khutt
	2	khatt-eetu	ta-khutt-u	Hat-khutt-u
	3	khatt-u	ya-khutt-u	Hay-khutt-u

bi- is added to the imperfect to make the habitual tense in the same way as *Ha-*.
Imperative: *khutt*(m), *khutti*(f), *khuttu*(pl)
Active Participle: *khaatti*(m), *khaatta*(f), *khaattiin*(pl)

Repeat the above tables till you know them by heart for *khatta*, and then drill the following verbs of the same kind:

gaṣṣa, yaguṣṣ 'to cut with scissors'; *gashsha, yagushsh* 'to sweep'; *laffa, yaliff* 'to turn, wrap'; *khashsha, yakhushsh* 'to enter'; *Habba, yaHibb* 'to like, love'.

Note that the past tense of verbs like *khatta* in the 3rd m. sg. resembles verbs like *khalla*. This is why it is important to learn both past and imperfect stems, since it is the imperfect that will show that these two verbs are of different kinds, i.e. the imperfect of *khatta* is *yakhutt* with no final vowel, whereas the imperfect of *khalla* is *yikhalli*, ending in a vowel.

One common verb which is a variation on *khatta* is *istaHamma, (istaHammeet), yistaHamm* 'to bathe oneself'. This is to *khatta* as *ista9mal* is to *daras*. Drill this verb also through the above tables.

As a further drill the teacher can name a pronoun and a verb, e.g. *ana, gaṣṣa,* and the student supply the correct form of the verb in the past tense, e.g. *gaṣṣeet.* Then do the same with the imperfect.

21.1.2 Repetition drill for verbs like *khatta*

Repeat the following sentences after the teacher:

al walad gaṣṣa l warag bee magaṣṣ ṣaghayyir, u ana gaṣṣeet al warag bee magaṣṣ kabiir.
al bitt khattat al kabaabi fi ṭ ṭarabeeza, u ana khatteet al kabaabi fi d doolaab.
al khaddaam gashsha l Hoosh bee mugshaasha ṭawiila, u ana gashsheet al beet bee mugshaasha giṣayra.
al mara laffat al malaabis bee sur9a, u ana laffeet al fasaatiin bi r raaHa.
ar raajil istaHamma fi l baHar, u ana istaHammeet fi l Hammaam.

21.1.3 More practice in verbs like *khatta*

Below are three lists: (a) the subject pronouns; (b) sentences containing some of the new verbs; and (c) time words indicating which tense of the verb is required:

a)		b)		c)	
	ana		*laffa l banṭaloon.*		*umbaariH* (past)
	inta		*khashsha l beet.*		*bukra* (future)
	inti		*khatta l magaṣṣ fi l farish.*		*daayman (bi-)*
	hu		*gaṣṣa l gumaash.*		*hassa9* (*gaa9id* with imperfect)
	hi		*istaHamma fi l baHar.*		
	niHna				
	intu				
	hum				

The teacher chooses an item from each list, e.g. *niHna, gaṣṣa l gumaash, hassa9* and the student replies with a sentence in the appropriate form, e.g. *gaa9diin naguṣṣ al gumaash hassa9.*

كلمات

نجض، ينجض
محشى
مالك؟
مقص، مقصات
قص، يقص
خت، يخت
فرش، فراش
معلقة، معالق
ضاق (ضقت)، يضوق
رز
هاكى
قش، يقش
حوش، حيشان

استحم، يستحم
كسلان، كسلانين
مقشاشة
جريدة، جرايد
اتذكر، يتذكر
كتاب، كتب
خش، يخش
كهربة
قطع، يقطع
قفل، يقفل
تلاجة، تلاجات
فرصة، فرص
حب، يحب
لف، يلف
بالراحة
حمام، حمامات

21.1.4 Conversation practice: Telling about what you did yesterday

Ask your teacher to tell you what they did yesterday between the time they got up and the time they went to bed. Record it and listen to it a couple of times at least.

Then create some sentences about what you did yesterday as you might tell it to a friend. Have the teacher record these for you so you can listen and mimic and work on memorising them.

21.2 Role play

Act out the parts of members of a family occupied in various activiities at home and talking to each other about what they are doing. See how long you can keep it up.

21.3 Vocabulary: kalmaat

najjaḍ, yinajjiḍ	to cook
maHshi	stuffed vegetables
maalik	what's the matter (see Notes on the dialogue)
magaṣṣ, magaṣṣaat	scissors
gaṣṣa, yaguṣṣ	to cut with scissors
khatta, yakhutt	to put
farish, furaash	bed (with bedding)
ma9laga, ma9aalig	spoon
ḍaag, (ḍugta), yaḍuug	to taste
ruzz	rice
haaki	here you are (see Notes on the dialogue)
gashsha, yagushsh	to sweep
Hoosh, Heeshaan	yard

istaHamma, yistaHamm	to bathe oneself
kaslaan, kaslaaniin	lazy
mugshaasha	broom
jariida, jaraayid	newspaper
itzakkar, yitzakkar	to remember
kitaab, kutub	book
khashsha, yakhushsh	to enter
kahraba	electricity
gaṭa9, yagṭa9	to go off
gafal, yagfil	to switch off
tallaaja, tallaajaat	refrigerator
furṣa, furaṣ	chance, occasion
Habba, yaHibb	to like, love
laffa, yaliff	to turn, wrap up
bi r raaHa	slowly, carefully
Hammaam, -aat	bathroom

الدرس الاتنين وعشرين

حوار : تأجير بيت

س : سيد البيت   م : مؤجر

م   واحد قال لى عندك بيوت للايجار.

س   صاح. عاوز تأجر بيت؟

م   ايوه، البيت بتاعنا صغير.

س   عاوز كم أوضة؟

م   تلاتة أوض وصالون.

س   عندى بيت بتلاتة أوض وقراش وجنينه سمحة.

م   فى ياتو حى؟

س   فى العمارات.

م   البيت دا مفروش ولا ما مفروش؟

س   ما مفروش. بعدين، عندى بيت تانى، ببنى فيه فى بحرى، حيكون مفروش.

م   بيجهز متين؟

س   ممكن لحدى شهرى تسعة.

م   والبيت القديم فيه مراوح ولا مكيف هوا؟

س   فيه مكيفين. لو عاوز تشوفه، ممكن أوديك.

م   طيب. نمشى.

تمرين

٢٢,١,١

ad daris al itneen u 9ishriin — Lesson 22

Hiwaar: ta'jiir beet — Dialogue: Renting a house

s:	siid al beet m: mu'ajjir	l:	landlord t: tenant
m:	waaHid gaal leey 9indak biyuut li l iijaar.	t:	Someone told me you have houses for rent
s:	ṣaaHH. 9aawz ta'ajjir beet?	l:	True. Do you want to rent a house?
m:	aiwa, al beet bitaa9na ṣaghayyir.	t:	Yes, our house is too small.
s:	9aawz kam ooḍa?	l:	How many rooms do you want?
m:	talaata uwaḍ u ṣaaluun.	t:	Three bedrooms and a lounge.
s:	9indi beet bee talaata uwaḍ u garraash u jineena samHa.	l:	I have a house with three bedrooms and a garage and a nice garden.
m:	fii yaatu Hayy?	t:	In which district?
s:	fi l 9amaaraat.	l:	In the New Extension.
m:	al beet da mafruush walla maa mafruush?	t:	Is that house furnished or unfurnished?
s:	maa mafruush. ba9deen, 9indi beet taani, babni fiihu fii baHri, Haykuun mafruush.	l:	Unfurnished. Then I am having another house built in Khartoum North that will be furnished.
m:	biyajhaz miteen?	t:	When will it be ready?
s:	mumkin liHaddi shahri tis9a.	l:	Possibly by September.
m:	w al beet al gadiim fiihu maraawiH walla mukayyif hawa?	t:	In the old house are there fans or an air cooler?
s:	fiihu mukayyifeen. law 9aawz tashuufu, mumkin awaddiik.	l:	There are two air coolers. If you want to see it, I can take you.
m:	ṭaiyib. namshi.	t:	Fine. Let's go.

Note on the dialogue

1. *yaatu* 'which' can come either before or after the noun it goes with, e.g. *yaatu walad?* or *al walad yaatu?* If it comes before the noun, the definite article is not needed and *yaatu* remains the same with masculine, feminine, and plural nouns, e.g. *yaatu Hilla?*, *yaatu naas?* If *yaatu* comes after the noun, the definite article is required and *yaatu* must agree in gender with the noun, e.g. *al walad yaatu?*; *al Hilla yaata?*; *an naas yaatum?*
2. When renting a house in Khartoum it is quite common to go through an agent or *samsaar.* If you rent a house through an agent, the normal practice is for the agent to receive the equivalent of a month's rent from both the landlord and the tenant. When you are looking for a house in a particular district you can ask local people to guide you to the nearest *samsaar.*
3. *9indi beet taani, babni fiihu fii baHri.* This is a relative clause, which translated literally is: 'I have another house (which) I am building it in Khartoum North'. This type of relative clause is explained in Lesson 27.1.2.

22.1 Drills: tamriin

22.1.1 Possessive phrases with *bitaa9* and *Hagg*

Revise *Hagg* as you learned it in Lesson 10.1.4. It was used there in the type of sentence 'something belongs to so-and-so.' *Hagg* and *bitaa9* are very frequently used in possessive phrases, e.g. 'my house' *al beet Haggi* or *al beet bitaa9i.* This kind of phrase is an alternative to a simple possessive phrase such as *beeti,* which also means 'my house'. How do they differ from each other? The following points should be noted:

a. There is no difference of meaning. *beeti* and *al beet Haggi (bitaa9i)* are the same.
b. The simple possessive phrase is always used with words referring to relatives and friends, parts of the body, and other things that can't normally be separated from oneself, e.g. name, nationality, etc. 'My father', is always *abuuy;* 'my name', is always *ismi,* and so on.

حقى	حقتى	بتاعى	بتاعتى
حقَك	حقتَك	بتاعَك	بتاعتَك
حقِك	حقتِك	بتاعِك	بتاعتِك
حقه	حقته	بتاعه	بتاعته
حقها	حقتها	بتاعها	بتاعتها
حقنا	حقتنا	بتاعنا	بتاعتنا
حقكم	حقتكم	بتاعكم	بتاعتكم
حقهم	حقتهم	بتاعهم	بتاعتهم

دا تلفونهم ...... دا التلفون بتاعهم (والى آخره)

دا تلفونهم	دى كورتكم
دى ورقته	دا دولابها
دى شنطتها	دا قردك
دا جلدى	دا حوشنا
دا جوازك	دى سفارتنا
دا عنوانهم	دا عفشهم
دى شتلتِك	دى اوضته
ديل كراسيها	ديل مراوحهم

٢٢,١,٢

سيد البيت ادى المؤجر المفتاح
ورينا احمد صورة
وريت صاحبى جلد جديد
اديتى اختك تلاتة شنط؟

c. The simple possessive phrase is also usual in expressions taken from the written language, such as those connected with government and administration, e.g. *maktab al busṭa, wizaarat al maaliiya,* and in certain other fixed phrases, e.g. *siid al beet.*
d. With all other words, in normal everyday conversation the possessive with *bitaa9* or *Hagg* is more common, although the simple possessive is possible, e.g. *al muftaaH bitaa9 al ooḍa di* is preferred over *muftaaH al ooḍa di; al kubbaaya Haggati* over *kubbaayti.*
e. The definite article is required in phrases with *bitaa9* or *Hagg,* in contrast to its absence in simple phrases, e.g. *al kuura Haggat aHmad* compared with *kuurt aHmad.*
f. *bitaa9* and *Hagg* agree in gender with the first noun, e.g. *al kursi Hagg (bitaa9) abuuy, al 9arabiiya Haggat (bitaa9at) abuuy*. The feminine is also used with plural nouns, e.g. *al karaasi Haggati* ('my chairs').

Tables for *Hagg* and *bitaa9* with the pronouns are given here. Repeat these tables after the teacher, one column at a time.

of me	Hagg-i	Haggat-i	bitaa9-i	bitaa9t-i
of you (m)	Hagg-ak	Haggat-ak	bitaa9-ak	bitaa9t-ak
of you (f)	Hagg-ik	Haggat-ik	bitaa9-ik	bitaa9t-ik
of him	Hagg-u	Haggat-u	bitaa9-u	bitaa9t-u
of her	Hagg-a	Haggat-a	bitaa9-a	bitaa9at-a
of me	Hagg-i	Haggat-i	bitaa9-i	bitaa9t-i
of us	Hagga-na	Haggat-na	bitaa9-na	bitaa9at-na
of you (pl)	Hagga-kum	Haggat-kum	bitaa9-kum	bitaa9at-kum
of them	Hagg-um	Haggat-um	bitaa9-um	bitaa9at-um

The sentences below contain some simple possessive phrases. The teacher should read these out and have the students replace the simple possessive phrases with ones using *bitaa9* or *Hagg.*

da talafoonum
di waragtu
di shanṭata
da jildi
da jawaazak
da 9unwaanum
di shatlatik
deel karaasiiha

di kuuratkum
da doolaaba
da girdak
da Hooshna
di safaaratna
da 9afashum
di ooṭṭu (*from* ooḍa; ḍ + t = ṭṭ)
deel maraawiHum

22.1.2 Verbs with two objects

The verbs *adda* 'to give' and *warra* 'to show' can take two objects, i.e. the thing that is given or shown, and the person to whom it is given or shown, e.g. *addeet al walad al kitaab* 'I gave the boy the book'.

In English we can put 'the boy' before 'the book,' as in the sentence above, or 'the book' before 'the boy,' as in the sentence 'I gave the book to the boy,' in which case we have to add 'to' before 'the boy.' The same is true if we replace the nouns with pronouns; e.g. we can say, 'I gave him it' or 'I gave it to him.' In Arabic too it's possible to vary the order of the words, but according to slightly different rules from the English ones.

Repeat the following sentences after the teacher:

A
a) siid al beet adda l mu'ajjir al muftaaH.
b) warreena aHmad ṣuura.
c) warreet ṣaaHbi jilid jadiid.
d) addeeti ukhtik talaata shinaṭ?

سيد البيت ادى المفتاح للمؤجر
ورينا صورة لاحمد
وريت جلد جديد لصاحبى
اديتى تلاتة شنط لاختك؟

سيد البيت اداه المفتاح
وريناه صورة
وريته جلد جديد
اديتيها تلاتة شنط؟

سيد البيت اداه المؤجر
وريناها احمد
وريته صاحبى
اديتيهم اختك؟

سيد البيت اداه ليه
وريناه ليها
وريته ليه
اديتيها ليهم؟

سيد البيت ادى المؤجر المفتاح
سيد البيت ادى المفتاح للمؤجر
سيد البيت اداه المفتاح
(والى آخره)

كلمات

سيد البيت
تأجير
مؤجر، مؤجرين

بحرى
جهز، يجهز
مروحة، مراوح

B a)   siid al beet adda l muftaaH li l mu'ajjir.
   b)   warreena ṣuura lee aHmad.
   c)   warreet jilid jadiid lee ṣaaHbi.
   d)   addeeti talaata <u>sh</u>inaṭ lee u<u>kh</u>tik?

C a)   siid al beet addaahu l muftaaH.
   b)   warreenaahu ṣuura.
   c)   warreetu jilid jadiid.
   d)   addeetiiha talaata <u>sh</u>inaṭ?

D a)   siid al beet addaahu l mu'ajjir.
   b)   warreenaaha aHmad.
   c)   warreetu ṣaaHbi.
   d)   addeetiihum u<u>kh</u>tik?

E a)   siid al beet addaahu leehu.
   b)   warreenaahu leeha.
   c)   warreetu leehu.
   d)   addeetiiha leehum?

Now repeat the sentences again, but this time take all the a)'s together, then all the b)'s, etc. For example:
   siid al beet adda l mu'ajjir al muftaaH.
   siid al beet adda l muftaaH li l mu'ajjir.

Note that where one of the objects is a pronoun and the other a noun, the pronoun always comes before the noun (see C and D). Where both are pronouns the person comes before the thing shown or given (see E).

22.1.3 Action drill

Put some objects on the table and practise using 'give.' For example, on the table are a cup, a watch, a book and a pen. The first person says, "Mary, give the cup to the teacher." Mary gives the cup to the teacher and says, "I have given it to him/her." The next person says, "John, give me the book." John gives the speaker the book and says "I am giving you the book." And so on.

22.1.4 Conversation practice: Your house

Ask your teacher to describe the house they live in. Listen carefully. Then prepare some sentences describing the house you live in now or some other house. You can mention the number of rooms and what kind of rooms they are, what sort of furniture you have, whether the house has a garden or yard or is a flat, and so on. Have your teacher record the sentences for you so you can listen and memorise them.

22.2 Role play

Act out the parts of someone trying to rent a house or flat from an agent. The prospective tenant may have favourable or unfavourable views of the house which the agent shows him. Probably he will ask questions about the rent, the water and electricity and so on.

22.3 Vocabulary: kalmaat

siid al beet	house-owner, landlord	baHri	Khartoum North
ta'jiir	renting	jahaz, yajhaz	to be ready
mu'ajjir, mu'ajjiriin	tenant	marwaHa, maraawiH	electric fan

ايجار، ايجارات
اجر، يأجر
قراش، قراشات
ياتو
حي، احيا
مفروش

مكيف هوا، مكيفات هوا
ودى (وديت)، يودى
ورى (وريت)، يورى
سمسار، سماسرة

iijaar, iijaaraat	rent
ajjar, yi'ajjir	to rent
garraash, garraashaat	garage
yaatu?	which? (see Notes on the dialogue)
Hayy, aHya	district of town
mafruush	furnished
mukayyif hawa, mukayyifaat hawa	air cooler
wadda, (waddeet), yiwaddi	to take someone to
warra, (warreet), yiwarri	to show
samsaar, samaasra	house agent

الدرس التلاتة وعشرين

حوار : العرس

ن : نورة   م : ماريا

ن   يا ماريا، شفتى عرس سودانى؟

م   لا. العرس السودانى كيف؟

ن   سمح خالص. العرس يومين. اول يوم العروس بتلبس ابيض زى العرس الاوربى. تانى يوم احسن من أول يوم. فيه عادات سودانية جميلة.

م   العادات السودانية زى شنو؟

ن   العروس بتلبس دهب كتير فى راسها وفى ايدينها وبترقص مع العريس. بعدين فى المسا هم بيقعدوا في عنقريب وام العروس بتجيب لبن. بيشربوا اللبن وبيبخوا بعض باللبن.

م   يا سلام، حكاية عجيبة. محل العرس دايما بيكون وين؟

ن   فى بيت ابو العروس.

م   بيباركوا للعروس كيف؟

ن   بيقولوا، مبروك. بيت مال وعيال.

تمرين

٢٣,١,١

أول، اولى
تانى، تانية
تالت، تالتة
رابع، رابعة

ad daris at talaata u 9i<u>sh</u>riin

Hiwaar: al 9iris

n: nuura   m: maria

n: ya maria, <u>sh</u>ufti 9iris suudaani?
m: la'. al 9iris as suudaani keef?
n: samiH <u>kh</u>aaliṣ. al 9iris yoomeen. awwal
yoom al 9aruus bitalbas abyaḍ zeey al 9iris al
uurubbi. taani yoom aHsan min awwal yoom.
fiihu 9aadaat suudaaniiya jamiila.

m: al 9aadaat as suudaaniiya zeey <u>sh</u>inuu?
n: al 9aruus bitalbas dahab katiir fii raasa u fii
iideena u bitarguṣ ma9a l 9ariis. ba9deen fi
l misa hum biyag9udu fii 9angareeb u umm
al 9aruus bitjiib laban. biya<u>sh</u>rabu l laban u
bibu<u>kh</u><u>kh</u>u ba9aḍ bi l laban.
m: ya salaam, Hikaaya 9ajiiba. maHall al 9iris
daayman bikuun ween?
n: fii beet abu l 9aruus.
m: bibaarku li l 9aruus keef?
n: biguulu, "mabruuk. beet maal wa 9iyaal."

Lesson 23

Dialogue: Weddings

N: Nura   M: Maria

N: Maria, have you seen a Sudanese wedding?
M: No; what's a Sudanese wedding like?
N: Very nice. A wedding lasts for two days.
On the first day the bride wears white like
a European wedding. The second day is
better than the first because of the beautiful
Sudanese customs.
M: What are these Sudanese customs?
N: The bride wears a lot of gold on her head and
arms and dances with the bridegroom. Then
in the evening they sit on an angareeb and
the bride's mother brings milk. They drink the
milk and spit it at each other.
M: Goodness me! That sounds strange. Where
does a wedding take place?
N: At the bride's father's house.
M: How do they congratulate the bride?
N: They say, "Congratulations. Wealth and
children to your house!"

Notes on the dialogue

Special greetings. In addition to the usual everyday greetings in Arabic, there are some greetings for special occasions. Here are some of the more common ones:

1. *mabruuk.* This greeting is roughly equivalent to 'congratulations' in English, it can be said to a newly married couple, the parents of a new baby, a person who has been successful in something, the owner of a new car, etc. The reply is, *allaa yibaarik fiik.*
2. *beet maal wa 9iyaal.* This expression is said to wish a bride and bridegroom a prosperous married life with lots of children.

The customs described above are those of one part of Sudan. People from other areas have different customs relating to marriage and weddings.

23.1 Drills: tamriin

23.1.1 The ordinal numbers: first, second, third

The ordinal numbers 1st to 10th are listed below. They have masculine and feminine forms like adjectives, which must agree with the nouns they qualify. These numbers may come before or after the nouns they go with, e.g. you can say, *awwal yoom* or *al yoom al awwal.* Note that if the number comes <u>before</u> the noun there is no definite article; whereas if it comes <u>after</u> the noun, the definite article is required with both noun and number just like any other adjective, and the number must agree in gender with the noun, e.g. *al yoom at taalit; al marra t taalta.*

1st	awwal, uula
2nd	taani, taanya
3rd	taalit, taalta
4th	raabi9, raab9a

خامس، خامسة
سادس، سادسة
سابع، سابعة
تامن، تامنة
تاسع، تاسعة
عاشر، عاشرة

شيل خامس قلم ...... شلت القلم الخامس (والى آخره)

٢٣,١,٢

الخدام بيخت السكاكين فى الطربيزة
...... الخدام كان بيخت السكاكين فى الطربيزة

العروس بتلبس دهب فى راسها (والى آخره)
الاولاد بيلعبوا كورة فى الحوش
بنستحم قبل العشا
انت بتستلم الجوابات من صندوق البسطة؟
الولد بيكوى الملابس بتاعتى
انت بتخيتى بالمكنة؟
بفهم العربى لكن ما بتكلم كويس
بتشتغلوا براكم
هو بيعرف غرب السودان احسن من ناس البلد
الناس هنا بيصطادوا تماسيح فى البحر

٢٣,١,٣

المرة ماشة السوق
...... المرة كانت ماشة السوق

انا راقد فى الاوضة براى (والى آخره)
الاطفال نايمين
انت ساكن مع جدك فى كوستى؟
انتِ عاوزة شاى بلبن؟
نحن ما عارفين الطريق
بتى خايفة من الفيل

5th	<u>kh</u>aamis, <u>kh</u>aamsa
6th	saadis, saadsa
7th	saabi9, saab9a
8th	taamin, taamna
9th	taasi9, taas9a
10th	9aa<u>sh</u>ir, 9aa<u>sh</u>ra

Line up ten pens and ten pieces of paper (or some other convenient objects, one set masculine and the other set feminine). The teacher can then tell a student to take one of the pens, e.g. *<u>sh</u>iil <u>kh</u>aamis galam*. The student obeys the order by picking up the fifth in line of the pens, and says as he does so, *<u>sh</u>ilta <u>kh</u>aamis galam* or *<u>sh</u>ilta l galam al <u>kh</u>aamis*.

In Sudanese Arabic the ordinal numbers over 10 are the same as the cardinal numbers, e.g. 'the twentieth tree' is *a<u>sh</u> <u>sh</u>ajara al 9i<u>sh</u>riin*, 'the forty-eighth line' is *al <u>kh</u>aṭṭ at tamanya u arba9iin*.

23.1.2 The past continuous tense

The present continuous tense is formed from *gaa9id* with the imperfect (see Lesson 6), e.g. *gaa9id agra* 'I am reading'. The past continuous tense is formed from the past of the verb 'to be' with the *bi*-form of the imperfect, e.g. *kunta bagra* 'I was reading'.

The past continuous tense can also be used with a past habitual meaning, e.g. *kunta bagu<u>shsh</u> al beet kulli yoom laakin hassa9 bagu<u>shsh</u>u marrateen fi l usbuu9 bass* 'I used to sweep the house every day but now I only sweep it twice a week'.

Below are sentences in the present habitual tense with *bi-*. The teacher should read out each sentence and let the student repeat the sentence in the past continuous. For example,

Teacher: *al <u>kh</u>addaam bi<u>kh</u>utt as sakaakiin fi ṭ ṭarabeeza.*
Student: *al <u>kh</u>addaam kaan bi<u>kh</u>utt as sakaakiin fi ṭ ṭarabeeza.*

al 9aruus bitalbas dahab fii raasa
al awlaad bil9abu kuura fi l Hoo<u>sh</u>
binistaHamm gabli l 9a<u>sh</u>a
inta bitistalm aj jawaabaat min ṣanduug al busṭa?
al walad biyakwi l malaabis bitaa9ti
inti bit<u>kh</u>ayyiti bi l makana?
bafham al 9arabi laakin maa batkallam kwaiyis
biti<u>sh</u>ta<u>gh</u>lu baraakum
hu biya9rif <u>gh</u>arb as suudaan aHsan min naas al balad
an naas hina bisṭaadu tamaasiiH fi l baHar

23.1.3 The past continuous with participles

Revise the active participle (see Lesson 15.1.1), especially the ones commonly used for the present continuous tense of their verbs. These participles are also used with *kaan* for the past continuous of their verbs, e.g. *ar raajil kaan waagif tiHt a<u>sh</u> <u>sh</u>ajara* 'the man was standing under the tree'.

Listed below are sentences containing active participles. The teacher should read these out one by one, and the students respond with the same sentence in the past continuous. For example,

Teacher: *al mara maa<u>sh</u>a s suug.*
Student: *al mara kaanat maa<u>sh</u>a s suug.*

ana raagid fi l ooḍa baraay
al aṭfaal naaymiin
inta saakin ma9a jiddak fii koosti?
inti 9aawza <u>sh</u>aay bee laban?
niHna maa 9aarfiin aṭ ṭariig
bitti <u>kh</u>aayfa min al fiil

هو جاى من الجنوب
انتوا ماسكين الكتب بتاعة مدرسنا
سيد الدكان قاعد فى الشارع

كلمات

عرس، اعراس	عريس، عرسان
عروس، عرايس	مسا
لبس، يلبس	عنقريب، عناقريب
اوربى	بخ، يبخ
عادة، عادات	بعض
جميل، جميلين	حكاية، حكايات
دهب	عجيب، عجيبين
راس، رسين	بارك، يبارك ل...
ايد، ايدين	مبروك
رقص، يرقص	مال وعيال

hu jaay min aj januub
intu maaskiin al kutub bitaa9at mudarrisna
siid ad dukkaan gaa9id fi sh shaari9

23.1.4 Conversation practice: 'How do you do this in Sudan?'

Perhaps you would like to know what the Sudanese customs are regarding a certain topic, such as the birth and naming of a new baby, or graduating from university. Ask your teacher to describe them for you and listen carefully. You could record the description.

With the teacher's help write some sentences about an interesting custom of your country. Ask the teacher to record the sentences for you so you can listen and memorise them.

23.2 Role play

Act out the parts of people involved in a wedding. Besides the bride and bridegroom there will be the bride's father or uncle as host welcoming guests and the women of the family cooking, not to mention relatives and friends coming to congratulate the couple.

23.3 Vocabulary: kalmaat

9iris, a9raas	wedding	9ariis, 9irsaan	bridegroom
9aruus, 9araayis	bride	misa (masc.)	evening
libis, yalbas	to put on, wear	9angareeb, 9anaagriib	rope bed
uurubbi	European	bakhkha, yabukhkh	to spit
9aada, 9aadaat	custom	ba9aḍ	each other
jamiil, -iin	beautiful	Hikaaya, Hikaayaat	story
dahab	gold	9ajiib, 9ajiibiin	strange
raas, risen	head	baarak, yibaarik li	to congratulate
iid, iideen (fem.)	hand	mabruuk	congratulations
ragaṣ, yarguṣ	to dance	maal wa 9iyaal	(see Dialogue note 2)

الدرس الاربعة وعشرين

حوار : السفر بالطيارة

ر : راكب　　م : موظف

ر　داير اعمل حجز لنيروبى فى الاسبوع الجاى.
م　عندك تذكرة؟
ر　ايوه.
م　ليكم نفر؟
ر　واحد بس.
م　انت داير مقعد جنب الشباك؟
ر　انا داير مقعد جنب الممر.
م　الطياره حقة يوم الاتنين ما فيها محل. يوم الخميس كويس معاك؟
ر　كويس. وزن العفش فى التذكرة لحدى كم؟
م　عشرين كيلو.
ر　ضرورى اعمل تأشيرة لكينيا ولا ما ضرورى؟
م　ضروري. امشي اطلب من السفارة باسرع ما يمكن.
ر　الطيارة حتقوم الساعة كم يوم الخميس؟
م　حتقوم الساعة تمنية الا تلت فى الصباح. لازم تجى المطار قبل ستة ونص.
ر　عندى صاحبى جاى من القاهرة الليلة. الطيارة بتاعة الساعة عشرة وربع جات؟
م　لسع. حتتأخر بساعة واحدة ونص.
ر　شكرا. انا ماشى الكفتيرة فى المطار، استنى شوية. انا خايف هو يجى وما يلقانى.

تمرين

٢٤,١,١

جيت	اجى	بجى
جيت	تجى	بتجى
جيتى	تجى	بتجى
جا	يجى	بيجى
جات	تجى	بتجى
جينا	نجى	بنجى
جيتوا	تجوا	بتجوا
جو	يجوا	بيجوا

ad daris al arba9a u 9i<u>sh</u>riin

Hiwaar: as safar bi ṭ ṭayyaara

Lesson 24

Dialogue: The plane journey

m: muwaẓẓaf   r: raakib

c: clerk   p: passenger

r: daayir a9mil Hajiz lee nayruubi fi l usbuu9 aj jaay.

p: I want to make a reservation to Nairobi for next week.

m: 9indak tazkara?

c: Have you got a ticket?

r: aiwa.

p: Yes.

m: lee kam nafar?

c: For how many people?

r: waaHid bass.

p: Only one.

m: inta daayir mag9ad jamb a<u>sh</u> <u>sh</u>ubbaak?

c: Do you want a window seat?

r: ana daayir mag9ad jamb al mamarr.

p: I would like a seat next to the aisle.

m: aṭ ṭayyaara Haggat yoom al itneen maa fiiha maHall. yoom al <u>kh</u>amiis kwaiyis ma9aak?

c: There's no room on the Monday plane. Is Thursday all right with you?

r: kwaiyis. wazn al 9afa<u>sh</u> fi t tazkara liHaddi kam?

p: Fine. What's the baggage allowance?

m: 9i<u>sh</u>riin kiilu.

c: 20 kilos.

r: ḍaruuri a9mil ta'<u>sh</u>iira lee kiinya walla maa ḍaruuri?

p: Do I need a visa for Kenya or not?

m: ḍaruuri. am<u>sh</u>i aṭlub min as safaara bee asra9 maa yumkin.

c: Yes. You should apply at the Kenyan embassy as soon as possible.

r: aṭ ṭayyaara Hatguum as saa9a kam yoom al <u>kh</u>amiis?

p: What time will the plane leave on Thursday?

m: Hatguum as saa9a tamanya illa tilit fi ṣ ṣabaaH. laazim taji l maṭaar gabli sitta u nuṣṣ.

c: It will leave at twenty to eight in the morning. You should be at the airport by half past six.

r: 9indi ṣaaHbi jaay min al <u>gh</u>aahira alleela. aṭ ṭayyaara bitaa9t as saa9a 9a<u>sh</u>ara u rubu9 jaat?

p: A friend of mine is coming from Cairo today. Has the 10:15 plane arrived?

m: lissa9. Hatit'a<u>khkh</u>ar bee saa9a waaHda u nuṣṣ.

c: Not yet. It will be an hour and a half late.

r: <u>sh</u>ukran. ana maa<u>sh</u>i l kafitiira fi l maṭaar, astanna <u>sh</u>waiya. ana <u>kh</u>aayif hu yaji u maa yilgaani.

p: Thank you. I'll go to the cafe in the airport and wait for a while. I am afraid he may arrive and not find me.

24.1 Drills: tamriin

24.1.1 The verb *jaa (jiit)* 'to come'

The verb *jaa (jiit)*, *yaji* is an unusual one that doesn't quite belong to any of the other groups of verbs. It has to be learned on its own. Tables for it are given below:

		Past	Imperfect	With *bi-*
Sing.	1	jiit	aji	baji
	2 m	jiit	taji	bitaji
	2 f	jiiti	taji	bitaji
	3 m	jaa	yaji	biyaji (or biiji)
	3 f	jaat	taji	bitaji
Plur.	1	jiina	naji	binaji
	2	jiitu	taju	bitaju
	3	joo	yaju	biyaju (or biiju)

تعال تعالى تعالوا
جاى جاية جايين

انا انتَ انتِ هو هى نحن انتوا هم

امبارح، لازم، دايما

دايما، هم ...... دايما هم بيجوا بيتنا (والى آخره)

٢٤,١,٢

طيارة، عنقريب، سكين، بيت، كتاب، زهرة، صاحب، ولد، زبونة، صاحبة

عجيب، ازرق، ابيض، كبير، المانى، انجليزى، حلو، كعب، صغير، جديد

زهرة، حلو ...... اخدت زهرتين حلوات من المشتل (والى آخره)

٢٤,١,٣

Imperative: *ta9aal, ta9aali, ta9aalu*
Active participle: *jaay, jaaya, jaayiin*

Drill the tables with the teacher until you know them by heart. Then the teacher should say one of the subject pronouns and one of the three words, *umbaariH, laazim, daayman*. The student responds with the appropriate form of the verb in a sentence, e.g. *daayman hum biyaju beetna*, 'They always come to our house'.

jaa occurs in some useful expressions:

a) it can be used in the sense of 'visit' or 'call on,' e.g. *jiitkum umbaariH laakin kuntu maa moojuudiin* 'I called on you yesterday but you weren't there'. In this context it does not need a preposition after it. And when inviting someone to visit you, you can say *ta9aal 9indana* 'come and see us'.
b) *jaa* is also used frequently in the sense of 'arrive' in preference to *wiṣil*, e.g. *abuuy jaa s saa9a Hidaashar* 'my father arrived at 11 o'clock'.

24.1.2 Adjectives with dual nouns

Revise duals of nouns (see Lesson 11.1.1) and the rules about adjectives with plural nouns (Lesson 11.1.2). Perhaps you remember the two ways in which adjectives form their plurals, either by adding an ending, e.g. *kwaiyis, kwaiysiin*, or by changing the vowels, e.g. *kabiir, kubaar*.

We introduce here the rules about adjectives with nouns in the dual. There are no special dual forms of the adjectives, so the plurals are used, but according to somewhat different rules from adjectives with plural nouns. Once again it has to be said that there is no standard practice and that you may hear alternatives to what is taught in this course. Fortunately one does not often have occasion to use adjectives with dual nouns.

1. Adjectives which form the plural by changing the vowels: the plural of such adjectives may occur with any noun in the dual, e.g. *raajleen kubaar* 'two big men'; *galameen Humur* 'two red pens'.
2. Adjectives which form their plural by adding the ending *-iin*:
   a) with nouns in the dual referring to male human beings use the usual plural, e.g. *raajleen kwaiysiin* 'two good men'; *mudarriseen shaaṭriin* 'two clever teachers'.
   b) with all other nouns in the dual use the feminine plural ending *-aat*, e.g. *bitteen kwaiysaat* 'two good girls'; *beeteen kabiiraat* 'two large houses'.

Here are two lists, one of nouns and one of adjectives. The teacher can pick an item from each list and the student make a sentence using them in the dual, e.g. *akhatta zahrateen Hilwaat min al mashtal* 'I got two lovely flowers from the nursery'.

ṭayyaara, 9angareeb, sikkiin, beet, kitaab, zahra, ṣaaHib, walad, zabuuna, ṣaaHba.

9ajiib, azrag, abyaḍ, kabiir, almaani, ingliizi, Hilu, ka9ab, ṣaghayyir, jadiid.

24.1.3 'Do you like...?'

People often discuss what they like and don't like or what they enjoy doing. In Arabic there are several different ways to express the idea of liking or enjoying a thing or an activity:

1. *ana baHibb* ______: you can use the verb *Habba, yaHibb* for 'like' in relation to something, e.g. *ana baHibb az zuhuur* 'I like flowers'; *inta bitHibb as samak?* 'Do you like fish?'

The following drill is for doing either in pairs or in a larger group. The first person says, *ana baHibb* ______, and the second person supplies an item which they like, e.g. *ana baHibb aj jidaad* 'I like chicken'. The second person then asks the first, *inta bitHibb shinuu?* or *inti bitHibbi shinuu?* The first person has to answer the question. Do this five or six times. Then the first person should ask *al*

ا　　انا بحب ......

ب　　انا بحب الفول سودانى. انت بتحب شنو؟

ا　　انا بحب الفول بجبنة. انتِ بتحبى شنو؟

ب　　انا بحب الخرطوم. المدرس بيحب شنو؟

ا　　المدرس بيحب الكورة. اولادك بيحبوا شنو؟

ب　　اولادى بيحبوا التلفزيون. (والى آخره)

ا　　انا برتاح ......

ب　　انا برتاح لصيد السمك. (والى آخره)

ا　　جنّه ......

ب　　جنّه عصيدة. (والى آخره)

كلمات

سفر	القاهرة
طيارة، طيارات	جا (جيت)، يجى
راكب، ركاب	اتأخر، يتاخر
حجز	استنى، يستنى
نفر، انفار	كفتيرة، كفتيرات
تذكرة، تذاكر	فول سودانى

mudarris biHibb <u>sh</u>inuu? or *u<u>kh</u>tik bitHibb <u>sh</u>inuu?* and the second person replies, so as to practice the other persons of the verb. If the group is larger you can go round the circle.

An exchange might go as follows:

First speaker:	ana baHibb...
Second speaker:	ana baHibb al fuul suudaani. inta bitHibb <u>sh</u>inuu?
First speaker:	ana baHibb al fuul bee jibna. inti bitHibbi <u>sh</u>inuu?
Second speaker:	ana baHibb al <u>kh</u>arṭuum. al mudarris biHibb <u>sh</u>inuu?
First speaker:	al mudarris biHibb al kuura. awlaadik biHibbu <u>sh</u>inuu?
Second speaker:	awlaadi biHibbu t tilivizyoon.

2. *ana bartaaH lee____*. If you want to say you enjoy a certain activity or it is your hobby you can use the verb *irtaaH, (irtiHta), yirtaaH* with the preposition lee followed by the thing you like doing, e.g. *ana bartaaH li l <u>kh</u>iyaata* 'I enjoy sewing'. Or perhaps fishing is your hobby. In that case you would say, *ana bartaaH lee ṣeed as samak* 'I enjoy fishing'.

    To practice this expression do the same as with 1, above.

3. *jinnu _____*.   Likings can be so strong as to seem like a craze to other people. Perhaps you are even prepared to admit that you are crazy about something. In that case the expression used in Arabic is *jinnu* 'his craze' or *jinni* 'my craze', 'I am crazy about,' e.g. *jinni musiigha* 'I am crazy about music', 'I really love music'; *jinna ragiṣ* 'she is mad on dancing'. Literally the word *jinn* means 'djinn' or 'genie', but in this context it is used as a figure of speech. It can also be applied to strong preferences in food and other things, e.g. *jinnu 9asiida. hu maa daayir kisra walla ruzz kullu kullu, 9asiida bass.* 'He is crazy about asida. He doesn't like kisra or rice at all, only asida'.

    Now try the same drill with *jinn* as you did for 1 and 2.

24.1.4 Conversation practice: Journeys

With the teacher's help prepare some questions you might want to ask a travel agent about journeys by air or train or other forms of transport. Have the teacher record them so you can listen and memorise.

24.1.5 Note on grammar

Use of the definite article: you may have noticed that Arabic sometimes has the definite article where English would use an indefinite article or a plural form of the noun. The rule is that Arabic uses the definite article to refer to abstract things, e.g. 'love,' or to something in general in contrast to a specific instance of that thing, e.g. *al <u>gh</u>anam biyaakl aṣ ṣafag* 'goats eat leaves'; *al 9iris as suudaani samiH* 'Sudanese weddings are nice'; *ana maa baHibb a<u>sh</u> <u>sh</u>u<u>gh</u>ul* 'I don't like work'.

24.2 Role play

Act out the parts of people making travel arrangements and then going to the airport to board a plane. There may be problems. You may have trouble getting on to the flight you want or the plane may be late or your baggage may be overweight.

24.3 Vocabulary: kalmaat

safar	travel, journey	al <u>gh</u>aahira	Cairo
ṭayyaara, ṭayyaaraat	aeroplane	jaa (jiit), yaji	to come, arrive
raakib, rukkaab	passenger	it'a<u>khkh</u>ar, yit'a<u>khkh</u>ar	to be late
Hajiz (no plural)	reservation	istanna, yistanna	to wait
nafar, anfaar	person, individual	kafitiira, -aat	cafe
tazkara, tazaakir	ticket	fuul suudaani	peanuts

مقعد، مقاعد
ممر
وزن
عفش
تأشيرة، تأشيرات
طلب، يطلب
باسرع ما ممكن
قام (قمت)، يقوم
مطار، مطارات

ارتاح (ارتحت)، يرتاح ل...
جنّ
مسيغة
صيد
صيد السمك
عصيدة

mag9ad, magaa9id	seat
mamarr	aisle in plane
wazin	weight
9afash	luggage
ta'shiira, -aat	visa
ṭalab, yaṭlub	request, apply for
bee asra9 maa yumkin	as soon as possible
gaam (gumta), yaguum	to depart (train, plane, etc.), get up
maṭaar, maṭaaraat	airport

irtaaH (irtiHta), yirtaaH lee	to enjoy (doing)
jinn	djinn, craze for something
musiigha	music
ṣeed	hunting
ṣeed as samak	fishing
9asiida	asida (dish of very thick sorghum porridge)

الدرس الخمسة وعشرين

حوار : الدكتور

د : دكتور   م : مريضة عجوزة   ا : ام ولد

د   اتفضلى اقعدى يا حاجة. بتشكى من شنو؟

م   انا ما كويسة يا دكتور، انا محمومة. عينينى بيوجعونى، ضهرى كمان بيوجعنى، وجسمى كله.

د   من متين انت عيانة؟

م   من بدرى. ما عارفة كم يوم.

د   عندك صداع؟

م   ايوه، صداع شديد.

د   اخدى الدوا دا واشربى منه تلاتة مرات فى اليوم بعد الاكل، ولازم ترتاحى.

م   ما بقدر آكل ابدا، يا دكتور. الوجع شديد.

د   معليش. اشربى موية كتيرة واكلى برتقان.

(هى بتطلع ومرة بتدخل مع ولدها)

ا   ولدى وقع من شجرة وكراعه اتعوقت.

د   (بيكشف على كراع الولد) ما مكسورة لكن فى ورم. حالفها، وما تخليه يمشى عليها.

ا   هو ما بيقدر يمشى هسع، بتوجعه شديد.

د   طيب. جيبيه تانى بعد تلاتة ايام.

ا   شكرا.

تمرين

٢٥,١,١

آكل	أوزن
تاكل	توزن
تاكلى	توزنى
ياكل	يوزن
تاكل	توزن

ad daris al khamsa u 9ishriin

Hiwaar: ad duktoor

d: duktoor   m: mariiḍa 9ajuuza
   u: umm walad

d: itfaḍḍali ag9udi ya Haajja. bita<u>sh</u>ki
   min <u>sh</u>inuu?
m: ana maa kwaiysa ya duktoor, ana
   maHmuuma. 9eeneeni biyooja9uuni, ḍahri
   kamaan biyooja9ni, u jismi kullu.
d: min miteen inti 9ayyaana?
m: min badri. maa 9aarfa kam yoom.

d: 9indik ṣudaa9?
m: aiwa, ṣudaa9 <u>sh</u>adiid.
d: u<u>kh</u>di d dawa da u a<u>sh</u>rabi minnu talaata
   marraat fi l yoom ba9d al akil, u
   laazim tirtaaHi.
m: maa bagdar aakul abadan, ya duktoor. al
   waja9 <u>sh</u>adiid.
d: ma9lee<u>sh</u>. a<u>sh</u>rabi mooya katiira u
   ukli burtukaan.

(hi biṭaṭla9 u mara bit<u>khush</u>sh ma9a walada)

u: waladi waga9 min <u>sh</u>ajara u
   kuraa9u it9awwagat.
d: (biyak<u>sh</u>if 9ala kuraa9 al walad)
   maa maksuura laakin fii waram. Haaliffaha,
   u maa ta<u>kh</u>alliihu yam<u>sh</u>i 9aleeha.
u: hu maa biyagdar yam<u>sh</u>i hassa9;
   bitooja9u <u>sh</u>adiid.
d: ṭaiyib. jiibiihu taani ba9ad talaata ayyaam.
u: <u>sh</u>ukran.

Lesson 25

Dialogue: The doctor

d: doctor   p: patient (old woman)
   b: boy's mother

d: Please sit down. What's your problem?

p: I'm not well, doctor, I've got a fever. My
   eyes hurt, my back hurts too, and my whole
   body.

d: Since when have you been ill?
p: For a long time. I don't know how
   many days.
d: Have you a headache?
p: Yes, a very bad headache.
d: Take this medicine and drink some three
   times a day after meals, and you
   should rest.
p: I can't eat at all, doctor. The pain is so bad.

d: Never mind. Drink plenty of water and
   eat oranges.

(She goes out and a woman comes in with
   her son.)
b: My son fell out of a tree and has injured his
   leg.
d: (examines the boy's leg)
   It's not broken but there's swelling. I'll
   bandage it and don't let him walk on it.
b: He can't walk at the moment because it
   hurts so.
d: O.K. Bring him back in three days' time.
b: Thank you.

Note on the dialogue

min badri means 'for a long time' in the sense of 'from a long time ago until now' and not in any other sense.

25.1 Drills: tamriin

25.1.1 Verbs like *akal* and *wazan*

Verbs beginning with *a* or *w* behave the same as other verbs in the past tense but are a little different in the imperfect. The list below gives the imperfect of *akal, yaakul* 'to eat'. and of *wazan, yoozin* 'to weigh'.

Sing.			
	1	aakul	oozin
	2 m	taakul	toozin
	2 f	taakli	toozni
	3 m	yaakul	yoozin
	3 f	taakul	toozin

ناكل	نوزن
تاكلوا	توزنوا
ياكلوا	يوزنوا

اكل أكلى اكلوا، اوزن اوزنى اوزنوا

ماكل ماكلة ماكلين، وازن وازنة وازنين

٢٥,١,٢

اقع	نقع
تقع	تقعوا
تقعى	
يقع	يقعوا
تقع	

ناكل، حتاخد، بيوزن، حيوصلوا، الِد، بيوجع، حتقعوا، بتاكلى، ترِد، أكل، بيوجعوا، حتلدى، بتاخد، اوزنى

بيوجع ...... ضهر المرة العجوزة بيوجعها (والى آخره)

٢٥,١,٣

الاذان الاول

صباح

ضهر

بعد الضهر

عصر

مغرب

مسا

ليل

Plur.	1	naakul	noozin
	2	taaklu	tooznu
	3	yaaklu	yooznu

Imperative: *ukul* (m), *ukli* (f), *uklu* (pl); *oozin* (m), *oozni* (f), *ooznu* (pl)
Active participle: *maakil* (m), *maakla* (f), *maakliin* (pl); *waazin* (m), *waazna* (f), *waazniin* (pl)

bi- and *Ha-* are added to the imperfect stem without change.

Like *akal* is *akhad, yaakhud.*
Like *wazan* are *wiṣil, yooṣal* and *waja9, yooja9*. Note that *waja9* only occurs in the 3rd person. Some people pronounce these verbs with *aw* instead of *oo*, e.g. *awzin.*

Drill the imperfect of *akal* and *wazan* and the other verbs like them.

25.1.2 Verbs like *waga9*

Unfortunately not all verbs beginning with *w* are like *wazan.* Some follow the pattern below in the table for the imperfect of *waga9, yaga9* 'to fall'.

Sing.	1	aga9	Plur.	1	naga9
	2 m	taga9		2	taga9u
	2 f	taga9i			
	3 m	yaga9		3	yaga9u
	3 f	taga9			

bi- and *Ha-* are added to the imperfect without change.

Like *waga9* are: *warad, yarid* ('to fetch water', 'take to water'); *wildat, talid* ('to give birth'). Note that *wildat* does not normally occur in the masculine for obvious reasons.

Drill *waga9* and the other verbs like it.

Note that it is only verbs on the pattern of *daras* that lose the *w* or change it to *oo*. Variations on the basic verb beginning with *w* are quite regular, e.g. *waṣṣal, yiwaṣṣil; warra, yiwarri,* etc.

Here is a list of verb forms. The teacher should pick words from the list and the students should make up sentences using them, e.g. Teacher: *biyooja9.* Student: *ḍahr al mara l 9ajuuza biyooja9a* 'The old woman's back hurts'.

naakul, Hataakhud, biyoozin, Hayooṣalu, alid, biyooja9, Hataga9u, bitaakli, tarid, ukul, biyooja9u, Hataldi, bitaakhud, oozni.

25.1.3 Times of the day

It is useful to know the times of the day in Arabic. The most common ones are given below:

al azaan al awwal	the first call to prayer (used to signify very early in the morning before dawn)
ṣabaaH	morning
ḍuhur	noon
ba9d aḍ ḍuhur	afternoon till about 4 p.m.
9asur	about 4 p.m. to dusk
mughrib	sunset
misa	evening
leel	night

انت بتعملى شنو فى الصباح؟	بفطر فى الصباح
ولدك بيعمل شنو فى الصباح؟	ولدى بيمشى المدرسة
(والى آخره)	

كلمات

دكتور ، دكاترة	وقع، يقع
دكتورة، دكتورات	كراع، كرعين
مريض، مرضانين	اتعوق، يتعوق
مريضة، مريضات	كشف، يكشف على
عجوز، عجايز	مكسور
شكى، يشكى	ورم
محموم، محمومين	لف، يلف
عين، عيون	وزن، يوزن
وجع، يوجع	وصل، يوصل
جسم، اجسام	ورد، يرد
صداع	ولدت، تلد
شديد	ضهر
اخد، ياخد	عصر
دوا، ادوية	مغرب
اكل، ياكل	ليل، ليالى
ابدا	اذان

To practice these times the teacher can ask the students, *inta bita9mil* (or *inti bita9mili*) *shinuu fi ṣ ṣabaaH?* 'What do you do in the morning?' (or at some other time of day), and the student should reply with an appropriate answer, e.g. *baftur fi ṣ ṣabaaH* 'I have breakfast in the morning'. The question could be about someone else, e.g. Teacher: *waladak biya9mil shinuu fi ṣ ṣabaaH?* Parent: *waladi biyamshi l madrasa* 'What does your son do in the morning?' 'My son goes to school'.

25.1.4 Conversation practice: When you are ill

Ask your teacher to describe some occasion when they or one of their relatives was ill. They can explain which part of the body hurt, how they went to the doctor or hospital and what the treatment was. Listen carefully. You could also record the description for listening later.

Then do the same thing about yourself. Describe some illness you have had, or someone you know, and where it hurt and so on.

25.2 Role play

Act out the parts of people in a doctor's waiting room or at the hospital discussing their symptoms and then going in one by one to see the doctor.

25.3 Vocabulary: kalmaat

duktoor, dakaatra	doctor (male)
duktoora, duktooraat	doctor (female)
mariiḍ, marḍaaniin	patient (male)
mariiḍa, mariiḍaat	patient (female)
9ajuuz, 9ajaayiz	old (person)
shaka, yashki	to complain
maHmuum, maHmuumiin	having a fever
9een (fem.), 9iyuun	eye
waja9, yooja9	to hurt (needs an object)
jisim, ajsaam	body
ṣudaa9	headache
shadiid	severe, strong
akhad, yaakhud	to take, get
dawa (masc.), adwiya	medicine
akal, yaakul	to eat
abadan	not at all, never
waga9, yaga9	to fall
kuraa9 (fem.), kir9een	leg and foot
it9awwag, yit9awwag	to be hurt, injured
kashaf, yakshif 9ala	to examine
maksuur	broken
waram	swelling
laffa, yaliff	to wrap, bind
wazan, yoozin	to weigh
wiṣil, yooṣal	to arrive
warad, yarid	to fetch water
wildat, talid	to give birth
ḍuhur	noon
9asur	late afternoon
mughrib	sunset
leel, layaali	night
azaan	call to prayer

اسئلة لمراجعة الدروس
من ٢١ الى ٢٥

١ الحوش بتاعكم اكبر من الحوش بتاع الجيران؟

٢ بتقص الورق بشنو؟

٣ بتقرا ياتو جريدة؟

٤ المراوح فى بيتك شغالة؟

٥ السودانيين بيباركوا للعروس والعريس كيف؟

٦ القطر حق وادى حلفا بيقوم يوم شنو؟

٧ اسم اليوم السابع فى الاسبوع شنو؟

٨ بتتغدى الساعة كم؟

٩ الدكتور بيوزن الاطفال الصغار؟

١٠ الغنم بتاكل شنو؟

١١ بترتاحوا بعد الضهر؟

١٢ المرضانين بيجوا الدكتور ولا الدكتور بيمشيهم؟

١٣ مشيت القاهرة؟ شفت شنو هناك؟

١٤ بتحب السفر؟

١٥ بتودى اولادك للمدرسة؟

١٦ لازم تدفع الايجار لسيد بيتك كل شهر؟

١٧ عندك عربية وقراش؟

١٨ الدكاكين بتاعة الدهب فى ياتو سوق؟

١٩ الناس هنا بياكلوا بمعلقة؟

٢٠ بتستحم قبل العشا ولا بعده؟

Revision questions for Lessons 21–25

Answer the following questions:

1. al Hoosh bitaa9kum akbar min al Hoosh bitaa9 aj jeeraan?
2. bitguṣṣ al warag bee shinuu?
3. bitagra yaatu jariida?
4. al maraawiH fii beetak shaghghaala?
5. as suudaaniiyiin bibaarku li l 9aruus w al 9ariis keef?
6. al gaṭar Hagg waadi Halfa biguum yoom shinuu?
7. ism al yoom as saabi9 fi l usbuu9 shinuu?
8. bititghadda s saa9a kam?
9. ad duktoor biyoozn al aṭfaal aṣ ṣughaar?
10. al ghanam bitaakul shinuu?
11. bitirtaaHu ba9d aḍ ḍuhur?
12. al marḍaaniin biyaju d duktoor walla d duktoor biyamshiihum?
13. masheet al ghaahira? shufta shinuu hinaak?
14. bitHibb as safar?
15. bitwaddi awlaadak li l madrasa?
16. laazim tadfa9 al iijaar lee siid beetak kulli shahar?
17. 9indak 9arabiiya u garraash?
18. ad dakaakiin bitaa9t ad dahab fii yaatu suug?
19. an naas hina biyaaklu bee ma9laga?
20. bitistaHamm gabli l 9asha walla ba9du?

الدرس الستة وعشرين

حوار : فى الخلا

م : مسافرين   ر : رحّل

م   السلام عليكم.

ر   وعليكم السلام. انتوا جايين من وين؟

م   جايين من الخرطوم. انتوا ساكنين فى المنطقة دى من بدرى؟

ر   لا. دى ما منطقتنا. نحن رحل. منطقتنا بعيدة من هنا. كل الارض الجنب البحر حقة ناس الحلة دى.

م   ناس الحلة بزرعوا شنو؟

ر   هم بزرعوا عيش وبصل.

م   قبيلتكم شنو؟

ر   نحن شايقية. عندنا جمال.

م   شفنا ناس راكبين حمير هناك فى الجبل. ديل من ناسكم؟

ر   ايوه، ديل ناسنا واردين للموية.

م   محل الموية قريب من هنا؟ بتجيبوها من الابيار؟

ر   بنجيبها من الابيار فى الصيف، لكن فى موية لسع فى الخيران بعد المطر. انتوا ماشين وين؟

م   ماشين النقعة نشوف الآثار. الدرب دا بودينا للنقعة؟

ر   ايوه، دا الدرب بتاع النقعة. امشوا طوالى جنب السكة حديد.

تمرين

٢٦,١,١

بقيت	بقينا
بقيت	بقيتوا
بقيتى	
بقى	بقوا
بقت	

لقيت لقيت لقيتى (والى آخره)، نسيت (والى آخره)

ad daris as sitta u 9ishriin — Lesson 26

Hiwaar: fi l khala — Dialogue: Out in the country

m:	musaafriin r: ruHHal	t:	travellers n: nomads
m:	as salaamu 9aleekum.	t:	Peace be upon you.
r:	u 9aleekum as salaam. intu jaayiin min ween?	n:	And peace upon you. Where have you come from?
m:	jaayiin min al kharṭuum. intu saakniin fi l manṭiga di min badri?	t:	We've come from Khartoum. Have you been living in this area for long?
r:	la'. di maa manṭigatna. niHna ruHHal. manṭigatna ba9iida min hina. kull al arḍ aj jamb al baHar Haggat naas al Hilla di.	n:	No. This is not our country. We are nomads. Our country is a long way from here. All the land beside the river belongs to the people of this village.
m:	naas al Hilla bizra9u shinuu?	t:	What do the village people grow?
r:	hum bizra9u 9eesh u baṣal.	n:	They grow sorghum and onions.
m:	gabiilatkum shinuu?	t:	What's your tribe?
r:	niHna shaaygiiya. 9indana jimaal.	n:	We are Shaigiya. We keep camels.
m:	shufna naas raakbiin Hamiir hinaak fi j jabal. deel min naaskum?	t:	We saw people riding donkeys on the hill there. Were those some of your people?
r:	aiwa; deel naasna waardiin li l mooya.	n:	Yes; those were our people going to fetch water.
m:	maHall al mooya gariib min hina? bitjiibuuha min al abyaar?	t:	Is the water near here? Do you get it from the wells?
r:	binjiiba min al abyaar fi ṣ ṣeef, laakin fii mooya lissa9 fi l kheeraan ba9d al maṭar. intu maashiin ween?	n:	We get it from the wells in summer, but there is still water in the streams after the rain. Where are you going?
m:	maashiin an nag9a nashuuf al aasaar. ad darib da biwaddiina li n nag9a?	t:	We're going to Naga to see the antiquities. Will this track lead us to Naga?
r:	aiwa, da d darib bitaa9 an nag9a. amshu ṭawwaali jamb as sikka Hadiid.	n:	Yes, this is the way to Naga. Go straight ahead beside the railway line.

Note on the dialogue

shaaygiiya: the Shaigiya are one of the larger Arabic-speaking tribes of Sudan. In Khartoum and the larger towns tribal distinctions may become blurred, but in rural areas they are very important.

26.1 Drills: tamriin

26.1.1 Verbs like *biga*

Revise verbs like *masha* and *gara* (see Lesson 17.1.1). There are a few verbs like *gara* but with *ii* in the past tense where *gara* has *ee*. They all have *i* in the first syllable. The past tense of *biga (bigiit), yabga* 'to become' is set out below. The imperfect and the imperative forms are the same as for *gara*.

Sing.	1	bigiit	Plur.	1	bigiina
	2 m	bigiit		2	bigiitu
	2 f	bigiiti			
	3 m	biga		3	bigu
	3 f	bigat			

Like *biga* are two other useful verbs: *liga (ligiit), yalga* 'to find', and *nisa (nisiit), yansa* 'to forget'.

انا انتَ انتِ هو هى نحن انتوا هم

هم، بقى ...... بقوا (والى آخره)

٢٦,١,٢

اقيف	نقيف
تقيف	تقيفوا
تقيفى	
يقيف	يقيفوا
تقيف	

اقيف اقيفى اقيفوا

٢٦,١,٣

هو جا الحلة وما لقى زول

هو بيوزن الفواكه وما بياكلها

هو داير ياخد الدوا ويبقى كويس

هو حيقيف فى الطربيزة وحيقع منها

انا انتَ انتِ هو هى نحن انتوا هم

هو بيوزن الفواكه وما بياكلها، انا ...... انا بوزن الفواكه وما باكلها

هو جا الحلة وما لقى زول، نحن ...... (والى آخره)

٢٦,١,٤

شجر كتير في الجنينة	دى شجرة واحدة	فى تلاتة شجرات قدام البيت بتاعنا
عندى بيض فى البيت	دى بيضة واحدة	لقيت اربعة بيضات فى الدولاب
فى بصل فى الدكان	دى بصلة واحدة	تلاتة بصلات وقعوا من القفة
الاولاد بياكلوا موز	دى موزة واحدة	القرد اكل خمسة موزات
سمك للبيع جنب البحر	دى سمكة واحدة	هى دايرة ستة سمكات
اشتريت ورق امبارح	دى ورقة واحدة	ادينى اربعة ورقات
ناس الحلة عندهم بقر	دى بقرة واحدة	جدى اشترا تمنية بقرات

Drill these three verbs in both the past and the imperfect. Then the teacher can say a subject pronoun at random and one of the three verbs. The student supplies the correct verb form. Do this first for the past and then for the imperfect, e.g. Teacher: *hum, biga*. Student: *bigu*.

26.1.2 *wagaf, yagiif* 'to stop, stand up'

The verb *wagaf* 'to stop, stand up' is odd in having a regular past tense like *daras* but an irregular imperfect. See the imperfect set out below:

Sing.	1	agiif	Plur.	1	nagiif
	2 m	tagiif		2	tagiifu
	2 f	tagiifi			
	3 m	yagiif		3	yagiifu
	3 f	tagiif			

The *a* drops out when *bi-* or *Ha-* is added, e.g. *bitgiif*.
Imperative: *agiif, agiifi, agiifu.*

The teacher should drill the imperfect of *wagaf* with the students and then test them with pronouns at random as for *biga,* etc.

26.1.3 A revision drill

Here are four sentences containing some of the new verbs you have learned in the last few lessons. The teacher should choose a sentence, read it out, then say a subject pronoun, e.g. ***hu biyoozn al fawaakih u maa biyaakula. ana.,*** and the student change the sentence to fit the pronoun, e.g. *ana boozin al fawaakih u maa baakula*

1. hu jaa l Hilla u maa liga zool.
2. hu biyoozn al fawaakih u maa biyaakula.
3. hu daayir yaakhud ad dawa u yabga kwaiyis.
4. hu Haygiif fi ṭ ṭarabeeza u Hayaga9 minnaha.

26.1.4 Collective nouns

In Arabic there are quite a number of nouns with collective meaning, e.g. *beeḍ* 'eggs', *shajar* 'trees', *warag* 'paper'. These nouns are masculine and go with masculine singular adjectives, verbs and pronouns.

Many of these collective nouns form a singular with singular meaning by adding the feminine ending *-a*, e.g. *beeḍa* 'an egg', *waraga* 'a piece of paper'. Many, but not all, of these nouns also have a plural, e.g. *shajaraat* 'trees', which is used with the numbers 3–10, e.g. *talaata beeḍaat* 'three eggs'.

A lot of words referring to kinds of fruit and vegetables and other foodstuffs are collective nouns, also plants and some animals. In the glossary at the back of this book these words are given in the collective form only and marked (coll.), e.g. *warag* (coll.).

Repeat the following sentences after the teacher. In the first column is the collective form, in the second column is the singular form and in the third column is the plural form.

Collective	**Singular**	**Plural**
shajar katiir fi j jineena	di shajara waaHda	fii talaata shajaraat giddaam al beet bitaa9na
9indi beeḍ fi l beet	di beeḍa waaHda	ligiit arba9a beeḍaat fi d doolaab
fii baṣal fi d dukkaan	di baṣala waaHda	talaata baṣalaat waga9u min al guffa
al awlaad biyaaklu mooz	di mooza waaHda	al girid akal khamsa moozaat
samak li l bee9 jamb al baHar	di samaka waaHda	hi daayra sitta samakaat
ishtareet warag umbaariH	di waraga waaHda	addiini arba9a waragaat
naas al Hilla 9indahum bagar	di bagara waaHda	jiddi ishtara tamanya bagaraat

٢٦,١,٥

شتا، صيف، خريف

الشتا كيف فى الخرطوم؟

الشتا كيف فى بلدك؟

كلمات

خلا	خور ، خيران
مسافر ، مسافرين	مطر
رحل	آثار
منطقة، مناطق	درب، دروب
بعيد، بعيدين	سكة حديد
ارض، اراضى	سكة
زرع، يزرع	حديد
عيش	بقى (بقيت)، يبقى
بصل	لقى (لقيت)، يلقى
قبيلة، قبايل	نسى (نسيت)، ينسى
حمار ، حمير	وقف، يقيف
حمارة، حمارات	شتا
بير ، ابيار	خريف
صيف	

26.1.5 Seasons of the year

In Khartoum there are three seasons of the year:

shita 'winter', the period between about October and April when the wind blows from the north and the weather is cooler. It is also very dry.

ṣeef 'summer' or 'hot season' from about the end of April to the end of June when temperatures rise into the upper thirties or forties and there tend to be a number of dust storms.

khariif 'rainy season' from July to September. This is the time when there is most likely to be rain, with greater humidity and clouds and a consequent drop in the temperature. The winds come from the south. It is also the time when the Nile is in flood.

Ask your teacher *ash shita keef fi l kharṭuum?* 'What is the winter like in Khartoum?' and the teacher should tell you in Arabic what it is like. Then the teacher can ask *ash shita keef fii baladak?* 'What is the winter like in your country?' and you can describe what winter is like in your country. Do the same with the other seasons.

26.1.6 Conversation practice: What do people do in the country?

Choose some topic to do with the rural areas, such as keeping livestock, growing food crops or sources of water. Prepare some questions in Arabic which you might want to ask people about the topic. For example, if you choose growing crops, you might ask, 'What do people grow in this district?' 'When do they plant?' 'When do they harvest the dura?' etc.

Your teacher may or may not know the answer to your questions but that doesn't matter. If you record and memorise the questions you will be able to ask them of the appropriate person at the appropriate time.

26.2 Role play

Act out the parts of people talking to people they meet while travelling in the country, asking them about their area, what is there and what they are doing. The travellers also need to explain what they are doing and where they are going.

26.3 Vocabulary: kalmaat

khala (masc.)	open country	khoor, kheeraan	stream-bed that is dry part of the year
musaafir, musaafriin	traveller, travelling		
ruHHal	nomads	maṭar	rain
manṭiga, manaaṭig	region, area	aasaar (pl)	antiquities
ba9iid, ba9iidiin	far, distant	darib, duruub	way, path
arḍ (fem.), araaḍi	land, earth	sikka Hadiid	railway
zara9, yazra9	to plant, grow	sikka	path, way
9eesh	sorghum (dura)	Hadiid	iron, metal
baṣal (coll.)	onions	biga (bigiit), yabga	to become
gabiila, gabaayil	tribe	liga (ligiit), yalga	to find
Humaar, Hamiir	donkey (male)	nisa (nisiit), yansa	to forget
Humaara, Humaaraat	donkey (female)	wagaf, yagiif	to stand up, stop
biir (fem.), abyaar	well (water)	shita	winter
ṣeef	summer	khariif	rainy season, spring

الدرس السبعة وعشرين

حوار : بيت الخليفة

ع : على ج : جون

ع شفت بيت الخليفة فى امدرمان؟

ج بيت الخليفة، دا شنو؟

ع دا بيت الخليفة عبدالله، السكن فيه زمن المهدية. هسع عملوه متحف وممكن تشوف فيه حاجات من الزمن داك زى الملابس حقة الدراويش فى جيش المهدى، وكمان اسلحة استعملوها فى حرب امدرمان.

ج الخليفة كان ساكن فيه مدة طويلة؟

ع هو كان ساكن فى البيت دا اربعة خمسة سنين لما كان حاكم السودان. الجيش بتاعه كان بيجى يقيف فى الميدان الجنب البيت وكان الخليفة بشوفه من محل عالى فوق البيت.

ج المتحف بيكون فاتح متين؟

ع كل يوم فى الصباح الا يوم الاتنين. داير تمشى؟

ج ايوه. انا فاضى يوم الخميس الجاى.

ع طيب. اجيك الساعة تسعة.

تمرين

٢٧,١,١

الناس الجو فى الصباح

الميدان الجنب البيت

ad daris as sab9a u 9ishriin — Lesson 27

Hiwaar: beet al khaliifa — Dialogue: The Caliph's house

9	9ali J: John	A:	Ali J: John
9:	shufta beet al khaliifa fii umdurmaan?	A:	Have you seen the Caliph's house in Omdurman?
J:	beet al khaliifa, da shinuu?	J:	The Caliph's house, what's that?
9:	da beet al khaliifa 9abdullaahi, as sakan fiihu zaman al mahdiiya. hassa9 9amaloohu matHaf u mumkin tashuuf fiihu Haajaat min az zaman daak zeey al malaabis Haggat ad daraawiish fii jeesh al mahdi, u kamaan asliHa ista9malooha fii Harib umdurmaan.	A:	It is the Caliph Abdullahi's house, which he lived in at the time of the Mahdiya. Now it has been made into a museum and you can see in it things from that time, such as the clothes of the dervishes in the Mahdi's army, and also weapons which were used at the battle of Omdurman.
J:	al khaliifa kaan saakin fiihu mudda ṭawwiila?	J:	Did the Caliph live in it for a long time?
9:	hu kaan saakin fi l beet da arba9a khamsa siniin lamman kaan Haakim as suudaan. aj jeesh bitaa9u kaan biiji yagiif fi l meedaan aj jamb al beet u kaan al khaliifa bishuufu min maHall 9aali foog al beet.	A:	He lived in that house for four or five years when he was ruling the Sudan. His army would come and stand in the square which is beside the house and the Caliph would look it over from a high place on top of the house.
J:	al matHaf bikuun faatiH miteen?	J:	When is the museum open?
9:	kulli yoom fi ṣ ṣabaaH illa yoom al itneen. daayir tamshi?	A:	Every day in the morning except Monday. Would you like to go?
J:	aiwa. ana faaḍi yoom al khamiis aj jaay.	J:	Yes. I'll be free next Thursday.
9:	ṭaiyib. ajiik as saa9a tis9a.	A:	O.K. I'll come for you at nine o'clock.

Notes on the dialogue

1. The Mahdi overthrew Turco-Egyptian sovereignty and ruled the Sudan from January to June 1885, when he died of an illness. He was succeeded by the Caliph Abdullahi, who ruled from 1885 to 1898. The whole period is known as the Mahdiya. The Caliph was defeated by an Anglo-Egyptian army under Kitchener at the Battle of Omdurman in 1898.
2. In Sudanese Arabic there is no special passive form of the verb. The third person plural can be used as the equivalent of an English passive in most contexts, e.g. 'these weapons were used in the battle of Omdurman' *ista9malu l asliHa deel fii Harib umdurmaan*; 'the plane was repaired' *ṣallaHu ṭ ṭayyaara*. Where an agent is expressed, the sentence can be switched around so that the agent becomes the subject, e.g. 'a lot of gold is worn by the bride' becomes *al 9aruus bitalbas dahab katiir,* literally 'the bride wears a lot of gold'.
3. In Arabic you say *arba9a khamsa siniin* where in English an 'or' is necessary between the numbers.

27.1 Drills: tamriin

27.1.1 Relative clauses

In Arabic the relative pronoun that corresponds to the English 'who,' 'which,' 'that' is *al,* just like the definite article, e.g. *an naas aj joo fi ṣ ṣabaaH* 'the people who arrived this morning'; *al meedaan aj jamb al beet* 'the square which is beside the house'.

Repeat the following Arabic sentences after the teacher:

الولد البيجيب البيض بيجى كل يوم خميس
المرة الولدت امبارح لسع راقدة فى البيت
الراجل الأجر بيتنا سافر الجنوب
ديل الاولاد الصغار الما بيمشوا المدرسة
دا الزول السرق القروش

شالوا الموية من البير ...... الموية الشالوها من البير
استعملوا الاسلحة ...... الاسلحة الاستعملوها

اخدنا موية من البير ...... البير الاخدنا منها موية

الجمال الشفناهم فى الدرب
الدوا الشربه الليلة
الصندوق الاخدته من السوق
البيت الالخليفة سكن فيه
السكين البتقطعى بيها اللحم
المرة الكلمتك عنها
الكتاب الشلته من المكتبة

٢٧,١,٢

ما فى زول بيعرف فرنساوى هنا
بشوف مكنيكى بيصلح عربيتى

٢٧,١,٣

الركاب اشتروا تذاكر .... الركاب الاشتروا تذاكر، التذاكر الالركاب اشتروها (والى آخره)

al walad al bijiib al beeḍ biiji kullu yoom <u>kh</u>amiis	*'The boy who brings the eggs comes every Thursday'.*
al mara l wildat umbaariH lissa9 raagda fi l beet	*'The woman who gave birth yesterday is still at home'.*
ar raajil al 'ajjar beetna saafar a<u>sh</u> <u>sh</u>imaal	*'The man who rented our house has gone to the North'.*
deel al awlaad aṣ ṣu<u>gh</u>aar al maa bim<u>sh</u>u l madrasa	*'Those are the small boys who don't go to school'.*
da z zool as sarag al guruu<u>sh</u>	*'That is the person who stole the money'.*

In all the examples given so far the relative pronoun refers to the subject of the relative clause. Whenever it refers to some other part of the clause a pronoun has to be added in the position that the noun would occupy if it had not already been mentioned, e.g.

> <u>sh</u>aalu l mooya min al biir → al mooya a<u>sh</u> <u>sh</u>aalooha min al biir *'the water which they took (it) from the well'*
> ista9malu al asliHa → al asliHa al ista9malooha *'the weapons which they used (them)'*

When this added pronoun is joined to a preposition it is often brought forward in the sentence, so that it follows the verb, e.g. *akhadna mooya min al biir → al biir al akhadna minnaha mooya* 'the well which we took (from it) water'

Repeat the following after the teacher:

> aj jimaal a<u>sh</u> <u>sh</u>ufnaahum fi d darib
> ad dawa a<u>sh</u> <u>sh</u>irbu alleela
> aṣ ṣanduug al a<u>kh</u>attu min as suug
> al beet al al <u>kh</u>aliifa sakan fiihu
> as sikkiin al bitagṭa9i beeha l laHam
> al mara al kallamtak 9ana
> al kitaab a<u>sh</u> <u>sh</u>iltu min al maktaba

27.1.2 Relative clauses with indefinite nouns

If you want to make a relative clause with an indefinite noun, you do not need the word *al*, e.g. *maa fii zool biya9rif faransaawi hina* 'There's no one here who knows French'; *ba<u>sh</u>uuf makaniiki biṣalliH 9arabiiyti* 'I'm looking for a mechanic who can repair my car'; *9indi beet taani, babni fiihu fii baHri* 'I have another house which I am building in Khartoum North'.

For practice in making relative clauses with indefinite nouns, translate the following sentences into Arabic:

> I want a woman who will work with me.
> We need a teacher who will teach English in our school.
> There is a man who makes furniture at the house over there.
> The hospital is looking for a doctor who cures skin diseases.
> He saw a dog eating bones.
> We saw pictures which he painted for his family.

27.1.3 Further drill on relative clauses

Make relative clauses out of the following sentences, e.g. *ar rukkaab i<u>sh</u>taru tazaakir* could be either *ar rukkaab al i<u>sh</u>taru tazaakir* or *at tazaakir al ar rukkaab i<u>sh</u>tarooha*.

الركاب اشتروا تذاكر
العرايس بيلبسوا دهب
انا قاعد اقرا الجريدة
كويتى فستان
دايره آخد الزهور
طبعوا الكتاب
هو بيبيع الجلود
لازم تملى اورنيك

الولد حيختّ الكراسى فى الاوضة ...... الاوضة الالولد حيختّ الكراسى فيها
فاطمة قصت شعرى بالمقص
شفت حاجات جميلة فى المتحف
لقوا اسلحة جديدة فى البيت
القلم وقع من الطربيزة
الباص بيقيف جنب المكتب
خالتى راقدة فى المستشفى

٢٧,١,٤

كانوا نايمين وواحد شال الراديو حقهم
ماشة اشترى قماش واخيت قميص بيه

.... والاولاد نزلوا
الدكتور نضف ايد البت و ....
.... وبترقص مع العريس
.... ونسا وكت الطيارة
.... واتأخرت

ar rukkaab ishtaru tazaakir
al 9araayis bilbasu dahab
ana gaa9id agra j jariida
kaweeti fustaan
daayra aakhud az zuhuur
ṭaba9u l kitaab
hu bibii9 aj juluud
laazim tamla urneek

Now look at the following list of sentences. These sentences all have a prepositional phrase of some kind at the end. Make new sentences according to the pattern *al walad Haykhutt al karaasi fi l ooḍa → al ooḍa al al walad Haykhutt al karaasi fiiha.*

al walad Haykhutt al karaasi fi l ooḍa
faaṭna gaṣṣat sha9ri bi l magaṣṣ
shufta Haajaat jamiila fi l matHaf
ligu asliHa jadiida fi l beet
al galam waga9 min aṭ ṭarabeeza
al baaṣ bigiif jamb al maktab
khaalti raagda fi l mustashfa

27.1.4 Clauses of time and purpose

In English and other European languages we use conjunctions indicating time and purpose very frequently, e.g. 'While they were asleep someone took their radio'; 'I am going to buy cloth so that I can sew a shirt.' The conjunctions underlined in the two previous sentences show the relationship between the two clauses they join together. Arabic also has conjunctions (see Lesson 30), but in a straightforward piece of narrative it often prefers to join clauses by 'and' and leave the relationship between them to be inferred from the context. For example,

'They were asleep and someone took their radio'. *kaanu naaymiin u waaHid shaal ar raadyu Haggahum.*
'I am going to buy cloth and I'll sew a shirt with it'. *maasha ashtari gumaash u akhayyit gamiiṣ beehu.*

Complete the translation of the following sentences into Arabic, doing away with the conjunctions as in the above examples:

'When the bus stopped the boys got off'.	*...w al awlaad nazalu.*
'The doctor cleaned the girl's hand before he bound it'.	*ad duktoor naḍḍaf iid al bitt u...*
'After the bride has put on gold she dances with the bridegroom'.	*...u bitarguṣ ma9a l 9ariis.*
'While he was reading the newspaper he forgot the time of the plane'.	*...u nisa wakit aṭ ṭayyaara.*
'I was late because I fell down on the way'.	*...u it'akhkharta.*

27.1.5 Conversation practice: Food and cooking

Revise the vocabulary you have learned during the course to do with food and buying or cooking it. Then ask your teacher what kinds of food they like and what they eat most often in their home. You could also ask who does the cooking or how a certain dish is cooked. Then reciprocate by telling the teacher what kinds of food you eat and so on.

كلمات

خليفة، خلفا
زمن
متحف، متاحف
درويش، دراويش
سلاح، اسلحة

حرب، حروب
لما
حاكم (حكم، يحكم)
ميدان، ميادين
عالى، عالين
فاضى، فاضين
باع، يبيع
سرق، يسرق
مكتبة، مكتبات

27.2 Role play

Act out the parts of people who are planning to visit the museum at the Caliph's house and then going there to visit. It would be good if you could actually visit this interesting museum in Omdurman, but before you go check when it is open.

Alternatively you could visit or pretend to visit one of the other museums in the city, such as the National Museum on Nile Avenue.

27.3 Vocabulary: kalmaat

khaliifa, khulafa (masc., but adds *t* in possessive phrases, etc., e.g. *khaliift al mahdi* 'successor of the Mahdi')	caliph, successor	Harib, Huruub	battle, war
		lamman	when
		Haakim (from *Hakam, yaHkum*)	ruling
		meedaan, meeyaadiin	public square
zaman	time, period	9aali, 9aaliyiin	high
matHaf, mataaHif	museum	faaḍi, faaḍiyiin	free, unoccupied
darwiish, daraawiish	dervish	baa9, yabii9	to sell
silaaH, asliHa	weapon	sarag, yasrug	to steal
		maktaba, -aat	library, bookshop

الدرس التمنية وعشرين

حوار: السفر

ى : يوسف   ك : كمال

ى   انتوا مسافرين ؟

ك   ايوه، ماشين الغرب بعد بكرة.

ى   حتمشوا بعربية ؟

ك   اذا كان الطيارة ماشة مرتى حتمشى بيها، اذا كان الطيارة ما ماشة هى حتسافر معاى بالعربية، لكن ما بتحب السفر بالعربات.

ى   السفر بياخد كم يوم لحدى الغرب ؟

ك   لو الطريق كويس بياخد يومين، لو فى هبوب كتيرة بياخد تلاتة اربعة ايام.

ى   اذا كان مرتك مشت بالطيارة انت حتسافر براك ؟

ك   لا. فى الطريق دا ما ممكن الواحد يسافر براه. لو العربية باظت ولا كان فى حادث لازم يكون معاه زول، عشان واحد يحرس العربية والتانى يفتش مساعدة.

ى   والله الطريق دا صعب.

ك   اى. الدرب صعب خالص. بيقطع صحرا ولازم نشيل موية واكل وبنزين كفاية لتلاتة ايام.

تمرين

٢٨,١,١

اذا كان مرتك مشت بالطيارة انت حتسافر براك؟

لو العربية باظت لازم يكون معاك زول.

ad daris at tamanya u 9ishriin — Lesson 28

Hiwaar: as safar — Dialogue: Travelling

y:	yuusif k: kamaal	Y:	Yusif K: Kamal
y:	intu musaafriin?	Y:	Are you going away?
k:	aiwa, maashiin al gharib ba9ad bukra.	K:	Yes, we're going to Western Sudan the day after tomorrow.
y:	Hatamshu bee 9arabiiya?	Y:	Are you going by car?
k:	iza kaan aṭ ṭayyaara maasha, marati Hatamshi beeha; iza kaan aṭ ṭayyaara maa maasha, hi Hatsaafir ma9aay bi l 9arabiiya, laakin maa bitHibb as safar bi l 9arabaat.	K:	If the plane flies, my wife will go by it; if the plane doesn't fly, she'll travel with me in the car, but she doesn't like car journeys.
y:	as safar biyaakhud kam yoom liHaddi al gharib?	Y:	How many days does the journey to the west take?
k:	law aṭ ṭariig kwaiyis biyaakhud yoomeen; law fii habuub katiira biyaakhud talaata arba9a ayyaam.	K:	If the road is good it takes two days; if there are a lot of dust storms it takes three or four days.
y:	iza kaan maratak mashat bi ṭ ṭayyaara, inta Hatsaafir baraak?	Y:	If your wife goes by plane, will you travel alone?
k:	la'. fi ṭ ṭariig da maa mumkin al waaHid yisaafir baraahu. law al 9arabiiya baaẓat walla kaan fii Haadis, laazim yakuun ma9aahu zool, 9ashaan waaHid yaHris al 9arabiiya w at taani yifattish musaa9ada.	K:	No. On that road one can't travel alone. If the car breaks down or there's an accident, there must be someone with one, so that one can guard the car while the other looks for help.
y:	wallaahi, aṭ ṭariig da ṣa9ab.	Y:	My goodness, that road is hard.
k:	ai, ad darib ṣa9ab khaaliṣ. biyagṭa9 ṣaHra u laazim nashiil mooya u akil u banziin kifaaya lee talaata ayyaam.	K:	Yes, the way is very difficult. It crosses desert and we have to carry enough water and food and petrol for three days.

28.1 Drills: tamriin

28.1.1 Conditional clauses

Conditional clauses are those that begin with 'if', e.g. 'if the plane flies my wife will go on it.' There are certain things to note in a conditional clause in Arabic.

There are a number of different words for 'if'—*law, kaan, iza, iza kaan*—which can be used interchangeably. This *kaan* should not be confused with the verb *kaan* 'to be'.

There are two types of conditional sentences in Sudanese Arabic, those that refer to the present or future, and those that refer to the past.

1. Present and future conditionals: If there is a verb (other than a participle) in the 'if' clause, it must be put in the past tense in Arabic, but the verb of the main clause of the sentence can be in whatever tense is required by the meaning. For example,

    iza kaan maratak mashat bi ṭ ṭayyaara, inta Hatsaafir baraak?
    If your wife goes by plane will you travel alone?

    law al 9arabiiya baaẓat, laazim yakuun ma9aak zool.
    If the car breaks down you will need someone with you.

كان ما لقيت باص اركب تكسى
كان مشيت البحر حاضربك
لو الطريق كويس السفر بياخد يومين
كان قابلته اسأله عن الشغل

لو كنت كلمتنى كنت مشيت معاكم

كان الطيارة مشت مرتى كانت مشت بيها

لو كنتوا مشيتوا الميدان امبارح كنتوا شفتوا جمال هناك
اذا سقيتى الشتلات ما كانت نشفت
اذا ما شرب الموية دى ما كان بقى عيان
لو ما ساعدنى كنت مت

٢٨,١,٢

...... كانت فهمت .... كان ذاكرت الدرس كانت فهمت
...... حتلقى ابوى هناك .... (والى آخره)
...... كنت لقيته قبل كدا
...... لازم نمشى بالقطر
...... اشرب موية كتيرة
...... كان سجل قون تانى
...... حتشترى لينا برتقان؟
...... ما كان ضربك
...... كنت مليت الاورنيك
...... كان حكم كل السودان
...... الناس بيشكوا طوالى

٢٨,١,٣

فيل ..... افيال (والى آخره)
مستشفى، اسلحة، جمل، خيران، دكتور ، مرضانين، اجسام، كرعين، راكب، راس، بيوت، دولاب، جريدة، سكاكين، مشتل، مشروع، جلد، شنطة، تمساح، اعمام، مهندسين، كوَر ، اسد، صاحب، جدّ، خبر ، جنينة، جزر ، فُسح، لون، اطفال، قميص، مدرسات

Repeat the following sentences after the teacher:

> kaan maa ligiit baaṣ, arkab taksi.
> kaan masheet al baHar, Haaḍrubak.
> law aṭ ṭariig kwaiyis, as safar biyaakhud yoomeen.
> kaan gaabaltu, as'alu 9an ash shughul.

2. Past conditionals: The verbs in both the 'if' clause and the main clause are in the past tense, and the past tense of the verb *kaan* 'to be' is added before the verb of the main clause; (it is often also added before the verb of the 'if' clause, but this makes no difference to the meaning). For example,

> *law kunta kallamtani, kunta masheet ma9aakum.*
> 'If you had told me I would have gone with you'.
>
> *kaan aṭ ṭayyaara mashat, marati kaanat mashat beeha.*
> 'If the plane had flown my wife would have gone on it'.

Repeat the following sentences after the teacher:

> law kuntu masheetu l meedaan umbaariH, kuntu shuftu jimaal hinaak.
> iza sageeti sh shatlaat maa kaanat nishfat.
> iza maa shirib al mooya di maa kaan biga 9ayyaan.
> law maa saa9adni, kunta mutta (*died*).

28.1.2 Further drill on the conditionals

Add suitable conditional clauses to complete the following sentences, e.g. *kaanat fihmat* → *kaan zaakarat ad daris kaanat fihmat.*

> ...Hatalga abuuy hinaak.
> ...kunta ligiitu gabli kida.
> ...laazim namshi bi l gaṭar.
> ...ashrab mooya katiira.
> ...kaan sajjal goon taani.
> ...Hatashtari leena burtukaan?
> ...maa kaan ḍarabak.
> ...kunta maleet al urneek.
> ...kaan Hakam kull as suudaan.
> ...an naas bishku ṭawwaali.

28.1.3 Revision of noun plurals

Below is a list of nouns in either singular or plural form. The teacher can test the students to see whether they recognise (a) what the word means and (b) whether the form is the singular or plural. Then the student gives the other form of the word, e.g. the teacher says, *"fiil,"* and the student responds, "elephant, singular, *afyaal.*"

> mustashfa, asliHa, jamal, kheeraan, duktoor, marḍaaniin, ajsaam, kir9een, raakib, raas, buyuut, doolaab, jariida, sakaakiin, mashtal, mashruu9, jilid, shanṭa, tumsaaH, a9maam, muhandisiin, kuwar, asad, ṣaaHib, jidd, khabar, jineena, juzur, fusaH, loon, aṭfaal, gamiiṣ, mudarrisaat

28.1.4 Conversation practice: Telling a story

Ask your teacher to tell a very short story, either a folk tale or an account of some personal experience. Record it and listen until you understand it all. Listen to the story-telling style.

كلمات

اذا (كان)
هبوب، هبايب
باظ، يبوظ
حادث، حوادث
حرس، يحرس
فتش، يفتش

مساعدة
صحرا، صحارى
بنزين
لو
قابل، يقابل

Then with the teacher's help write a short story in Arabic or a short account of a personal experience and try telling it. If it gives you more confidence, ask the teacher to record the story and then you memorise it before telling it.

28.2 Role play

Act the parts of people travelling by car, either in the city or making a long journey across country. Lots of things can happen on the roads. Your car might break down or be in an accident. You may meet people or animals on the road. Policemen may stop you and ask for your licence.

28.3 Vocabulary: kalmaat

iza (kaan)	if	musaa9ada	help
habuub, habaayib	wind, dust-storm	ṣaHra, ṣaHaari	desert
baaẓ, yabuuẓ	to break down	banziin	petrol, gasoline
Haadis, Hawaadis	accident	law	if
Haras, yaHris	to guard	gaabal, yigaabil	to meet (someone)
fattash, yifattish	to look for		

الدرس التسعة وعشرين

حوار : المصور

س : سوداني   خ : خواجة

س   السبب الخلاك تجي السودان شنو؟

خ   عاوز آخد صور عن تاريخ السودان. هسع قاعد اصور البيوت القديمة في سواكن. سواكن جميلة خالص، لكن الحاجة البطالة فيها، الناس مرقوا منها والبيوت الجميلة مكسرة.

س   انت براك ولا معاك ناس تانيين؟

خ   نحن اربعة نفر. واحد قاعد يصور الآثار في منطقة كريمة وواحد في قصر السلطان علي دينار في الفاشر وواحد مسؤول من المجموعة. عاوزين نسوي فلم.

س   الفلم دا، بتعملوه لشنو؟

خ   عشان نوريه في التلفزيون في بلدنا.

س   ما ممكن نشوفه في تلفزيونا هنا؟

خ   دا حسب ناسكم هنا.

س   الحكومة هي البتدفع ليكم قروش للشغل دا؟

خ   ايوه. حكومتنا بتدينا مواهي وحكومة السودان بتدينا مواصلات ومرشدين.

تمرين

٢٩,١,١

غسل	مغسِل مغسِلة مغسِلين
سافر	مسافر مسافرة مسافرين
اشترى	مشتري مشترية مشترين
انكسر	منكسر منكسرة

ad daris at tis9a u 9ishriin — Lesson 29

Hiwaar: al muṣawwir — Dialogue: The photographer

s:	suudaani k: khawaaja	S:	Sudanese f: foreigner
s:	as sabab al khallaak taji s suudaan shinuu?	S:	What was the reason which made you come to Sudan?
k:	9aawz aakhud ṣuwar 9an taariikh as suudaan. hassa9 gaa9id aṣawwir al biyuut al gadiima fii sawaakin. sawaakin jamiila khaaliṣ, laakin al Haaja l baṭṭaala fiiha, an naas maragu minnaha w al biyuut aj jamiila makassara.	f:	I want to take pictures on the history of the Sudan. At present I am photographing the old houses in Suakin. Suakin is very beautiful, but unfortunately the people have left and the beautiful houses are broken down.
s:	inta baraak walla ma9aak naas taanyiin?	S:	Are you alone or are there other people with you?
k:	niHna arba9a nafar. waaHid gaa9id yiṣawwir al aasaar fii manṭigat kariima u waaHid fii gaṣr as sulṭaan 9ali diinaar fi l faashir u waaHid mas'uul min al majmuu9a. 9aawziin nasawwi filim.	f:	There are four of us. One is photographing the ancient monuments in the Karima area, one is at the palace of the sultan Ali Dinar in El Fasher and one is responsible for our group. We want to make a film.
s:	al filim da, bita9miluuhu lee shinuu?	S:	What are you making this film for?
k:	9ashaan nawarriihu fi t tilivizyoon fii baladna.	f:	So that we can show it on the television in our country.
s:	maa mumkin nashuufu fii tilivizyoonna hina?	S:	Can't we see it on our television here?
k:	da Hasab naaskum hina.	f:	That's up to your people here.
s:	al Hukuuma hi al bitadfa9 leekum guruush li sh shughul da?	S:	Is it the government that pays you for this work?
k:	aiwa. Hukuumatna bitaddiina mawaahi u Hukuumt as suudaan bitaddiina muwaaṣalaat u murshidiin.	f:	Yes. Our government gives us salaries and the government of the Sudan provides us with transport and guides.

29.1 Drills: tamriin

29.1.1 More on active participles

In Lessons 15 and 23 you learned the use of certain common active participles in the present and past continuous tenses. In this lesson the active participles of other verbs are dealt with. There are two things to be learned about them: 1) their formation, which is regular; and 2) their use, which varies considerably from verb to verb.

1. Formation: You are already familiar with the form of the active participles of verbs like *daras, shaaf, gara* and *khatta,* that is, *daaris, shaayif, gaari* and *khaatti.* They have *aa* in the first syllable and *i* in the second, with feminine and plural forms as for *saakin, saakna, saakniin.*

For other verbs, namely those like *ghassal, saafar, ishtaghal, inkasar, itkallam, ista9mal,* the active participle is formed on the following pattern.

ghassal	→	mughassil, -a, -iin
saafar	→	musaafir, -a, -iin
ishtaghal	→	active participle of this verb not used, but ishtara → mushtari, -a, -iin
inkasar	→	minkasir, -a

اتكلم	متكلم متكلمة متكلمين
استعمل	مستعمِل مستعمِلة مستعمِلين

كتب .... كاتب كاتبة كاتبين

باظ ... (والى آخره)

بنى شال غير نضف شكى شرب رقص قام لبس دخل قش دق ضاق

٢٩,١,٣

ماسك	ماسكة	ماسكين
ماسكنى	ماسكانى	ماسكنّى
ماسكَك	ماسكاك	ماسكنَك
ماسكِك	ماسكاكى	ماسكنِك
ماسكه	ماسكاه	ماسكنه
ماسكها	ماسكاها	ماسكنها
ماسكنا	ماسكانا	ماسكنا
ماسككم	ماسكاكم	ماسكنكم
ماسكهم	ماسكاهم	ماسكنهم

itkallam	→	mutkallim, -a, -iin
ista9mal	→	musta9mil, -a, -iin

2. Use: Because the usage of the active participles differs from verb to verb, it is necessary to learn the meaning of each one you come across separately.

One common use is similar to the '-ing' form of English verbs, e.g. *shufta naas jaaybiin karaasi* 'I saw people bringing chairs'. See Dialogue 26 for examples of this usage: *shufna naas raakbiin Hamiir hinaak* 'we saw people riding donkeys there', and *deel naasna waardiin li l mooya* 'those are our people going to fetch water'.

For some verbs the active participle is used with a slightly different meaning from the bi- form, e.g. ana gaayil.... 'I think...', but ana baguul 'I say'; ana shaayif 'I am looking at', but ana bashuuf 'I will look for'.

For yet other verbs the active participle has more of a future meaning, e.g. *ana musaafir bukra* 'I will be going away tomorrow'.

In some cases the active participle has become a noun and is no longer used with any verbal meaning, e.g. *kaatib* (from *katab* 'to write') means 'a clerk', *mushtari* 'buyer'. Active participles in this last category tend to have different plurals, e.g. *raakib, rukkaab* 'passenger'.

Form active participles for the following verbs: *katab, baaẓ, bana, shaal, ghayyar, naḍḍaf, shaka, shirib, ragaṣ, gaam, libis, dakhal, gashsha, dagga, ḍaag.*

29.1.2 Using active participles

Translate the following sentences into Arabic, using an active participle in each sentence.

Those are our children playing in the water.
I saw a lion sleeping beside the road.
The people sitting on the chairs got up quickly.
Leela heard Yusuf telephone Hassan.
I am looking for a pen.
Is she using the soap which I gave her?
We found him lying on the ground.
He fell (while) taking a box from on top of the cupboard.
The woman holding a baby is their daughter.

29.1.3 Active participles with pronoun objects

Since the active participles are parts of verbs they can take objects. When these objects are pronouns they are attached to the participle as in the case of other verbs (see Lesson 18 for object pronouns).

However, the active participles of verbs like *daras* undergo a few changes when pronouns are attached to them, as you can see in the tables below.

maasik	maaska	maaskiin
maasikni	maaskaani	maaskinni
maaskak	maaskaak	maaskinnak
maaskik	maaskaaki	maaskinnik
maasku	maaskaahu	maaskinnu
maasika	maaskaaha	maaskinnaha
maasikna	maaskaana	maaskinna
maasikkum	maaskaakum	maaskinnakum
maasikum	maaskaahum	maaskinnahum

Note that:

a) the *i* of the masc. sing. is lost according to the rules on the loss of *i* learned in Lesson 16.1.4.
b) the final *a* of the fem. sing. is lengthened.
c) the *iin* ending of the plural is changed to *inn* plus an extra *a* before pronouns beginning with a consonant other than *n*. Pronouns beginning with *n* are assimilated to the participle, e.g. *maaskiin* plus *ni* becomes *maaskinni.*

الرجال كانوا جايبين طربيزات ..... الرجال كانوا جايبنهم

انا ما عارف خالك ..... (والى آخره)
انت ضاربة الحمار دا لشنو؟
شوف الولد دا شايل الدولاب
شافوا ناس وازنين البطاطس
اختى لابسة الهدوم حقتى

ناس الحله شافونا.
لشنو ضربتنى كدا؟
ما عرفتك كل كل.
بتى الصغيرة سمعتكم فى الصالون.
امِك مسكتك عشان العربات.

٢٩,١,٤

كتب	مكتوب مكتوبة
كسر	مكسور مكسورة
مسك	ممسوك ممسوكة
لبس	ملبوس ملبوسة
قص	مقصوص مقصوصة
بنى	مبنى مبنية
نسا	منسى منسية
كسّر	مكسَر مكسَرة
ساعد	مساعَد مساعَدة
استعمل	مستعمَل مستعمَلة

سمع قش سكن قفل فتح دقّ

Repeat the tables above after the teacher. Then try the same thing with the active participles of *shaaf* and *ḍarab*.

Now change the object nouns in the following sentences into pronouns, e.g. *ar rujaal kaanu jaaybiin ṭarabeezaat → ar rujaal kaanu jaaybinnahum.*

ana maa 9aarif khaalak.
inti ḍaarba al Humaar da lee shinuu?
shuuf al walad da shaayil al guruush.
shaafu naas waazniin al baṭaaṭis.
ukhti laabsa l hiduum Haggati.

Change the following sentences into the present, using the participle:

naas al Hilla shaafoona.
lee shinuu ḍarabtani kida?
maa 9iriftak kullu kullu.
bitti ṣ ṣaghaayra sim9atkum fi ṣ ṣaaluun.
ummik masakatik 9ashaan al 9arabaat.

29.1.4 Passive participles

Passive participles are formed from the verb on a regular pattern and are equivalent to the past participles like 'written' in English. However they are used much less frequently than in English, so the important thing is to be able to recognise them when you hear them used. Below are examples of the passive participles of the different kinds of verbs:

katab:	maktuub, maktuuba	written
kasar:	maksuur, maksuura	broken
masak:	mamsuuk, mamsuuka	held
libis:	malbuus, malbuusa	worn
gaṣṣa:	magṣuuṣ, magṣuuṣa	cut
bana:	mabni, mabniiya	built
nisa:	mansi, mansiiya	forgotten
kassar:	makassar, makassara	broken, fragmented
saa9ad:	musaa9ad, musaa9ada	helped
ista9mal:	musta9mal, musta9mala	used, second-hand

Form passive participles for the following verbs: *simi9, gashsha, sakan, gafal, fataH, dagga.*

29.1.5 Conversation practice: Making a speech

With the teacher's help make up a speech which you might give at an occasion where you are asked to say a few words of appreciation or of congratulations to people who have just achieved something, such as passing a test or earning a degree or completing a project. Have your teacher record it for listening and memorisation.

كلمات

مصور ، مصورين
سبب، اسباب
تاريخ
بطال، بطالين
مكسر
قصر ، قصور
سلطان، سلاطين

مسؤول من
مجموعة، مجموعات
فلم، افلام
لشنو؟
تلفزيون، تلفزيونات
حكومة، حكومات
ماهية، مواهى
مرشد، مرشدين

29.2 Role play

Either act out the parts of people who are making a film of something in Sudan and who are hoping to have their film shown on television;
or pretend you are interviewing someone about a job taking photographs for your organisation or business. You will discuss their past experience, what hours they will work and where, and what their salary will be.

29.3 Vocabulary: kalmaat

muṣawwir, muṣawwiriin	photographer	mas'uul min	responsible for
sabab, asbaab	reason, cause	majmuu9a, majmuu9aat	group of people associated formally
taariikh	history		
baṭṭaal, baṭṭaaliin	bad	filim, aflaam	film
makassar	broken, crumbling (from *kassar* 'to break into pieces')	lee shinuu?	why? what for?
		tilivizyoon, tilivizyoonaat	television
		Hukuuma, Hukuumaat	government
gaṣir, guṣuur	palace	maahiiya, mawaahi	wages, salary
sulṭaan, salaaṭiin	sultan, ruler	murshid, murshidiin	guide

الدرس التلاتين

حوار : العيد

ف : فيليب ا : احمد

ف يانو عيد أكبر فى السودان؟

ا عيد الضحية فى شهر الحج. الناس المشوا الحج بيضبحوا خرفان هناك فى مكة. الناس الما مشوا الحج بيضبحوا خرفان فى بيوتهم. لما يضبحوا الخرفان بيدوا بعض اللحم للمساكين.

ف بيزوروا بعض كتير فى الوكت دا؟

ا اول يوم فى العيد بنقعد فى البيت لكن تانى يوم بنطلع نزور الاهل والاصحاب وبعد ما الناس يرجعوا من الحج بنزورهم كمان.

ف كنت قايل العيد الكبير هو عيد رمضان.

ا عيد الفطر برضو عيد كبير. شفت، المسلمين بيصوموا فى رمضان من الاذان الاول لحدى المغرب وحرام الواحد ياكل ويشرب اي حاجة الا بعد المغرب. عشان كدا بيكون عندنا عيد لما شهر الصوم ينتهى.

تمرين

٣٠,١,١

ad daris at talaatiin

Hiwaar: al 9iid

P: Philip a: aHmad

P: yaatu 9iid akbar fii s suudaan?
a: 9iid aḍ ḍaHiiya fii shahr al Hajj. an naas al mashu l Hajj biḍbaHu khurfaan hinaak fii makka. an naas al maa mashu l Hajj biḍbaHu khurfaan fii biyuutum. lamman yiḍbaHu l khurfaan biddu ba9ḍ al laHam li l masaakiin.
P: bizuuru ba9aḍ katiir fi l wakit da?
a: awwal yoom fi l 9iid binag9ud fi l beet laakin taani yoom binaṭla9 nazuur al ahal w al aṣHaab u ba9d maa n naas yarja9u min al Hajj binzuurum kamaan.
P: kunta gaayil al 9iid al kabiir hu 9iid ramaḍaan.
a: 9iid al faṭur barḍu 9iid kabiir. shufta, al muslimiin biṣuumu fii ramaḍaan min al azaan al awwal liHaddi l mughrib u Haraam al waaHid yaakul u yashrab eeyi Haaja illa ba9d al mughrib. 9ashaan kida bikuun 9indana 9iid lamman shahr aṣ ṣoom yintahi.

Lesson 30

Dialogue: The festival

P: Philip A: Ahmad

P: Which festival is the biggest one in the Sudan?
A: The festival of the sacrifice in the month of pilgrimage. The people who have gone on pilgrimage kill sheep there in Mecca. The people who haven't gone on pilgrimage kill sheep at home. When they kill the sheep part of the meat is given to the poor.
P: Do they visit each other a lot at that time?
A: On the first day of the festival we stay at home but on the second day we go out visiting family and friends, and after people return from pilgrimage we visit them too.
P: I thought the big festival was the Ramadan festival.
A: The festival of fast-breaking is also a big festival. You see, Muslims fast during Ramadan from the first call to prayer up to sunset, and it is forbidden to eat or drink anything except after sunset. So we have a festival when the month of fasting ends.

Note on the dialogue

At the big festivals, whether Muslim or Christian, it is common to wish your friends *kulli sana w inta ṭaiyib (inti ṭayba)* 'Many happy returns of the day.' The reply is *w inta ṭaiyib (inti ṭayba).* Another festival greeting is *batmanna leek 9iid sa9iid* 'I wish you a happy festival.'

Visiting friends and relatives is a big part of festivals. You may well be invited to join your neighbours in their celebrations and it is quite in order to call on them to wish them a happy festival and take them a gift. Besides the two mentioned in the dialogue, the other important festivals celebrated in Sudan are the *muulid* (birthday of the prophet Muhammad) for Muslims, and for Christians Easter (*9iid al giyaama*) and Christmas (*9iid al miilaad*).

30.1 Drills: tamriin

30.1.1 Clauses beginning with conjunctions

In Lesson 27.1.4 you learned that in straightforward narrative Arabic prefers to join clauses with 'and,' where English would have a conjunction such as 'when' or 'so that.' However, there are also contexts in which other conjunctions are needed, especially in answer to questions about the time or purpose of an action, e.g. Question: "When did she go out?" *hi maragat miteen?* Answer: "After we had lunch" *ba9d maa itghaddeena.*

When the conjunctions are followed by the imperfect it is usually the imperfect without *bi-*.

The most common conjunctions are the following:

بعد ما
قبل ما، قبال ما
لحدى ما، لغاية ما
منما
لما
لانو
عشان
عشان

الناس بيدوا لحم للمساكين متين؟
بيزوروا الحجاج والحاجات متين؟
لشنو المسلمين بياكلوا بالليل فى رمضان؟
بتغسلوا العدة متين؟
انت شغال من متين؟
حتبيع العفش حقك متين؟
الشجر نشف لشنو؟
حتقعد فى السودان لحدى متين؟
متين الخليفة سكن فى بيته فى امدرمان؟
بتنضفوا الصالون قبل شنو؟

٣٠,١,٢

انا انتَ انتِ هو هى نحن انتوا هم
دفع غيّر جاب اختار بدا خلى نادى خفض لف اتذكر وقف جا
هم، دفع ....عاوزهم يدفعوا القروش (والى آخره)

٣٠,١,٣

اخد زرع خاف نجض رسم نام قش ادى كوى بنى جهز ودى
بقى، خاف .... بقيت اخاف منه (والى آخره)

ba9d maa:	after	
gabli/gubbaal maa:	before	(always followed by the imperfect, never by the past tense)
liHaddi/lighaayat maa:	until	
mimmaa:	since	
lamman:	when	
laanu:	because	
9ashaan:	because	(may be followed by the imperfect with *bi-*)
9ashaan:	so that	

Answer the following questions with a sentence that includes a clause beginning with one of the conjunctions from the list above, e.g. Question: *bitamshi l maktab miteen?* Answer: *bamshi l maktab ba9d maa afṭur.*

an naas biddu laHam li l masaakiin miteen?
bizuuru l Hujjaaj w al Haajjaat miteen?
lee shinuu l muslimiin biyaaklu bi l leel fii ramaḍaan?
bitghassilu l 9idda miteen?
inta shaghghaal min miteen?
Hatbii9 al 9afash Haggak miteen?
ash shajar nishif lee shinuu?
Hatag9ud fi s suudaan liHaddi miteen?
miteen al khaliifa sakan fii beetu fii umdurmaan?
bitnaḍḍifu ṣ ṣaaluun gabli shinuu?

30.1.2 Further use of *9aawz* and *daayir*

9aawz and *daayir* with the imperfect were introduced in Lesson 8. However when the subject of the imperfect verb is different from that of *9aawz* or *daayir*, as in 'I want you to go to the market,' then it takes the form of an object pronoun joined to *9aawz,* e.g. *9aawzak tamshi s suug.*

Drill: the teacher should pick one of the subject pronouns and a verb from the following list and the student should use them in a sentence of the 'I want....' type (this will serve as revision of the verbs), e.g. *hum, dafa9 → 9aawzum yadfa9u l guruush.*

dafa9, ghayyar, jaab, ikhtaar, bada, khalla, naada, khaffaḍ, laffa, itzakkar, wagaf, jaa.

30.1.3 Further use of *daayir* and *biga*

daayir with the imperfect can also be used with the meaning 'to be about to do something,' e.g. *hu daayir yiṣalliH 9arabiiytak,* 'he is about to repair your car'.

You have met *biga* meaning 'to become,' but another use of it is with a following verb in the imperfect, meaning 'to begin,' e.g. *bigiit ajri,* 'I began to run'.

For a final revision of the verbs the teacher should say *daayir* or *biga* and one of the following list, and the student should make up a sentence using them.

akhad, zara9, khaaf, najjaḍ, rasam, naam, gashsha, adda, kawa, bana, jahaz, wadda.

30.1.4 Conversation practice: Festivals

Choose a festival which you yourself or your family celebrate, and compose a description of it with your teacher's help, including the purpose of the celebration, what people do to celebrate and how many days it lasts. You could also describe any special foods associated with the festival and what sort of gifts, if any, are exchanged. Then have your teacher record it for listening and memorisation.

كلمات

عيد، اعياد
حج
ضبح، يضبح
خروف، خرفان
بعض
مسكين، مساكين
زار، يزور
قايل
مسلم، مسلمين
صام، يصوم

حرام
اى حاجة
الا
صوم
انتهى، ينتهى
المولد
عيد القيامة
عيد الميلاد
دفع، يدفع
اتمنى، يتمنى

30.2 Role play

Some Sudanese friends are celebrating a festival and they tell you about it and invite you to come to their house to celebrate with them.

30.3 Vocabulary: kalmaat

9iid, a9yaad	festival	Haraam	forbidden on religious grounds
Hajj	pilgrimage	eeyi Haaja	anything
ḍabaH, yaḍbaH	to kill an animal, slaughter	illa	except
kharuuf, khurfaan	sheep	ṣoom	fasting
ba9aḍ	some	intaha, yintahi	to end
miskiin, masaakiin	poor	al muulid	Mulid (the Prophet's birthday)
zaar, yazuur	to visit	9iid al giyaama	Easter
gaayil....	I think....	9iid al miilaad	Christmas
muslim, muslimiin	Muslim	dafa9, yadfa9	to pay
ṣaam, yaṣuum	to fast	itmanna, yitmanna	to wish, hope

Postscript

You have finished this course but you have not finished learning Sudanese Arabic. If you want to become really fluent, spend as much time as you can with Sudanese, listening to their conversation and noting down new words and expressions. At this stage it is also very helpful to record conversations or speeches or stories and listen to them repeatedly at home, in order to grasp the intonation patterns of the language. Listen to the colloquial Arabic programmes on the radio and television and hire a Sudanese to take you for a conversation class once or twice a week, at which you discuss a subject that you have prepared beforehand. You will discover some further points of grammar not covered in this beginners' course, and, of course, a lot more vocabulary. Your reward will be an entrance into and appreciation of Sudanese culture in a way that is impossible without a knowledge of the language.

English - Arabic glossary

This glossary contains:

- all the words contained in this course with the exception of greetings and other expressions that cannot be translated literally;
- additional words of frequent use, especially names of foodstuffs in the markets.

Abbreviations

adj	adjective	m	masculine
coll	collective	nn	noun
conj	conjunction	pl	plural
f	feminine	vb	verb

A

able to	gidir, yagdar
about, concerning	9an
above	foog
abroad	barra
accident	Haadis, Hawaadis
according to	Hasab
address	9unwaan, 9anaawiin
aeroplane	ṭayyaara, -aat
afraid, to be	khaaf, (khufta), yakhaaf
after	ba9ad
afternoon (noon to 4 p.m.)	ba9d aḍ ḍuhur
afternoon (4 p.m. to dusk)	9asur
again	taani
agree	samaH, yasmaH; ittafag (ma9a)
agricultural	ziraa9i, -iya
agriculture	ziraa9a
air	hawa (m)
air cooler	mukayyif hawa, mukayyifaat hawa
airport	maṭaar, -aat
aisle (in plane)	mamarr
all	kull, kulli
alone	bara
alright	ṭaiyib, -iin
also	kamaan; barḍu
always	daayman
America	amriika
and	u, w
animal	Hayawaan, -aat
antiquities	aasaar
anything	eeyi Haaja
apples	tuffaaH (coll)
apricots	mishmish (coll)
Arabic (adj)	9arabi, -iyiin
Arabic (language)	9arabi
area	manṭiga, manaaṭig
army	jeesh, jiyuush
around	Hawl
arrival	wuṣuul
arrive	wiṣil, yooṣal; jaa, yaji

B

back (nn)	ḍahar
bad	ka9ab, -iin; baṭṭaal, -iin
bag (of paper or polythene)	kiis, akyaas
bag (handbag or satchel)	shanṭa, shinaṭ
bakery	ṭaabuuna, ṭawaabiin
ball (for game)	kuura, kuwar
bananas	mooz (coll)
bandage, bind (vb)	laffa, yaliff
basket	guffa, gufaf
bathe oneself	istaHamma, yistaHamm
bathroom	Hammaam, -aat
battery	baṭṭaariiya, -aat
battle	Harib, Huruub
be	kaan, (kunta), yakuun
beans (broad beans)	fuul maṣri
beans (green beans)	faṣuulya
beat (vb)	ḍarab, yaḍrub
beautiful	jamiil, -iin; samiH, -iin
because	9ashaan
become	biga, yabga
bed (with bedding)	farish, furaash
bed (bedstead)	sariir, saraayir
bed (rope bed)	9angareeb, 9anaagriib
bedroom	ooṭṭ an noom
bees	naHal (coll)
beer	biira
beetroots	banjar (coll)
before	gabli; gubbaal
begin	bada, yabda
behind	wara
belly	baṭun (f), buṭuun

belonging to	Hagg, Haggat
below	tiHit
beside	jamb
better	aHsan
between	been
big	kabiir, kubaar
birds	ṭeer (coll)
birth, to give	wildat, talid
black	aswad, sooda, suud
blackboard	sabbuura, -aat
blue	azrag, zarga, zurug
body	jisim, ajsaam
book (nn)	kitaab, kutub
bookshop	maktaba, -aat
booking	Hajiz (no plural)
born	mawluud, -iin
boss	mudiir, mudiiriin
bougainvillea	jahannamiiya
box	ṣanduug, ṣanaadiig
boy	walad, awlaad
bread	9eesh
break (vb)	kasar, yaksur
break in pieces	kassar
break down, stop working	baaẓ, yabuuẓ
breakfast (nn)	faṭuur
breakfast (vb)	faṭar, yafṭur
bride	9aruus, 9araayis
bridegroom	9ariis, 9irsaan
bridge (nn)	kubri, kabaari
bring	jaab, (jibta), yajiib
Britain	bariṭaanya
broken	maksuur
broken in pieces	makassar
broken down, not working	baayiẓ
broken, to be; break of itself	inkasar, yinkasir
brother	akhu, akhwaan
brown	bunni, -iyiin
brown-skinned	asmar, samra, sumur
build	bana, yabni
bus	baaṣ, -aat; baṣ, -aat
busy	mashghuul
but	laakin
butcher	jazzaar, -iin
butter	zibda
buy	ishtara, yishtari
by	bee, bi

C

cabbage	karnab, karaanib
cafe	kafitiira, -aat
Cairo	al ghaahira
caliph	khaliifa (m), khulafa
call (vb)	naada, yinaadi
prayer call	azaan
camel	jamal, jimaal
candle	sham9a, shumuu9
canopy	ṣeewaan, -aat
car	9arabiiya, 9arabaat (or 9arabiiyaat)
carefully	bi r raaHa
carrots	jazar (coll)
carry	shaal, (shilta), yashiil
cat (male)	kadiis, kadaayis
cat (female)	kadiisa, -aat
cattle	bagar (coll)
celery	karaafis
centre-forward	sintir firwid
chair	kursi, karaasi
chance, opportunity	furṣa, furaṣ
change (for money)	fakka
change (vb)	ghayyar, yighayyir
charcoal	faHam
chat (vb)	itwannas, yitwannas
cheap	rakhiiṣ, rukhaaṣ
cheese	jibna
chickens	jidaad (coll)
child (small)	ṭifil, aṭfaal
children	awlaad; wileedaat
choose	ikhtaar, (ikhtirta), yikhtaar
Christmas	9iid al miilaad
church	kaniisa, kanaayis
cigarette	sijaara, sajaayir
cinnamon	girfa
civil servant; male	muwaẓẓaf, -iin
civil servant; female	muwaẓẓafa, -aat
class (period)	Hiṣṣa, Hiṣaṣ
clean (vb)	naḍḍaf, yinaḍḍif
clean (adj)	naḍiif, nuḍaaf
clerk	kaatib, kataba
clever	shaaṭir, -iin
clothes	hiduum; malaabis
coffee (the drink)	gahwa
coffee (the beans)	bunn
cold (adj)	baarid
collect	istalam, yistalim
color	loon, alwaan
come	jaa, yaji
come here!	ta9aal
company (commercial)	sharika, -aat
complain	shaka, yashki
computer	kombyuutar, kombyuutaraat
conference	mu'tamar, mu'tamaraat
congratulate	baarak, yibaarik li
congratulations	mabruuk
connect (telephone)	waṣṣal
consultant	mustashaar
continually	ṭawwaali

cook (preparing meal)	ṭabakh, yaṭbukh
cook (specific)	najjaḍ
correct (adj)	ṣaaHH
cotton	guṭun
country	balad (m or f), buldaan
countryside	khala (m)
courtyard	Hoosh, Heeshaan
cover (vb)	ghaṭṭa, yighaṭṭi
craze (for something)	jinn
crocodile	tumsaaH, tamaasiiH
cucumber (smooth variety)	khiyaar (coll)
cucumber (grooved)	9ajjuur (coll)
cup	kubbaaya, kabaabi
cupboard	doolaab, dawaaliib
custom	9aada, -aat (or 9awaayid)
customer; male	zabuun, zabaayin
customer; female	zabuuna, -aat
cut (vb); with knife	gaṭa9, yagṭa9
cut (vb); with scissors	gaṣṣa, yaguṣṣ
cut off (on telephone)	mafṣuul

D

dance (vb)	ragaṣ, yarguṣ
date (of month)	taariikh, tawaariikh
dates (fruit)	balaH (coll); tamur (coll)
daughter	bitt, banaat
day	yoom, ayyaam
day after tomorrow	ba9ad bukra
day before yesterday	awwal umbaariH
delicious	laziiz
depart	gaam, (gumta), yaguum
dervish	darwiish, daraawiish
desert	ṣaHra, ṣaHaari
dialling tone	Haraara
dialogue	Hiwaar
die	maat, (mutta), yamuut
die (formal word)	itwaffa, yitwaffa
difficult	ṣa9ab, -iin
difficulty	mushkila, mashaakil
dinar	diinaar
director	mudiir, mudiiriin
dirty	waskhaan, -iin
dish	ṣaHan, ṣuHuun
district	Hayy, aHya
djinn	jinn
do	9amal, ya9mil
doctor, physician	duktoor, dakaatra
dog	kalib, kilaab
donkey (male)	Humaar, Hamiir
donkey (female)	Humaara, -aat
door	baab, abwaab
dozen	dasta, disat
draw (vb)	rasam, yarsum
drawer (of desk)	duruj, adraaj
dress, put on	libis, yalbas
dress (nn)	fustaan, fasaatiin
drink (vb)	shirib, yashrab
drink (nn)	sharaab
driver	sawwaag, -iin
dry (adj)	naashif
dry, to become dry	nishif, yanshaf
dry, to dry something	nashshaf
durra	9eesh
dust	turaab
dust storm	habuub, habaayib

E

each other	ba9aḍ
eager	mushtaag, -iin
ear	aḍaan, iḍneen
early	badri
earth, land	arḍ (f), araaḍi
east	sharig
Easter	9iid al giyaama
eastern	shargi
easy	saahil
eat	akal, yaakul
ebony	baabaanuus
eggs	beeḍ (coll)
Egypt	maṣir
electricity	kahraba
elephant	fiil, afyaal
email	jawaab iliktrooni
embassy	safaara, -aat
embroider	ṭarraz, yiṭarriz
embroidery	taṭriiz
empty	faaḍi, -iin
end (vb)	intaha, yintahi
end (nn)	nihaaya
engaged (busy)	mashghuul
engine	makana, -aat
engineer	muhandis, -iin
England	ingiltara
English (language)	ingliizi
English (adj)	ingliizi, -iyiin
to enjoy (doing)	irtaaH (irtiHta), yirtaaH lee
enough	kifaaya
enter	khashsha, yakhushsh; dakhal, yadkhul
envelope	ẓarif, ẓuruuf
European	uurubbi, -iyiin
even, even if	Hatta
evening	misa (m)

examine, look at	kashaf, yakshif (9ala)
for example	masalan
excellent	mumtaaz, -iin
expensive	ghaali, -iin
explain	waḍḍaH
eye	9een, 9iyuun

F

face (nn)	washsh, wushuush
fall (vb)	waga9, yaga9
family, relatives	ahal; usra, usar
fan (electric)	marwaHa, maraawiH
far, distant	ba9iid, -iin
fast (vb)	ṣaam, (ṣumta), yaṣuum
fasting	ṣoom
fat (adj)	samiin, sumaan
father	abu, ubbahaat (or abwaat)
ferry	banṭoon, -aat
festival	9iid, a9yaad
fetch water	warad, yarid
feverish	maHmuum, -iin
few	shwaiya; basiiṭ
figs	tiin (coll)
fill	mala, yamla
filling	mali
film (nn)	filim, aflaam
find	liga, yalga
fine	tamaam
finished	khalaaṣ
fire	naar (f), niiraan
fish	samak (coll)
floor, tiles	balaaṭ
flour	dagiig
white flour	dagiiga fiina
flower (ornamental)	zahra, zuhuur
fly (housefly)	ḍubbaan (coll)
fold (vb)	ṭabbag
follow	taba9, yatba9
food	akil
foot	gadam (f), agdaam
on foot	bee rijleen
football	kuura
for, to	lee, li
for, for (a price)	bee, bi
forbidden (on religious grounds)	Haraam
foreigner (male)	khawaaja, -aat
foreigner (female)	khawaajiiya, -aat
forget	nisa, yansa
fork	shooka, shuwak
form (official)	urneek, araaniik
France	faransa
French	faransi, -iyiin
free (unoccupied)	faaḍi, -iin
fried	muHammar
friend (male)	ṣaaHib, aṣHaab
friend (female)	ṣaaHba, -aat
from	min
fruit	fawaakih
full	malyaan
funeral	bika
furnished	mafruush
furniture	9afash

G

game	la9ba, -aat
garage	garraash, -aat
garden	jineena, janaayin
garlic	tuum
gasoline	banziin
gate	baab, abwaab
Germany	almaanya
German	almaani, -iyiin
get, obtain	akhad, yaakhud
get on (bus, etc.)	rikib, yarkab
get off, out (bus, etc.)	nazal, yanzil
get up	gaam, (gumta), yaguum
gift	hadiiya, hadaaya
ginger	zanjabiil
giraffe	zaraaf (coll)
girl	bitt, banaat
give	adda, yaddi
glass (drinking)	kubbaaya, kabaabi
glass (substance)	gizaaz
glasses (spectacles)	naḍḍaara, -aat
go	masha, yamshi
go for a walk	itfassaH
go out	marag, yamrug; ṭala9, yaṭla9
go up, over	ṭala9, yaṭla9
goal, score	goon, agwaan
goats	ghanam (coll)
God	allaa
gold	dahab
good	kwaiyis, -iin
goods, merchandise	buḍaa9a
government	Hukuuma, -aat
grandfather	jidd, juduud
grandmother	Habbooba, -aat
grapefruit	'grapefruit' (Arabic term not used)
grass	Hashiish
green	akhdar, khadra, khudur
grilled	mashwi
group of people	jamaa9a, -aat

group of people (associated formally)	majmuu9a, -aat
guard (vb)	Haras, yaHris
guard (nn)	ghafiir, ghufara
guavas	jawaafa (coll)
guest (male)	ḍeef, ḍuyuuf (or ḍeefaan)
guest (female)	ḍeefa, -aat
guide (nn)	murshid, -iin

H

hair	sha9ar (coll)
half	nuṣṣ, anṣaaṣ
half (in a football game)	shooṭ
hand	iid (f), iideen
handle	iid (f), iideen
happy	mabṣuut, -iin
have	9ind
head	raas, riseen
headache	ṣudaa9
health	ṣaHHa
hear	simi9, yasma9
heat	Harr
heavy	tagiil, tugaal
help (vb)	saa9ad
help (nn)	musaa9ada
here	hina
high	9aali, -iin
hill	jabal, jibaal
history	taariikh
hit (vb)	ḍarab, yaḍrub; dagga, yadugg
hold	masak, yamsik
honey	9asal an naHal
hope (vb)	itmanna, yitmanna
horse	Huṣaan, Haṣiin
hospital	mustashfa (m), -yaat
hot	Haarr; sukhun
hour	saa9a, -aat
house	beet, biyuut
house agent	samsaar, samaasra
house-owner	siid al beet; ṣaaHib al beet
how?	keef
how many? how much?	kam
hunt (vb)	iṣṭaad, (iṣṭitta), yiṣṭaad
hurt	waja9, yooja9
husband	raajil, rujaal; zooj, azwaaj

I

ice	talij
if	iza; law; in
ill	9ayyaan, -iin
immediately	ṭawwaali
in	fii, fi
in front of	giddaam
injured, to be	it9awwag
iron (vb)	kawa, yakwi
iron (nn)	makwa
island	jaziira, juzur
ivory	9aaj

J

jam	marabba
jelabiya	jallaabiiya, jalaaliib
journey	safar
juice	9aṣiir
jump (vb)	naṭṭa, yanuṭṭ
just	saakit

K

kebab	kabaab
key	muftaaH, mafaatiiH
Khartoum	al kharṭuum
kill	katal, yaktil
kilo	kiilu (no plural)
kind, sort	noo9, anwaa9
kitchen	maṭbakh, maṭaabikh
kitchen utensils	9idda
knife	sikkiin (f), sakaakiin
knock (vb)	dagga, yadugg
know	9irif, ya9rif
Korea	kuuriiya

L

land	arḍ (f), araaḍi
landlord	siid al beet
language	lugha, -aat
last	aakhir
lastly	akhiiran
later	ba9deen
late, to be	it'akhkhar
laugh	ḍiHik, yaḍHak
lawyer	muHaami, -iin
lazy	kaslaan, -iin
leaf	ṣafag (coll)
learn	it9allam
leather	jilid
leave (something somewhere)	khalla, yikhalli
Lebanon	lubnaan
left (direction)	shimaal
leg	kuraa9 (f), kir9een
lentils	9adas
lesson	daris, duruus
let, allow	khalla, yikhalli
letter (post)	jawaab, -aat

lettuce	khass (coll)
library	maktaba, -aat
license	rukhṣa, rukhaṣ
lie down	ragad, yargud
light (artificial)	nuur, anwaar
light (in weight)	khafiif, -iin
like (vb)	Habba, yaHibb
like (prep)	zeey
like this	kida
limes	leemuun (coll)
line	khaṭṭ, khuṭuuṭ
lining	buṭaana
list (nn)	lista, -aat
listen	simi9, yasma9
little, a	shwaiya
live, dwell	sakan, yaskun
liver	kibda, kibad
long	ṭawiil, ṭuwaal
to be a long time	ṭawwal
look	shaaf, (shufta), yashuuf
look for	fattash; kaas, (kusta), yakuus
lose	rawwaH, yirawwiH
loss, at a (in price)	khasraan
love (vb)	Habba, yaHibb
low	waaṭi, -iin
luggage	9afash
lunch	ghada (m)

M

machine	makana, -aat
machine, sewing machine	makanat khiyaata
madam (polite)	sitt, sittaat
mail (air mail)	al bariid aj jawi
make	9amal, ya9mil; sawwa, yisawwi
man	raajil, rujaal
mangoes	manga (coll)
many	katiir, kutaar
market	suug, aswaag
marrow (vegetable), courgette	koosa
marry, get married	itzawwaj
married	mutzawwij, -iin
match (football)	mubaara, -yaat
matches	kibriit (coll)
material, cloth	gumaash
meaning	ma9na, ma9aani (m)
meat	laHam; laHma
beef	laHam bagari
mutton	laHam daani
minced meat	mafruum
mechanic	makaniiki, makaniikiiya
medicine	dawa (m), adwiya
meet someone	laaga, yilaagi
meet each other	itlaagu, yitlaagu; itgaabal
melon (cantaloupe)	shammaam (coll)
melon (watermelon)	baṭṭiikh (coll)
memorise	zaakar
menu	lista, -aat
merchant	taajir, tujjaar
messenger	muraasla, muraasaliin
milk	laban
mill	ṭaaHuuna, ṭawaaHiin
ministry	wizaara, -aat
mint (herb)	na9na9
minute	dagiiga, dagaayig
money	guruush
monkey	girid, guruud
month	shahar, shuhuur
moon	gamar
morning	ṣabaaH
mosque	jaami9, jawaami9
mother	umm, ummahaat
mountain	jabal, jibaal
mouth, opening	khashum, khushuum
much	katiir
museum	matHaf, mataaHif
music	musiigha
Muslim	muslim, -iin

N

name	isim, asaami (or usuum)
nationality	jinis, ajnaas
near	gariib, -iin
necessary	ḍaruuri
neighbor (male)	jaar, jeeraan
neighbor (female)	jaara, -aat
never	abadan
new	jadiid, judaad
news	khabar, akhbaar
newspaper	jariida, jaraayid
night	leela, leeyaali
night time	leel
Nile, the	an niil
no	la'
nomads	ruHHal
noon	ḍuhur
north	shimaal
northern	shimaali
not	maa; mush
not yet	lissa9
notebook	noota, nuwat
now	hassa9; hassi
number	nimra, nimar
nursery (plants)	mashatal, mashaatil

O

occasion	furṣa, furaṣ
occupation	waẓiifa
of course	ṭab9an
office	maktab, makaatib
often	katiir
oil	zeet
okra (ladies fingers)	baamya
Omdurman	umdurmaan
old (of people)	9ajuuz, 9ajaayiz; kabiir, kubaar
old (of things)	gadiim, gudaam
on	fii, fi; 9ala
onions	baṣal (coll)
only	bass
open (vb)	fataH, yaftaH
or	walla
oranges	burtukaan (coll)
original	aṣli
originally	aṣlan
outing, stroll	fusHa, fusaH
outside	barra
over, above	foog
overloaded	maHmuul, -iin
owner	siid, siyaad; ṣaaHib, aṣHaab

P

packet	9ilba, 9ilab
pain	waja9, awjaa9
palace	gaṣir, guṣuur
pancakes, Sudanese	kisra
paper	warag (coll)
paper (document)	waraga, awraag
parsley	bagduunis
party (entertainment)	Hafla, -aat
passenger	raakib, rukkaab
passport	jawaaz, -aat
patient (ill) (male)	mariiḍ, marḍaaniin
patient (ill) (female)	mariiḍa, -aat
pay	dafa9, yadfa9
peanuts	fuul suudaani
peanut butter	fuul madguug
pen	galam, aglaam
pencil	galam (ruṣaaṣ), aglaam
people	naas
pepper	filfil (coll)
pepper (hot red pepper)	shaṭṭa
performance	mustawa (m)
perhaps	yimkin
person	zool; nafar, anfaar
petrol	banziin
photograph (vb)	ṣawwar
photograph (nn)	ṣuura, ṣuwar
photographer	muṣawwir, -iin
picture	ṣuura, ṣuwar
piece	giṭ9a, giṭa9; Hitta, Hitat
pigeons	Hamaam (coll)
pile	koom, akwaam
pilgrim (male)	Haajj, Hujjaaj
pilgrim (female)	Haajja, -aat
pilgrimage	Hajj
go on pilgrimage	masha l Hajj
pink	bambi, -iyiin
place	maHall, -aat; makaan, -aat
plant (vb)	zara9, yazra9
plant (nn)	shatla, -aat; nabat, -aat
plate	ṣaHan, ṣuHuun
play (vb)	li9ib, yal9ab
player	laa9ib, -iin
pleasant, nice	Hilu, -iin
please	law samaHta
poor	miskiin, masaakiin
possible	mumkin
post box	ṣanduug al busṭa
post office	maktab al busṭa
potatoes	baṭaaṭis (f)
sweet potatoes	bambay
pound (money)	jineeh (plural not used)
10 Sudanese pounds	diinaar
pour	kabba, yakubb
practice	tamriin
pray	ṣalla, yiṣalli
prayer call	azaan
present (adj)	moojuud, -iin
price	si9ir
print (vb)	ṭaba9, yaṭba9
print out (from computer) (vb)	ṭalla9, yiṭalli9 fii waraga
problem	mushkila, mashaakil
project	mashruu9, mashaarii9
pull	jarra, yajirr
pumpkin	gara9 (coll)
push	dafar, yadfar
put, place	khatta, yakhutt
put into	dakhkhal
put on (clothing)	libis, yalbas

Q

quarter	rubu9, arbaa9
question (nn)	su'aal, as'ila
quickly	bee sur9a; guwaam

R

radio	raadyu (or raadi), rawaadi
radishes	fijil (coll)
railway	sikka Hadiid
rain	maṭar, amṭaar
rainy season	khariif
raisins	zabiib (coll)
read	gara, yagra
ready (of things)	jaahiz
ready (of people)	musta9idd, -iin
ready, to be	jahaz, yajhaz
reason	sabab, asbaab
receipt	waṣil, waṣuulaat
red	aHmar, Hamra, Humur
reduce the price	khaffaḍ
refrigerator	tallaaja, -aat
region	manṭiga, manaaṭig
remember	itzakkar
rent (vb)	ajjar, yi'ajjir
rent (nn)	iijaar, -aat
renting (nn)	ta'jiir
repair; improve	ṣallaH
reservation (booking)	Hajiz (no plural)
residence (private house)	manzil
responsible (for)	mas'uul, -iin (min)
rest (vb)	irtaaH, (irtiHta), yirtaaH
rest, remainder	baagi
restaurant	maṭ9am, maṭaa9im
return	raja9, yarja9
revenue stamp	damgha, -aat
rice	ruzz
ride (vb)	rikib, yarkab
right (direction)	yamiin
river	baHar, buHuur
river-bed (seasonally dry)	khoor, kheeraan
room	ooḍa, uwaḍ
rope	Habil, Hubaal
rose (or any other showy flower)	warda, warid
ruling	Haakim, -iin
run (vb)	jara, yajri

S

salad	salaṭa
sale, for sale	li l bee9
salt	miliH
sausages	sujuuk
say	gaal, (gutta), yaguul
scheme	mashruu9, mashaarii9
school	madrasa, madaaris
scissors	magaṣṣ, -aat
score (vb)	sajjal
sea	baHar
seat	mag9ad, magaa9id
secretary	sikirteera, -aat
see	shaaf, (shufta), yashuuf
sell	baa9, (bi9ta), yabii9
send	rassal
servant (male)	khaddaam, -iin
servant (female)	khaddaama, -aat
sesame	simsim
severely, strongly	shadiid
sew	khayyat
sewing	khiyaata
sheep	kharuuf, khurfaan
sheet	milaaya, -aat
shirt	gamiiṣ, gumṣaan
shoe	jazma, jizam
shop	dukkaan, dakaakiin
shopkeeper	siid ad dukkaan
short	giṣayyir, guṣaar
show (vb)	warra, yiwarri
shut	gafal, yagfil
sing	ghanna, yighanni
sir, Mr.	seeyid
sister	ukhut, ukhwaat
sit down	ga9ad, yag9ud
sitting room	ṣaaluun, ṣawaaliin
skin, hide	jilid, juluud
sky	sama
slaughter	ḍabaH, yaḍbaH
sleep (vb)	naam, (numta), yanuum
sleep (nn)	noom
slowly	bi r raaHa
small	ṣaghayyir, ṣughaar
smile (vb)	ḍiHik, yaḍHak
so-so	kida kida
so that	9ashaan
soap	ṣaabuun
some	ba9aḍ
sometimes	marraat; aHyaanan
son	walad, awlaad
song	ughniiya, aghaani
soon	ba9ad shwaiya
sorghum, guinea-corn	9eesh
sorry, very	mut'assir
soup	shoorba
south	januub
southern	januubi
speak	itkallam
special	makhṣuuṣ, -iin
specialist	mustashaar
spit	bakhkha, yabukhkh
splendid	tamaam

spoon	ma9laga, ma9aalig
spring (season)	khariif
sprinkle	rashsha, yarushsh
square (public)	meedaan, meeyaadiin
squash (pumpkin)	gara9 (coll)
squash (zucchini)	koosa
stadium	istaad, -aat
stamp (postage)	ṭaab9a, ṭawaabi9
stamp (revenue)	damgha, -aat
stand up	wagaf, yagiif
standard	mustawa (m)
stay (vb)	ga9ad, yag9ud
steal	sarag, yasrug
stew	mulaaH
stomach	baṭun (f), buṭuun
stop oneself	wagaf, yagiif
stop something	waggaf
storeroom	makhzan
story	Hikaaya, -aat; giṣṣa, giṣaṣ
straight on	ṭawwaali
strange	9ajiib, -iin
street	shaari9, shawaari9
study (vb)	daras, yadrus
Sudan, the	as suudaan
Sudanese	suudaani, -iyiin
sugar	sukkar
suitcase	shanṭa, shinaṭ
sultan, ruler	sulṭaan, salaaṭiin
summer	ṣeef
sun	shamis, -aat (f)
sunset	mughrib
supper	9asha (m)
sweep	gashsha, yagushsh
sweeping	mugshaasha
sweet (adj)	Hilu, -iin
sweet (nn)	Halaawa, Halawiyaat
swelling	waram
switch off	gafal, yagfil
switch on	fataH, yaftaH

T

table	ṭarabeeza, -aat
take	shaal, (shilta), yashiil; akhad, yaakhud
take someone somewhere	wadda, yiwaddi
tailor	tarzi, tarziya; khayyaat, -iin
talk (vb)	itkallam
talking, speech	kalaam
tall	ṭawiil, ṭuwaal
taste (vb)	ḍaag, (ḍugta), yaḍuug
taxi	taksi (or taks), takaasi
tea	shaay
teach	darras
teacher (male)	mudarris, -iin; ustaaz, asaatiza
teacher (female)	mudarrisa, -aat; ustaaza, -aat
telephone	talafoon, -aat
to phone someone	ḍarab lee waaHid talafoon
television	tilivizyoon, -aat
tell	kallam
tenant	mu'ajjir, -iin
than	min
that	daak, diik
the	al
there	hinaak
there is, are	fii
these	deel
thing	Haaja, -aat; shi
third (nn)	tilit, atlaat
this	da, di
those	deelaak
throw	rama, yarmi
ticket	tazkara, tazaakir
time, long time ago	zamaan
time, number of times	marra, -aat
time, past time	zaman
time, period of time	mudda, mudad
time, point in time	wakit
tin can	9ilba, 9ilab
tired	ta9baan, -iin
to	lee, li; 9ala
tobe	toob, tiyaab (or teebaan)
today	alleela
together	sawa
toilet, w.c.	adbakhaana, -aat
tomatoes	ṭamaaṭim (f)
tomorrow	bukra; baakir
tooth	sinn, asnaan (or sinuun)
total	jumla, jumal
towel	bishkiir, bashaakiir
town	madiina, mudun
tradition	9aada, -aat (or 9awaayid)
train	gaṭar, gaṭraat
transport	muwaaṣalaat
travel (vb)	saafar
travel (nn)	safar
traveller	musaafir, -iin
trees	shajar (coll); shidar (coll)
tribe	gabiila, gabaayil

trousers	banṭaloon, banaaṭliin
true	ṣaaHH
turn	laffa, yaliff
type (vb)	ṭaba9, yaṭba9

U

uncle (paternal)	9amm, a9maam
uncle (maternal)	khaal, kheelaan
under	tiHit
understand	fihim, yafham
university	jaam9a, -aat
until	liHaddi; lighaayat
use (vb)	ista9mal
useful	mufiid, -iin

V

vegetables	khudrawaat; khadaar
stuffed vegetables	maHshi
very	jiddan; khaaliṣ; shadiid
village	Hilla, Hilaal
visa	ta'shiira, -aat
visit (vb)	zaar, (zurta), yazuur
visit (nn)	ziyaara
visitor (male)	ḍeef, ḍuyuuf
visitor (female)	ḍeefa, -aat

W

wages	maahiiya, mawaahi
wait (vb)	istanna, yistanna; rija, yarja
waiter	walad
walk, stroll	fusHa, fusaH
walk, go for a walk	itfassaH
want	9aawz, -iin; daayir, -iin
war	Harib, Huruub
warm up	sakhkhan
wash	ghassal
watch (time piece)	saa9a, -aat
water (nn)	mooya
water (vb)	saga, yasgi
way, path	darib, duruub; ṭariig, ṭurug
weapon	silaaH, asliHa
wear	libis, yalbas
weather	joo
wedding	9iris, 9urusaat
week	usbuu9, asaabii9
weep, cry	baka, yabki
weigh	wazan, yoozin
weight	wazin
welcome	marHaba
well (water)	biir (f), abyaar
west	gharib
western	gharbi
wet	leeyin, -iin
what?	shinuu
wheat	gamiH
when? (question)	miteen
when (conj)	lamman
where?	ween
which?	yaatu, yaata, yaatum
white	abyaḍ, beeḍa, buyuḍ
who?	minuu
why?	lee shinuu
win	ghalab, yaghlib
wind	habuub, habaayib; hawa (m), ahwiya
window	shubbaak, shabaabiik
wing	janaaH, ajnaHa
winter	shita
wish (vb)	itmanna, yitmanna
with	ma9a
woman	mara, niswaan
word	kalma, -aat
work (vb)	ishtaghal
work (nn)	shughul
working	shaghghaal, -iin
wrap up	laffa, yaliff
write	katab, yaktib
written	maktuub
wrong, mistaken	ghalṭaan, -iin

Y

yard	Hoosh, Heeshaan
year	sana, siniin
yeast	khamiira
yellow	aṣfar, ṣafra, ṣufur
yes	aiwa, ai
yesterday	umbaariH; amis
yet	lissa9
yoghurt	zabaadi

Z

zero	ṣifir

Days of the week

Sunday	yoom al aHad
Monday	yoom al itneen
Tuesday	yoom at talaata
Wednesday	yoom al arbi9a
Thursday	yoom al khamiis
Friday	yoom aj jum9a
Saturday	yoom as sabit

Times of the day

first call to prayer	al azaan al awwal
morning	ṣabaaH
noon	ḍuhur
early/mid afternoon	ba9d aḍ ḍuhur
late afternoon	9asur
sunset	mughrib
evening	misa
night	leel

Cardinal numbers

0	ṣifir
1	waaHid, -a
2	itneen
3	talaata
4	arba9a
5	khamsa
6	sitta
7	sab9a
8	tamanya
9	tis9a
10	9ashara
11	Hidaashar
12	iṭnaashar
13	talaṭṭaashar
14	arba9ṭaashar
15	khamuṣṭaashar
16	siṭṭaashar
17	saba9ṭaashar
18	tamanṭaashar
19	tisa9ṭaashar
20	9ishriin
21	waaHid u 9ishriin
22	itneen u 9ishriin
30	talaatiin
40	arba9iin
50	khamsiin
60	sittiin
70	sab9iin
80	tamaniin
90	tis9iin
100	miiya
101	miiya u waaHid
125	miiya khamsa u 9ishriin
200	miiyteen
300	tultumiiya
400	urbu9umiiya
500	khumsumiiya
600	suttumiiya
700	sub9umiiya
800	tumnumiiya
900	tus9umiiya
1000	alf
2000	alfeen
3000	talaata alf
100,000	miiyat alf

one year	sana waaHda
two years	sanateen
three years	talaata siniin
ten years	9ashara siniin
eleven years	Hidaashar sana
100 years	miiyat sana

Ordinal numbers

first	awwal, -a
second	taani, -ya
third	taalit, -a
fourth	raabi9, -a
fifth	khaamis, -a
sixth	saadis, -a
seventh	saabi9, -a
eighth	taamin, -a
ninth	taasi9, -a
tenth	9aashir, -a

(From 11th on up, the cardinal form is usually used, although the ordinal can be formed by suffixing *-aawi, -aawiya* to the cardinal form.)

Fractions

half	nuṣṣ, anṣaaṣ
third	tilit, atlaat
fourth	rubu9, arbaa9
fifth	khumus, akhmaas
sixth	sudus, asdaas
seventh	subu9, asbaa9
eighth	tumun, atmaan
ninth	tusu9, atsaa9
tenth	9ushur, a9shaar
¼	rubu9
¾	talaata arbaa9

An alternate way of expressing these fractions, and which must be used for denominators greater than ten, is as follows:

¼	waaHid 9ala arba9a
¾	talaata 9ala arba9a
2/11	itneen 9ala Hidaashar

Arabic - English glossary

a

aa<u>kh</u>ir	last
aasaar	antiquities
abadan	not at all; never
abu, ubbahaat (or abwaat)	father (see Lesson 12.1.3)
abwaab	pl. of baab
abwaat	pl. of abu
abyaar	pl. of biir
abyaḍ, beeḍa, buyuḍ	white
adba<u>kh</u>aana, -aat	toilet; w.c.
adda, yaddi	to give
adraaj	pl. of duruj
adwiya	pl. of dawa
aḍaan, iḍneen	ear
aflaam	pl. of filim
afyaal	pl. of fiil
agdaam	pl. of gadam
aglaam	pl. of galam
agwaan	pl. of goon
a<u>gh</u>aani	pl. of u<u>gh</u>niiya
ahal	family, relatives
ahlan (wa sahlan)	welcome (a greeting)
ahwiya	pl. of hawa
aHmar, Hamra, Humur	red
aHsan	better
aHya	pl. of Hayy
aHyaanan	sometimes
ai, aiwa	yes
ajjar, yi'ajjir	to rent
ajnaas	pl. of jinis
ajnaHa	pl. of janaaH
ajsaam	pl. of jisim
akal, yaakul	to eat
akil	food
aktar	more
bi l aktar	more so
akwaam	pl. of koom
akyaas	pl. of kiis
a<u>kh</u>ad, yaa<u>kh</u>ud	to take
a<u>kh</u>baar	pl. of <u>kh</u>abar
a<u>kh</u>dar, <u>kh</u>adra, <u>kh</u>udur	green
a<u>kh</u>iiran	lastly, recently
a<u>kh</u>u, a<u>kh</u>waan	brother
a<u>kh</u>waal	pl. of <u>kh</u>aal
a<u>kh</u>waan	pl. of a<u>kh</u>u
al	the
allaa	God
allaa yibaarik fiik; allaa yisallimak	(see Lesson 7.1.1)
alleela	today
almaani, -iyiin	German
almaanya	Germany
alwaan	pl. of loon
amis	yesterday
amriika	America
amṭaar	pl. of maṭar
ana	I
anfaar	pl. of nafar
anṣaaṣ	pl. of nuṣṣ
anwaar	pl. of nuur
anwaa9	pl. of noo9
araaḍi	pl. of arḍ
araaniik	pl. of urneek
arbaa9	pl. of rubu9
arḍ (f), araaḍi	land, earth
asaabii9	pl. of usbuu9
asaami	pl. of isim
asaatiza	pl. of ustaaz
asbaab	pl. of sabab
asliHa	pl. of silaaH
asmar, samra, sumur	brown-skinned
asnaan	pl. of sinn
aswaag	pl. of suug
aswad, sooda, suud	black
aswad (coll. nn)	aubergine; eggplant
as'ila	pl. of su'aal
aṣfar, ṣafra, ṣufur	yellow
aṣHaab	pl. of ṣaaHib
aṣlan	originally
aṣli	original, real
atlaat	pl. of tilit
aṭfaal	pl. of ṭifil
awjaa9	pl. of waja9
awlaad	pl. of walad; children
awraag	pl. of waraga
awwal, -a	first
awwal umbaariH	day before yesterday
ayyaam	pl. of yoom
azaan	call to prayer
azrag, zarga, zurug	blue
azwaaj	pl. of zooj
a9maam	pl. of 9amm
a9yaad	pl. of 9iid

b

baab, abwaab	door, gate
baabaanuus	ebony
baagi	remainder, rest
baakir	tomorrow
baamya	okra, 'ladies fingers'
baarak, yibaarik,	to congratulate
allaa yibaarik fiik	(see Lesson 7.1.1)
baarid	cold (adj)
baaṣ, -aat	bus (nn)
baayiẓ, -iin	not working, broken down
baaẓ, yabuuẓ	to break down, stop working
baa9, (bi9ta), yabii9	to sell
bada, yabda	to begin
badri	early
bagar (coll)	cattle
bagari, laHam bagari	beef
bagduunis	parsley
baHar, buHuur	sea, river
baHri	North Khartoum
baka, yabki	to weep, cry
bakhkha, yabukhkh	to spit
balaaṭ	floor, tiles
balad (m or f), buldaan	country
balaH (coll)	dates (fruit)
bambay	sweet potatoes
bambi, -iyiin	pink
bana, yabni	to build
banaat	pl. of bitt
banaaṭliin	pl. of banṭaloon
banjar (coll)	beetroot
banṭaloon, banaaṭliin	trousers
banṭoon, -aat	ferry (nn)
banziin	petrol, gasoline
bara-	alone (see Lesson 16.1.3)
al baraka fiikum	(see Lesson 13, Dialogue note 2)
barḍu	also
bariid	mail (nn)
al bariid aj jawi	air mail
bariṭaanya	Britain
barra	outside, abroad
basiiṭ	a little, few
bass	only
baṣ, -aat	bus (nn)
baṣal (coll)	onions
bashaakiir	pl. of bishkiir
baṭaaṭis (f)	potatoes
baṭṭaal, -iin	bad
baṭṭaariiya, -aat	battery
baṭṭiikh (coll)	watermelon
baṭun (f), buṭuun	belly, stomach (nn)
ba9ad, ba9d	after
ba9aḍ	each other; some
ba9deen	later, and then...
ba9iid	distant, far
bee, bi	by, for
beeḍ (coll)	eggs
beeḍa (adj)	f. of abyaḍ
beeḍa (nn)	an egg
been	between
beet, biyuut	house (nn)
siid al beet; ṣaaHib al beet	landlord, houseowner
beet maal wa 9iyaal	(see Lesson 23, Dialogue note 2)
bi, bee	by, for
biga, yabga	to become
biir, abyaar	well (nn)
biira	beer
bee9, li l bee9	for sale
bika	funeral
bishkiir, bashaakiir	towel
bitaa9, -at	(see Lesson 22.1.1)
bitt, banaat	girl, daughter
biyuut	pl. of beet
buḍaa9a	goods, merchandise
buHuur	pl. of baHar
bukra	tomorrow
ba9ad bukra	day after tomorrow
buldaan	pl. of balad
bunn	coffee beans
bunni, -iyiin	brown
burtukaan (coll)	oranges
busṭa, maktab al busṭa	post office
ṣanduug al busṭa	post office box
buṭaana, -aat	lining
buṭuun	pl. of baṭun
buyuḍ	pl. of abyaḍ

d

da (m)	this, that
daak (m)	that
daani, laHam daani	mutton
daayir, -iin	to want
daayman	often, always
dafar, yadfar	to push
dafa9, yadfa9	to pay
dagaayig	pl. of dagiiga
dagga, yadugg	to knock, hit
dagiig	flour
dagiiga, dagaayig	minute (nn)
dagiiga fiina	white flour
dahab	gold

dakaakiin	pl. of dukkaan
dakaatra	pl. of duktoor
dakhal, yadkhul	to enter
dakhkhal, yidakhkhil	to put into, insert
damgha, -aat	revenue stamp
9amal damgha	to affix a revenue stamp
daraawiish	pl. of darwiish
daras, yadrus	to study
darib, duruub	path, way
daris, duruus	lesson
darras, yidarris	to teach
darwiish, daraawiish	dervish
dasta, disat	dozen
dawa (m), adwiya	medicine
dawaaliib	pl. of doolaab
deel	these
deelaak	those
di (f)	this, that
diik (f)	that
diinaar	dinar, 10 Sudanese pounds
disat	pl. of dasta
doolaab, dawaaliib	cupboard, wardrobe
dukkaan, dakaakiin	shop (nn)
siid ad dukkaan	shopkeeper
duktoor, dakaatra	(male) doctor
duktoora, -aat	female doctor
duruj, adraaj	drawer (of desk)
duruub	pl. of darib
duruus	pl. of daris

ḍ

ḍaag, (ḍugta), yaḍuug	to taste
ḍabaH, yaḍbaH	to slaughter, kill (an animal)
ḍahar	back (nn)
ḍarab, yaḍrub	to hit, beat
ḍarab lee waaHid talafoon	to phone someone
ḍaruuri	necessary
ḍeef, ḍuyuuf (or ḍeefaan)	male visitor, guest
ḍeefa, -aat	female visitor, guest
ḍeefaan	pl. of ḍeef
ḍiHik, yaḍHak	to smile, laugh
ḍubbaan (coll)	housefly
ḍuhur	noon
ba9d aḍ ḍuhur	early/mid afternoon
ḍuyuuf	pl. of ḍeef

e

eeyi Haaja	anything

f

faaḍi, -iin	empty, free, unoccupied
faat	(see Lesson 15, Grammar note 2)
faHam	charcoal
fakka (nn)	change (money)
Faransa	France
faransi, -iyiin	French
farish, furaash	bed (with bedding)
fasaatiin	pl. of fustaan
faṣuulya	green beans
fataH, yaftaH	to open
fattash, yifattish	to look for
faṭar, yafṭur	to have breakfast
faṭuur	breakfast (nn)
fawaakih	fruit
fi, fii	at, in, on
fihim, yafham	to understand
fii	there is, there are
fii, fi	at, in, on
fiil, afyaal	elephant
fijil (coll)	radishes
filfil (coll)	pepper
filim, aflaam	film (nn)
foog	over, above, on
furaash	pl. of farish
furaṣ	pl. of furṣa
furṣa, furaṣ	opportunity, chance, occasion
fusaH	pl. of fusHa
fusHa, fusaH	outing, stroll, walk
fustaan, fasaatiin	dress (nn)
fuul, fuul maṣri	broad beans
fuul suudaani	peanuts
fuul madguug	peanut butter

g

gaabal, yigaabal	to meet (someone)
gaal, (gutta), yaguul	to say
gaam, (gumta), yaguum	to depart, get up
gaayil, ana gaayil...	I think...
gabaayil	pl. of gabiila
gabiila, gabaayil	tribe
gabli	before, ago
gabli kida	before this
gadam (f), agdaam	foot
gadiim, gudaam	old (of things)
gafal, yagfil	to shut, switch off
gahwa	coffee (the drink)
galam, aglaam	pen, pencil
gamar	moon

gamiH	wheat
gamiiṣ, gumṣaan	shirt
gara, yagra	to read
gara9 (coll)	pumpkin, squash
gariib, -iin	near
garraash, -aat	garage
gaṣir, guṣuur	palace
gaṣṣa, yaguṣṣ	to cut (with scissors)
gashsha, yagushsh	to sweep
gaṭar, -aat	train (nn)
gaṭa9, yagṭa9	to cut (with a knife), go off (electricity)
ga9ad, yag9ud	to sit down, stay
giddaam	ahead, further, in front (of)
gidir, yagdar	to be able
girfa	cinnamon
girid, guruud	monkey
giṣaṣ	pl. of giṣṣa
giṣayyir, guṣaar	short
giṣṣa, giṣaṣ	story (tale)
giṭa9	pl. of giṭ9a
giṭ9a, giṭa9	piece
gizaaz	glass (substance)
goon, agwaan	goal, score (nn)
gubbaal	before
gudaam	pl. of gadiim
gufaf	pl. of guffa
guffa, gufaf	basket
gumaash	material, cloth
gumṣaan	pl. of gamiiṣ
guruud	pl. of girid
guruush (pl.)	money
guṣaar	pl. of giṣayyir
guṣuur	pl. of gaṣir
guṭun	cotton
guwaam	quickly

gh

ghafiir, ghufara	guard (nn)
ghaali, -iin	expensive
al ghaahira	Cairo
ghaa9at aṣ ṣadaagha	Friendship Hall
ghada (m)	lunch (nn)
ghalab, yaghlib	to win
ghalṭaan, -iin	mistaken, wrong
ghanam (coll)	goats
ghanna, yighanni	to sing
gharbi, -iyiin	western
gharib	west
ghassal, yighassil	to wash
ghaṭṭa, yighaṭṭi	to cover
ghayyar, yighayyir	to change
ghufara	pl. of ghafiir

h

haa-	(see Lesson 21, Dialogue note 2)
habaayib	pl. of habuub
habuub, habaayib	wind, dust-storm
hadiiya, hadaaya	gift
hassa9, hassi	now, just, just now
hawa (m), ahwiya	air, wind
hi	she
hiduum	clothes
hina	here
hinaak	there
hu	he
hum	they

H

Haadis, Hawaadis	accident
Haaḍir	okay (response to a command or request)
Haaja, -aat	thing
eeyi Haaja	anything
Haajj, Hujjaaj	a man who has made the pilgrimage to Mecca
Haajja, -aat	a woman who has made the pilgrimage to Mecca
Haakim, -iin	ruling (vb)
Haarr	hot
Habba, yaHibb	to like, love
Habbooba, -aat	grandmother
Habil, Hubaal	rope (nn)
Hadiid,	
sikka Hadiid	railway
Hafla, -aat	party (celebration)
Hagg, -at	(see Lesson 10.1.4; Lesson 22.1.1)
Hajiz	reservation, booking
Hajj	pilgrimage
masha l Hajj	to go on pilgrimage
Halaawa, Halawiyaat	sweet (nn)
Halawiyaat	pl. of Halaawa
Hamaam (coll)	pigeons
al Hamdulilla	(see Lesson 1.1.1 greetings)
Hamiir	pl. of Humaar
Hammaam, -aat	bathroom
Hamra	f. of aHmar
Haraam	forbidden on religious grounds
Haraara	dialling tone
Haras, yaHris	to guard
Harib, Huruub	battle, war (nn)

Harr	heat (nn)
Hasab	according to, depending on
Haṣiin	pl. of Huṣaan
Hashiish	grass
Hatta	even, even if
Hawaadis	pl. of Haadis
Hawl	around, surrounding
Hayawaan, -aat	animal
Hayy, aHya	district of town
Heeshaan	pl. of Hoosh
Hikaaya, -aat	story, tale
Hilaal (or Hilal)	pl. of Hilla
Hilla, Hilaal (or Hilal)	village
Hilu, -iin	sweet, nice, pleasant
Hiṣaṣ	pl. of Hiṣṣa
Hiṣṣa, Hiṣaṣ	class period
Hitat	pl. of Hitta
Hitta, Hitat	piece
Hiwaar	conversation, dialogue
Hoosh, Heeshaan	yard, courtyard
Hubaal	pl. of Habil
Hujjaaj	pl. of Haajj
Hukuuma, -aat	government
Humaar, Hamiir	(male) donkey
Humaara, -aat	female donkey
Humur	pl. of aHmar
Huruub	pl. of Harib
Huṣaan, Haṣiin	horse

i

iḍneen	pl. of aḍaan
iid (f), -een	hand, handle (nn)
iijaar, -aat	rent (nn)
ikhtaar, yikhtaar	choose
iliktrooni, jawaab iliktrooni	email
illa	except
in	if
ingiltara	England
ingliizi	English (language)
ingliizi, -iyiin	English (adj)
inkasar, yinkasir	to become broken
inta	you (m. sg.)
intaha, yintahi	to end
inti	you (f. sg.)
intu	you (pl.)
irtaaH, (irtiHta), yirtaaH	to rest
irtaaH, (irtiHta), yirtaaH lee	to enjoy (doing)
isim, asaami (or usuum)	name (nn)
istaad, -aat	stadium
istaHamma, yistaHamm	to bathe (oneself)
istalam, yistalim	to collect
istanna, yistanna	to wait
ista9mal, yista9mal	to use
iṣṭaad, (iṣṭitta), yiṣṭaad	to hunt
ishtaghal, yishtaghil	to work
ishtara, yishtari	to buy
itfaḍḍal	(see Lesson 2.1.1)
itfassaH, yitfassaH	to go for a walk, stroll
itgaabal, yitgaabal	to meet each other
itghadda, yitghadda	to have lunch
itkallam, yitkallam	to speak, talk
itlaagu, yitlaagu	to meet each other
itmanna, yitmanna	to wish, hope
ittafag, yittafig (ma9a)	to agree (with)
itwaffa, yitwaffa	to die (formal word)
itwannas, yitwannas	to chat
itzakkar, yitzakkar	to remember
itzawwaj, yitzawwaj	to get married
it9allam, yit9allam	to learn
it9awwag, yit9awwag	to become hurt, injured
it'akhkhar, yit'akhkhar	to be late
iza, iza kaan	if
izzeey al Haal, izzeeyyak	(see Lesson 7.1.1; Lesson 1.1.1)

j

jaa, yaji	to come, arrive
jaab, (jibta), yajiib	to bring
jaahiz, -a	ready, ready-made (of things)
jaami9, jawaami9	mosque
jaam9a, -aat	university
jaar, jeeraan	(male) neighbor
jaara, -aat	female neighbor
jaay	(see Lesson 15, Notes on grammar)
jabal, jibaal	hill, mountain
jadiid, judaad	new
jahannamiiya	bougainvillea
jahaz, yajhaz	to be ready
jalaaliib	pl. of jallaabiiya
jallaabiiya, jalaaliib	jelabiya
jamaa9a, -aat	group of people
jamal, jimaal	camel
jamb	near, beside
jamiil, -iin	beautiful
janaaH, ajnaHa	wing
janaayin	pl. of jineena
januub	south
januubi	southern
jara, yajri	to run
jaraayid	pl. of jariida
jariida, jaraayid	newspaper
jarra, yajirr	to pull
jawaab, -aat	letter (post)
jawaab iliktrooni	email
jawaafa (coll)	guavas

jawaami9	pl. of jaami9
jawaaz, -aat	passport
jawi, al bariid aj jawi	air mail
jazaayir	pl. of jaziira
jazar (coll)	carrots
jaziira, juzur (or jazaayir)	island
jazma, jizam	shoe (nn)
jazzaar, -iin	butcher
jeeraan	pl. of jaar
jeesh, jiyuush	army
jibaal	pl. of jabal
jibna	cheese
jidaad (coll)	chickens
jidd, juduud	grandfather
jiddan	very
jilid, juluud	skin, hide, leather
jimaal	pl. of jamal
jineeh	pound (money)
jineena, janaayin	garden (nn)
jinis, ajnaas	nationality
jinn, djinn	craze for something
jisim, ajsaam	body
jiyuush	pl. of jeesh
jizam	pl. of jazma
joo (nn)	weather
joo (vb)	they came
judaad	pl. of jadiid
juduud	pl. of jidd
juluud	pl. of jilid
jumal	pl. of jumla
jumla, jumal	total (nn)
juzur	pl. of jaziira

k

kaan	if
kaan, (kunta), yakuun	to be
kaas, yakuus	to look for
kaatib, kataba	clerk
kabaab	kebab
kabaabi	pl. of kubbaaya
kabaari	pl. of kubri
kabba, yakubb	to pour
kabiir, kubaar	old (of people), big
kadaayis	pl. of kadiis
kadiis, kadaayis	male cat
kadiisa, -aat	female cat
kafitiira, -aat	cafe
kahraba	electricity
kalaam	talking, speech
kalib, kilaab	dog (nn)
kallam, yikallim	to talk to, tell
kalma, -aat	word
kam	how many? how much?
kamaan	also
kanaayis	pl. of kaniisa
kaniisa, kanaayis	church
karaafis	celery
karaanib	pl. of karnab
karaasi	pl. of kursi
karnab, karaanib	cabbage
kasar, yaksur	to break
kaslaan, -iin	lazy
kassar, yikassir	to break in pieces
kashaf, yakshif 9ala	to examine
katab, yaktib	to write
kataba	pl. of kaatib
katal, yaktil	to kill
katiir, -iin (or kutaar)	much, many; often; a lot
kawa, yakwi	to iron
ka9ab, -iin	bad
keef	how?
kibad	pl. of kibda
kibda, kibad	liver
kibriit (coll)	matches
kida	like that, like this; and so on
gabli kida	before this
kida kida	so-so
mush kida?	isn't that so?
kifaaya	enough
kiilu	kilogram, kilometer
kiis, akyaas	plastic or paper bag
kilaab	pl. of kalib
kir9een	pl. of kuraa9
kisra	Sudanese pancakes
kitaab, kutub	book (nn)
kombyuutar, kombyuutaraat	computer
koom, akwaam	pile (nn)
koosa	courgette, marrow, zucchini, Italian squash
kubaar	pl. of kabiir
kubbaaya, kabaabi	cup, drinking glass
kubri, kabaari	bridge (nn)
kull, kulli	all, every
kullu kullu	at all
kuraa9 (f), kir9een	leg (including the foot)
kursi, karaasi	chair (nn)
kutaar	pl. of katiir
kutub	pl. of kitaab
kuura, kuwar	ball, football
kuuriiya	Korea
kuwar	pl. of kuura
kwaiyis, -iin	good, well

kh

khaaf, (khufta), yakhaaf	to be afraid

khaal, kheelaan (or akhwaal)	maternal uncle
khaala, -aat	maternal aunt
khaaliṣ	very
khaamis	fifth (adj)
khabar, akhbaar	news
khadaadiim	pl. of khaddaam
khadaar	vegetables
khaddaam, -iin (or khadaadiim)	male servant
khaddaama, -aat	female servant
khadra	f. of akhdar
khaffaḍ, yikhaffiḍ	to reduce the price
khafiif, -iin (adj)	light (in weight)
khala (m)	open country, countryside
khalaaṣ	finished
khaliifa (m), khulafa	caliph, successor
khalla, yikhalli	to leave (something), let, allow
khamiira	yeast, raising agent
khamsa	five
khamsiin	fifty
khariif	rainy season, spring
al kharṭuum	Khartoum
kharuuf, khurfaan	sheep
khass (coll)	lettuce
khasraan	at a loss (in price)
khashum, khushuum	mouth (nn)
khashsha, yakhushsh	to enter
khatta, yakhutt	to put, place
khaṭṭ, khuṭuuṭ	line
khawaaja, -aat	male foreigner
khawaajiiya, -aat	female foreigner
khayyaat, -iin	tailor
khayyat, yikhayyit	to sew
kheelaan	pl. of khaal
kheer, bee kheer	well (adj)
kheeraan	pl. of khoor
khiyaar (coll)	smooth cucumber
khiyaata	sewing (nn)
makanat khiyaata	sewing machine
khoor, kheeraan	stream bed (of a seasonal stream)
khudrawaat	vegetables
khudur	pl. of akhdar
khulafa	pl. of khaliifa
khurfaan	pl. of kharuuf
khushuum	pl. of khashum
khuṭuuṭ	pl. of khaṭṭ

l

laaga, yilaagi	to meet (someone)
laakin	but, however
laa9ib, -iin	player
laban	milk
laffa, yaliff	to turn, wrap up, bind, bandage
laHam (or laHma)	meat
laHam bagari	beef
laHam daani	mutton
laHam mafruum	minced meat (ground meat)
lamman	when (conj)
law	if
law samaHta	please, if you please
laziiz, -a	delicious
la9ba, -aat	a game
la'	no
lee, li	for, to
lee, lee shinu	why? what for?
leel	night time
leela, leeyaali	night
leemuun (coll)	lemons, limes
leeyaali	pl. of leela
leeyin, -iin	wet (adj)
li, lee	for to
libis, yalbas	to put on, wear, dress
liga, yalga	to find
lighaayat	until
liHaddi	until, to
lissa9	still, yet (as a reply); not yet
lista, -aat	menu, list
li9ib, yal9ab	to play
loon, alwaan	colour (nn)
lubnaan	Lebanon
lugha, -aat	language

m

maa	not
maahiiya, mawaahi	wages, salary
maal, beet maal wa 9iyaal	(see Lesson 23, Dialogue note 2)
maal-	(see Lesson 21, Dialogue note 1)
maat, (mutta), yamuut	to die
mabruuk	congratulations!
mabṣuut, -iin	happy
madaaris	pl. of madrasa
madiina, mudun	town
madrasa, madaaris	school
mafaatiiH	pl. of muftaaH
mafruum, laHam mafruum	minced meat
mafruush	furnished
magaṣṣ, -aat	scissors
mag9ad, magaa9id	seat

maHall, -aat	place (nn)
maHmuul, -iin	overloaded (with responsibilities)
maHmuum, -iin	having a fever, feverish
maHshi	stuffed vegetables
majlis ash sha9b	the People's Assembly
majmuu9a, -aat	group of people associated formally
makaan, -aat	place (nn)
makaatib	pl. of maktab
makana, -aat	engine, machine
makanat khiyaata	sewing machine
makaniiki, -iya	mechanic
maksuur	broken
maktab, makaatib	office
maktab al busṭa	post office
maktaba, -aat	library, bookshop
maktuub, -a	written
makwa (m)	iron, ironing (nn)
makhṣuuṣ, -iin	special
makhzan	storeroom
mala, yamla	to fill, fill in
malaabis	clothes
mali	filling, filling in (nn)
malyaan	full
mamarr	aisle in plane
manaaṭig	pl. of manṭiga
manga (coll)	mangoes
manṭiga, manaaṭig	area, region
manzil	residence (private house)
mara, niswaan	woman
maraawiH	pl. of marwaHa
marabba	jam (food)
marag, yamrug	to go out
marḍaaniin	pl. of mariiḍ
marHaba	welcome
mariiḍ, marḍaaniin	male patient
mariiḍa, -aat	female patient
marra, -aat	time, instance
marraat	sometimes
marwaHa, maraawiH	electric fan
masaakiin	pl. of miskiin
masak, yamsik	to hold
masalan	for example
mas'uul, -iin (min)	responsible (for)
maṣir	Egypt
masha, yamshi	to go
masha l Hajj	to go on pilgrimmage
mashaakil	pl. of mushkila
mashaarii9	pl. of mashruu9
mashaatil	pl. of mashtal
mashghuul	busy, engaged
mashruu9, mashaarii9	scheme, project
mashtal, mashaatil	nursery (plants)
mashwi	grilled
mataaHif	pl. of matHaf
matHaf, mataaHif	museum
maṭaabikh	pl. of maṭbakh
maṭaar, -aat	airport
maṭaa9im	pl. of maṭ9am
maṭar, amṭaar	rain (nn)
maṭbakh, maṭaabikh	kitchen
maṭ9am, maṭaa9im	restaurant
mawaahi	pl. of maahiiya
mawluud, -iin	born
ma9a	with
ma9aalig	pl. of ma9laga
ma9laga, ma9aalig	spoon (nn)
ma9leesh	sorry, never mind
ma9na, ma9aani (m)	meaning
meedaan, meeyaadiin	public square
meeyaadiin	pl. of meedaan
milaaya, -aat	sheet
miliH	salt (nn)
min	from, among, than
minuu	who?
misa (m)	evening
miskiin, masaakiin	poor
mishmish (coll)	apricots
miteen	when?
moojuud, -iin	available, here, present
mooya	water (nn)
mooz (coll)	bananas
mubaara, -yaat	match (football)
mudad	pl. of mudda
mudarris, -iin	male teacher
mudarrisa, -aat	female teacher
mudda, mudad	period of time
mudiir, mudiiriin	director, boss
mudun	pl. of madiina
mufiid, -iin	useful
muftaaH, mafaatiiH	key (nn)
al mugran	the Mogran
mugshaasha	sweeping (nn)
mughrib	sunset
muhandis, -iin	engineer (nn)
muHaami, -iin	lawyer
muHammar, -a	fried
mukassar	broken in pieces, crumbling
mukayyif, -aat, mukayyif hawa	air cooler, air conditioner
mulaaH	stew (nn)
mumkin	possible
mumtaaz, -iin	excellent
muraasla, muraasaliin	messenger
murshid, -iin	guide
musaafir, -iin	traveller, travelling

musaa9ada	help (nn)
musiigha	music
muslim, -iin	Muslim
mustashaar	consultant, specialist
mustashfa (m), -yaat	hospital
mustawa (m)	standard, performance, level
musta9idd, -iin	ready (people)
muṣawwir, -iin	photographer
mush	not
mush kida?	isn't that so?
mushkila, mashaakil	problem, difficulty
mushtaag, -iin	eager, longing
mutzawwij, -iin	married
mut'assir	very sorry
al muulid	Mulid (the Prophet's birthday)
muwaaṣalaat	transport, transportation
muwaẓẓaf, -iin	male civil servant, official
muwaẓẓafa, -aat	female civil servant, official
mu'ajjir, -iin	tenant
mu'tamar, mu'tamaraat	conference

n

naada, yinaadi	to call
naam, (numta), yanuum	to sleep
naar (f), niiraan	fire (nn)
naas	people (nn)
naashif	dry (adj)
nabat, -aat	plant (nn)
naḍḍaara, -aat	glasses, spectacles
naḍḍaf, yinaḍḍif	to clean
naḍiif, nuḍaaf	clean (adj)
nafar, anfaar	person, individual
naHal (coll)	bees
9asal an naHal	honey
najjaḍ, yinajjiḍ	to cook
nashshaf, yinashshif	to dry something
naṭṭa, yanuṭṭ	to jump
nazal, yanzil	to get out, off
na9am	yes? pardon?
na9na9	mint (herb)
nihaaya	end (nn)
niHna	we
an niil	the Nile
niiraan	pl. of naar
nimar	pl. of nimra
nimra, nimar	number
nisa, yansa	to forget
niswaan	pl. of mara
nishif, yanshaf	to become dry
noom	sleep (nn)
noota, nuwat	notebook
noo9, anwaa9	kind, type, sort
nuḍaaf	pl. of naḍiif
nuṣṣ, anṣaaṣ	half
nuur, anwaar	light (nn)
nuwat	pl. of noota

o

ooḍa, uwaḍ	a room
ooṭṭ an noom	bedroom

r

raabi9	fourth (adj)
raadi (or raadyu), rawaadi	radio
raaHa, bi r raaHa	carefully, slowly
raajil, rujaal	man, husband
raakib, rukkaab	passenger
raas, riseen	head
ragad, yargud	to lie down
ragaṣ, yarguṣ	to dance
raja9, yarja9	to return
rakhiiṣ, rukhaaṣ	cheap, inexpensive
rama, yarmi	to throw
rashsha, yarushsh	to sprinkle
rasam, yarsum	to draw
rassal, yirassil	to send
rawaadi	pl. of raadi (or raadyu)
rawwaH, yirawwiH	to lose
rija, yarja	to wait
rijleen, bee rijleen	on foot
rikib, yarkab	to ride, get on
riseen	pl. of raas
rubu9, arbaa9	quarter, fourth (nn)
ruHHal	nomads
rujaal	pl. of raajil
rukkaab	pl. of raakib
rukhaaṣ	pl. of rakhiiṣ
rukhaṣ	pl. of rukhṣa
rukhṣa, rukhaṣ	licence (nn)
ruzz	rice

s

saabi9	seventh (adj)
saadis	sixth (adj)
saafar, yisaafir	to travel
saahil	easy
saakin, -iin	living, dwelling (vb)
saakit	just, only

saa9a, -aat	hour, watch (time-piece)
saa9ad, yisaa9id	to help
sabab, asbaab	reason, cause (nn)
sabbuura, -aat	blackboard
safaara, -aat	embassy
safar	journey, travel (nn)
saga, yasgi	to irrigate, water
sajaayir	pl. of sijaara
sajjal, yisajjil	to record, score, register
sakaakiin	pl. of sikkiin
sakan, yaskun	to live, dwell
sakhkhan, yisakhkhin	to become warm, warm up
salaam, ya salaam	goodness me
as salaamu 9aleekum	(see Lesson 1.1.1)
salaama, ma9a s salaama	good-bye
salaaṭiin	pl. of sulṭaan
salaṭa	salad
sama	sky
samaasra	pl. of samsaar
samaH, yasmaH	to agree
law samaHta...	please..., if you please...
samak (coll)	fish (nn)
samiH, -iin	beautiful, pleasant
samiin, sumaan	fat (adj)
samra	f. of asmar
samsaar, samaasra	house agent
sana, siniin	year
saraayir	pl. of sariir
sarag, yasrug	to steal
sariir, saraayir	bedstead
sawa	together
sawwa, yisawwi	to make
sawwaag, -iin	driver
sa'al, yas'al	to ask a question
seeyid	sir, Mr.
siid, siyaad	owner
siid ad dukkaan	shopkeeper
sijaara, sajaayir	cigarette
sikirteera, -aat	secretary
sikka Hadiid	railway
sikkiin (f), sakaakiin	knife (nn)
silaaH, asliHa	weapon
simi9, yasma9	to hear, listen
simsim	sesame
siniin	pl. of sana
sinn, asnaan (or sinuun)	tooth, tusk
sintir firwid	center forward
sinuun	pl. of sinn
sitt, sittaat	madam, lady
sitta	six
sittiin	sixty
siyaad	pl. of siid
si9ir	price
sooda	f. of aswad
sujuuk	sausages
sukkar	sugar (nn)
sukhun	hot
sulṭaan, salaaṭiin	sultan, chief, ruler
sumaan	pl. of samiin
sumur	pl. of asmar
sur9a, bee sur9a	quickly
suud	pl. of aswad
as suudaan	Sudan
suudaani, -iin	male Sudanese
suudaaniiya, -aat	female Sudanese
suug, aswaag	market, shops
su'aal, as'ila	question (nn)

Ṣ

ṣaaHba, -aat	female friend
ṣaaHH	true
ṣaaHib, aṣHaab	male friend, owner
ṣaaluun, ṣawaaliin	living room
ṣaam, (ṣumta), yaṣuum	to fast
ṣabaaH	morning
ṣabaaH al kheer	good morning
ṣabaaH an nuur	(the reply to ṣabaaH al kheer)
ṣaabuun	soap
ṣadaagha, ghaa9at aṣ ṣadaagha	Friendship Hall
ṣafag (coll)	leaves
ṣafra	f. of aṣfar
ṣaghayyir, ṣughaar	small
ṣaHaari	pl. of ṣaHra
ṣaHan, ṣuHuun	dish, plate
ṣaHHa	health
ṣaHra, ṣaHaari	desert
ṣalla, yiṣalli	to pray
ṣallaH, yiṣalliH	to improve, repair
ṣanaadiig	pl. of ṣanduug
ṣanduug, ṣanaadiig	box
ṣanduug al busṭa	post box
ṣawaaliin	pl. of ṣaaluun
ṣawwar, yiṣawwir	to take a picture, photograph
ṣa9ab, -iin	difficult
ṣeef	summer
ṣeewaan, -aat	canopy, awning
ṣifir	zero, nil
ṣoom	fasting (nn)
ṣudaa9	headache
ṣufur	pl. of aṣfar
ṣughaar	pl. of ṣaghayyir
ṣuHuun	pl. of ṣaHan

ṣuura, ṣuwar	picture, photograph (nn)
ṣuwar	pl. of ṣuura

sh

shaaf, (shufta), yashuuf	to look at, see
shaal, (shilta), yashiil	to take, carry
shaari9, shawaari9	street
shaaṭir, -iin	clever
shaay	tea
shabaabiik	pl. of shubbaak
shadiid	severely, strongly, very
shaghghaal, -iin	working
shahar, shuhuur	month
shajar (coll)	trees
shaka, yashki	to complain
shamis (f), -aat	sun
shammaam (coll)	cantaloupe, melon
sham9a, shumuu9	candle
shanṭa, shinaṭ	handbag, suitcase, satchel
sharaab	drink (nn)
shargi, -iyiin	eastern
sharig	east
sharika, -aat	company (commercial)
shatla, -aat	seedling, plant
shaṭṭa	hot red pepper
shawaari9	pl. of shaari9
sha9ar (coll)	hair
sha9b,	
majlis ash sha9b	the People's Assembly
shi	thing
shidar (coll)	trees
shimaal	left, north
shimaali	northern
shinaṭ	pl. of shanṭa
shinuu	what?
shirib, yashrab	to drink
shita	winter
shooka, shuwak	fork
shoorba	soup
shooṭ	half (football match)
shubbaak, shabaabiik	window
shughul	work (nn)
shuhuur	pl. of shahar
shukran,	thank you
shukran jaziilan	thank you very much
shumuu9	pl. of sham9a
shuwak	pl. of shooka
shwaiya	a little, a little while

t

taajir, tujjaar	merchant
taalit, -a	third (adj)
taani, -ya, -iin	again, more, second, other
taariikh, tawaariikh	history, date
taba9, yatba9	to follow
tagiil, tugaal	heavy
takaasi	pl. of taks or taksi
taksi (or taks), takaasi	taxi
talaata	three
talafoon, -aat	telephone
ḍarab lee waaHid talafoon	to phone someone
talij	ice (nn)
tallaaja, -aat	refrigerator
tamaam	fine, splendid!
tamaasiiH	pl. of tumsaaH
tamaniin	eighty
tamriin	practice, drills
tamur (coll)	dates (fruit)
tarzi, tarziya	tailor
taṭriiz	embroidery
tawaariikh	pl. of taariikh
tazaakir	pl. of tazkara
tazkara, tazaakir	ticket
ta9aal	come!
ta9baan, -iin	tired
ta'jiir	renting (nn)
ta'shiira, -aat	visa
teebaan	pl. of toob
tiHit	under, below
tiin (coll)	figs
tilit, atlaat	third (nn)
tilivizyoon, -aat	television
tiyaab	pl. of toob
toob, tiyaab (or teebaan)	tobe
tuffaaH (coll)	apples
tugaal	pl. of tagiil
tujjaar	pl. of taajir
tumsaaH, tamaasiiH	crocodile
turaab	dust, dust-storm
tuum	garlic
tuuti	Tuti Island

ṭ

ṭaabuuna, ṭawaabiin	bakery
ṭaab9a, ṭawaabi9	postage stamp
ṭaaHuuna, ṭawaaHiin	mill (nn)
ṭabakh, yaṭbukh	to prepare a meal, cook
ṭaba9, yaṭba9	to type, print
ṭabbag, yiṭabbig	to fold
ṭab9an	of course, certainly
ṭaiyib, -iin	alright, okay

ṭalab, yaṭlub	to request, ask for
ṭala9, yaṭla9	to go out, go up, go over, exceed
ṭalla9, yiṭalli9 fii waraga	to print out (from computer)
ṭamaaṭim (f)	tomatoes
ṭarabeeza, -aat	table (nn)
ṭariig, ṭurug	way, path
ṭarraz, yiṭarriz	to embroider
ṭawaabiin	pl. of ṭaabuuna
ṭawaabi9	pl. of ṭaab9a
ṭawaaHiin	pl. of ṭaaHuuna
ṭawiil, ṭuwaal	long, tall
ṭawwaali	continually, straight on, at once, immediately
ṭawwal, yiṭawwil	(a person) to be a long time
ṭayyaara, -aat	aeroplane
ṭeer (coll)	birds
ṭifil, aṭfaal	child
ṭuwaal	pl. of ṭawiil
ṭurug	pl. of ṭariig

u

u, w	and
ubbahaat	pl. of abu
ughniiya, aghaani	song
ukhwaat	pl. of ukhut
ukhut, ukhwaat	sister
umbaariH	yesterday
awwal umbaariH	day before yesterday
umdurmaan	Omdurman
umm, -ahaat	mother (see Lesson 12.1.1)
urneek, araaniik	official form
usar	pl. of usra
usbuu9, asaabii9	week
usra, usar	family
ustaaz, asaatiza	male teacher
ustaaza, -aat	female teacher
usuum	pl. of isim
uurubbi, -iyiin	European
uwaḍ	pl. of ooḍa

w

w, u	and
waaHid, -a	one
waaṭi, -iin	low (adj)
wadda, tiwaddi	to take someone to
waḍḍaH, yiwaḍḍiH	to explain, clarify
wagaf, yagiif	to stand up, stop (oneself)
waga9, yaga9	to fall
waggaf, yiwaggif	to stop (something)
waja9, awjaa9	pain (nn)
waja9, yooja9	to hurt someone or something
wakit	time (nn)
walad, awlaad	boy, son
walla	or
wallaahi	really (literally: my God!)
wara	behind (prep)
warad, yarid	to fetch water
warag (coll)	paper
waraga, awraag	document, paper
waram	swelling (nn)
warda, warid	rose (nn)
warid	pl. of warda
warra, yiwarri	to show
waskhaan, -iin	dirty
waṣṣal, yiwaṣṣil	to connect (telephone)
washsh, wushuush	face (nn)
wazan, yoozin	to weigh
wazin	weight
waẓiifa	occupation
ween	where?
wildat, talid	to give birth, have a child
wileedaat	children
wiṣil, yooṣal	to arrive
waṣil, waṣuulaat	receipt
wizaara, -aat	ministry
wizaarat al maaliiya	the Ministry of Finance
wuṣuul	arrival
wushuush	pl. of washsh

y

yaatu, -a, -um	which?
yamiin	right (direction)
ya9ni	that is to say
yimkin	perhaps, maybe
yoom, ayyaam	day
yumma	Mummy, Mommy

z

zaakar, yizaakir	to memorize
zaar, (zurta), yazuur	to visit
zabaadi	yoghurt
zabaayin	pl. of zabuun
zabiib (coll)	raisins
zabuun, zabaayin	male customer
zabuuna, -aat	female customer
zahra, zuhuur	flower (ornamental), plant
zamaan	long ago
zaman	past time, period

zanjabiil	ginger
zaraaf (coll)	giraffe
zara9, yazra9	to plant, grow
zarga	f. of azrag
zeet	oil (nn)
zeey	like (adj)
zibda	butter (adj)
ziraa9a	agriculture
ziraa9i, -iyiin	agriculturalist
ziyaara	visit (nn)
zooj, azwaaj	husband
zooja, -aat	wife
zool	person
zuhuur	pl. of zahra
zurug	pl. of azrag

ẓ

ẓarif, ẓuruuf	envelope (nn)
ẓuruuf	pl. of ẓarif

9

9aada, -aat (or 9awaayid)	custom, tradition
9aaj	ivory
9aali, -iin	high
9aashir	tenth (adj)
9aawz, -iin	want (vb)
9adas	lentils
9afash	furniture, luggage
9afwan	you're welcome (response to shukran)
9ajaayiz	pl. of 9ajuuz
9ajiib, -iin	strange
9ajjuur	grooved cucumber
9ajuuz, 9ajaayiz	old (person)
9ala	on, to
9amaara	high building
al 9amaaraat	the New Extension
9amal, ya9mil	to make, do
9amal damgha	to affix a revenue stamp
9amm, a9maam	paternal uncle
9amma, -aat	paternal aunt
9an	about, concerning
9anaagriib	pl. of 9angareeb
9anaawiin	pl. of 9unwaan
9angareeb, 9anaagriib	rope bed
9arabaat	pl. of 9arabiiya
9arabi	Arabic (language)
9arabi, -iyiin	Arabic (adj)
9arabiiya, -aat (or 9arabaat)	car
9ariis, 9irsaan	bridegroom
9aruus, 9araayis	bride
9asal an naHal	honey
9asiida	asida (dish of very thick sorghum porridge)
9asur	later afternoon
9aṣiir	juice
9asha (m)	supper, evening meal
9ashaan	because (of), so that
9awaayid	pl. of 9aada
9ayyaan, -iin	sick, ill
9een (f), 9iyuun	eye (nn)
9eesh	bread, durra, sorghum, guinea corn
9idda	kitchen utensils
9iid, a9yaad	festival, feast
9iid al giyaama	Easter
9iid al miilaad	Christmas
9ilab	pl. of 9ilba
9ilba, 9ilab	tin can, packet
9ind-	have (see Lesson 16.1.2)
9irif, ya9rif	to know
9iris, a9raas	wedding
9irsaan	pl. of 9ariis
9ishriin	twenty
9iyuun	pl. of 9een

Lightning Source UK Ltd.
Milton Keynes UK
UKHW051248281118
333081UK00009B/255/P

9 781556 713781